12-25-08

To Our Dear Staci,

We hope this recipe book helps
you pass on the traditions of our
Greek cuisine

Our family has been known for
wonderful cooks. Please teach and
share them with your beautiful family
and carry on the traditions

With all our Love, Kisses and Hugs
Nanny Sal & Uncle Dick
"Stay Sweet"

Vefa Alexiadou

Greek Pastries and Desserts

Thessaloniki, Greece. 1991

The Author

Vefa Alexiadou is Greece's leading cooking authority today. A gifted cook who comes from a line of gifted cooks, she has modernized Greek cooking using contemporary methods and equipment while retaining authentic flavor. A graduate of the University of Thessaloniki in Chemistry, she also took classes in Nutrition at the University of California at Berkeley. Her love of cooking motivated her to visit many foreign countries and to study culinary arts, food styling, table decorating and the hygiene of food. Her Chemistry background enables her to combine scientific know-how with her culinary talent. As a regular on Greece's most popular morning TV show, she has passed on the heritage of Greek cookery to hundreds of thousands of Greek women. Vefa Alexiadou's articles and recipes appear in the four major Greek women's magazines: «Health and Beauty», «Ekini» (She), «Kuzina» and «Home Decoration and Architecture», as well as in numerous other publications and newspapers. She is the author, stylist, and publisher of her best-selling cookbooks: «Invitation to Dinner», «Invitation to Cocktails», «Invitation to Tea», «Invitation to a Children's Party», «Greek Cuisine», «Greek Pastries and Desserts», and «Festive Cuisine».

1997 Third edition

© *1989 Vefa Alexiadou*

Nevrokopiou 16, Thessaloniki, 546 38, Greece

Telephone - 031-213-219 or 031-341-846

ISBN 960-85018-7-3

REGISTRATION No TX 3 380 543

Editor and Publisher: Vefa Alexiadou, Thessaloniki, Greece
Cover Photographer: Pierre Couteau, Athens
Cover Artist: Kostis Kolios, Athens
Photography: Zacharias Anastassiadis, Chrissa Nikoleri, Thessaloniki
Typesetting: Fotron S.A., Athens
Color Separation: A. Bastas, D. Plessas S.A., Athens
Montage: Andreas Androulakis, Athens
Printing: Pergamos S.A., Athens
Book Binding: K. Papadakis S.A., Athens

In memory of my mother

*For the happy years of growing up
full of love and family warmth*

4

Sweet Memories

Writing this book brought back a flood of memories. Each sweet, each delicacy reminded me of scenes, voices, and stories out of my childhood, buried I thought with the passing years.

I recall how longingly I waited every afternoon for Mr. Yannis, the street vendor. As he turned the corner of my house, he would be shouting his wares in the loud, piercing voice that brought all the children running: "Samali from Constantinople! A drachma a piece!". Then he would set up the folding table he carried under his arm, placing on it the "Sini", a huge flat tray with the golden-brown delicacy, decorated with almonds and drenched in heavy syrup. The sight of it transfixed our eyes and made our mouths water. On other days, Mr. Yannis might have "pastelli with honey" (a sesame seed bar), traditional candies or rich, creamy homemade ice cream, depending on the season.

Nostalgia overtakes me and I am engulfed in sadness when I think of the old customs which created in us a sense of community and belonging, and realize they are slowly fading away, with only a few women of my generation still clinging to them. I remember how my mother, each year on St. Barbara's feast day, December 4th, dished out a special wheat pudding into glass bowls, sprinkling it with cinnamon, cloves and walnuts. How eager we children were to take part in the religious tradition of distributing that "Varvara", as it was called, to friends' homes in the neighborhood, not only because we were rewarded with sweets, and even sometimes with coins.

Another tradition I remember was St. John's Bonfire on the day before the Saint's name day, June 23rd. The girls in my neighborhood took turns jumping over the bonfire as the boys teased them, reciting little verses. When the flame died down it was time to bake the pita, a sweet, round bread without salt, kneaded and shaped by three newlyweds. When it was ready, each single girl received a slice to hide under her pillow in hopes it would reveal in her dreams the identity of her future husband.

The wedding cake, cut by the bride and groom, was a foreign custom which became common in Greece after the Second World War. Sweets traditionally served at a Greek wedding were made by the bride herself, to show her culinary skills to her new husband. During the week preceding the wedding, the groom-to-be would spend a whole day in the home of the bride, during which time she called on all her skills to convince him what a perfect housewife and good cook he was getting.

In Pelion where I grew up, as well as in other parts of Greece, the bride made Baklava for her wedding. Crisp, golden-brown, in thick honey syrup, cut into little diamond-shaped pieces, and decorated with cloves, the enormous pan accompanied the bride to the church. The wedding festivities and celebratory meal usually took place immediately after the ceremony in the village square by the church.

"Kourabiedes" and "meringues" were other wedding delicacies, often given to the guests in the church, along with sugared almonds called "koufeta". Siatista was famous for "saliaria", a traditional sweet prepared by the bride-to-be for her engagement party and sent by her to her future mother-in-law to "sweeten her up" and show off her baking skills. In Katerini even today the mother-in-law breaks a sweet, round loaf over the head of the bride when she crosses the threshold of her new home, upon returning from church, a custom which is believed to ensure the coming of

grandchildren. In other areas, the bride breaks a pomegranate so that her home will be filled with children. In Roumeli, the mother-in-law feeds the bride walnuts in honey so that her life with her new husband will be sweet. She also prepares a sweet bread with a raised design on it and sprinkles it with confectioners' sugar after baking. The "preventa", as this bread is called, is placed on a silver tray covered with white lace and taken to the church. Later it is given to the guests at the wedding dinner.

Very early in the morning of New Year's Day the women in Roumeli used to take various sweets and home grown fruit, grains, and nuts, such as walnuts, figs, wheat and corn to the "korita", a basin carved out of stone, into which they put a little of each as a symbolic offering so that the harvest would be plentiful in the new year.

When I was a child, going to the annual market (fair) in Volos, my favorite sweet was "halva" from the town of Farsala. In my childish eyes, that "halva", with its glistening surface, was the most heavenly sweet in the world. Even today, all my diet resolutions are forgotten at the sight of that delightful temptation.

Remembering wartime food shortages during the German occupation, I can still taste the cornbread with carob syrup and raisins we ate. It was all we could afford then, and most of the time, we did not even have raisins to put in it, but even that austerity food had its own deliciousness. I wish I had a slice right now as I write this. Later, during my school years in Salonika, the memory of munching on hot, crisp rings of bread covered with sesame seeds (koulouria), and a piece of kaseri cheese during class break, is still with me. In those times we had none of the modern snacks and sandwiches one finds in school canteens now, but now what I crave are those simple homemade treats of the old days.

I still remember walking in Aristotelous Square on hot summer evenings, past outdoor movie houses and rows of shops selling "loukoumades" (tiny hot Greek Honey Donuts), the air filled with the aroma of the freshly made goodies, cinnamon and honey. There were old coffee shops along the seaside, a bit further on from the harbor to the White Tower, and pastry shops serving goat milk "dondurma" ice cream with sour cherry syrup and roasted almonds. If only I could recapture the taste of that incredible ice cream, and watch again the little boats sailing off to Perea, Baxe and Aghia Triada.

How many sweet memories, how many cherished old customs from the not so far away past, a time when people were happy with the little they had, before they ever began chasing after the luxuries of today.

Vefa Alexiadou

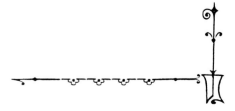

Contents

5 Jams and Compotes

6 Syrup Pastries and Desserts

7 Cookies and Confections

8 Religion and Tradition

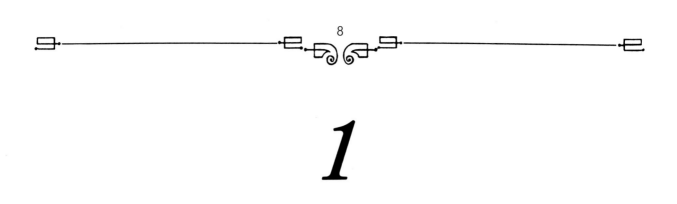

1

Preserved Fruits
(Glika Koutaliou)

The traditional welcome to a guest, even nowadays in almost all the Greek villages and in many cities, is an offering of fruits preserved in heavy syrup. The fruit is placed on a tiny crystal plate and served on a silver or copper tray covered with crocheted lace or embroidered linen. The Greek hostess proudly offers her homemade fruits along with a crystal glass of iced water, so much appreciated after the taste of the syrupy, crisp, aromatic fruit. Colorful, glossy and delectable, gleaming on the crystal plate, the preserved fruit is pleasing to the eye and the palate. After a long journey through the countryside, while relaxing in the shade of a vine-covered Greek courtyard, the enjoyment of this delicacy is like being in an oasis of coolness and joy. The Greek custom of welcoming a visitor to ones home with the preserved fruit is beautiful in its simplicity.

If you have only experienced store-bought Greek preserved fruits and found them too sweet, you will be surprised at how much more flavor they have when you make them yourself.

General Instructions

To preserve fruits in heavy syrup choose very young under-ripe, unblemished, good quality, small fruits. Soft and sensitive fruits, must be soaked in lime water to help in keeping their shape and crispness. To make lime water, mix 2 tablespoons hydrated lime with 2 quarts of water, until the liquid resembles milk. Then strain it through a fine sieve. If hydrated lime is not available, take a lime stone, and soak it in water for a few days. Cover the fruit with the lime water and let it soak for 1-4 hours.

Larger fruits, like figs, Seville oranges, should be pierced in several places and left to soak, plunged in water containing 1 tablespoon citric acid. The citric acid penetrates the fruit thoroughly, preventing crystallization. Also $1/2$ teaspoon citric acid added towards the end of cooking prevents the syrup from crystallizing. Citric acid can be substituted by adding either the strained juice of one lemon or $1/2$ cup glucose (corn syrup). However, the use of too much glucose, will affect the taste.

Bitter fruits, such as Seville oranges, figs, oranges and walnuts, should be treated to eliminate the bitterness. Put the fruit into a pan, pour boiling water to cover and boil for 5-10 minutes. Then strain. Repeat the procedure 2-3 times if necessary. Weigh the fruit and allow the same weight of sugar, unless otherwise specified. The fruit should be stoned or cored before weighing. Dissolve the sugar in water, stirring over low heat. Put the lid on the pan for a minute, to allow the steam to dissolve any sugar splashed on the sides of the pan. When the sugar is completely dissolved, cook for 5-10 minutes without stirring to make a thick syrup. Drop in the fruit, and cook for 15 minutes, skimming occasionally. Allow the fruits to stand, in the syrup,

Tiny Mandarins in Syrup, page 14

overnight. The next day cook over medium heat, stirring occasionally to prevent burning, until the fruit is soft and translucent and the syrup is set. If the fruit is cooked before the syrup is ready, transfer it to jars with a slotted spoon and continue to cook the syrup until the setting point is reached. Pour the syrup over the fruits in the jars. This procedure keeps the fruit intact and preserves the aroma.

To test for setting, dip a spoon into the syrup vertically and allow excess syrup to drip off. When drops begin to form, hold the spoon over a small dish. If the drops spread on the plate, the syrup is not set. When drops remain intact, the syrup is set. You may flavor the preserve adding vanilla, cloves, cinnamon sticks or geranium according to the fruit and to your own preference. Stir in the flavoring just before removing from the heat.

If almonds are used, blanch and, if desired, roast them before adding. Insert them into the half-cooked fruits, after wetting with a little lemon juice to prevent crystallizing. Allow the preserved fruit to cool, slightly, before ladling it into sterilized jars, and let it cool completely before sealing and storing. Store it in a dry, cool and dark place or, preferably, in the refrigerator if it is to be kept for a long time.

If the preserve has been kept for a period of time and the syrup looks watery, pour it off and boil until it is reset. Return it to the fruits. If the preserved fruit crystallizes, transfer to a pan, add a little glucose and cook over low heat for a while. Pot and store again. If mold should form on the surface, carefully remove and discard it. The remaining preserve is edible. It may be necessary to reset the syrup, as the preserves usually form mold when the syrup is not properly set.

Figs in Syrup, page 11

Figs or Eggplants in Syrup
(Siko i Melitzanaki Gliko)

Yields 25-30 pieces
Preparation time 24 hours
Cooking time approximately 1 hour

25-30 small, young green figs (2 lbs)
lime water (see General Instructions, page 9)
1 small piece copper sulphate, the size of a pea (available from drug stores)
1 tablespoon citric acid
2$^1/_2$ lbs sugar
4 cups water
8-10 cloves or 1 teaspoon vanilla (optional)
1/2 teaspoon citric acid
2 tablespoons lemon juice
1/2 cup glucose (corn syrup)

Select the figs and preserve them at the beginning of May, when the fruit is very young and tender, and the seeds have not developed yet. Peel and put the figs in a bowl. Pour over enough lime water to cover, and let them soak for one hour. Strain and rinse them several times. Eliminate the bitterness by boiling in water 3 times, according to the general instructions (page 9). Add the copper sulphate during the second boiling, to preserve the bright, green color. Cool the fruit slightly. Pierce each fig with a skewer through the stem end and squeeze it carefully to remove the excess water. Dissolve the citric acid in cold water, enough to cover the figs, and pour it over them. Let them stand for about 1 hour, so that the citric acid will penetrate the fruit thoroughly and prevent crystallization. (Otherwise, when cooking the fruit, add $^1/_2$ teaspoon citric acid at the beginning and not towards the end). Strain the figs and dry on absorbent paper. Put the sugar and water in a heavy-bottomed pan and cook, covered, for about 10 minutes. Add the figs and cook, uncovered, over low heat for 15 minutes, removing any scum that comes to the surface. Leave them overnight in the syrup. The next day, cook again until the figs are soft and translucent and the syrup is completely set. If the figs get soft before the setting point is reached, remove them from the syrup with a slotted spoon and thicken the syrup by boiling a little longer. Add the figs along with the flavoring and glucose. Cook for a few minutes longer, testing for setting. While still hot, put the figs into sterilized jars and cover with the syrup. Seal and store in a dark, cool place or preferably in the refrigerator. Use the same recipe to preserve tiny, young eggplants.

Tomatoes in Syrup
(Domataki Gliko)

Yields 2 lbs
Preparation time 24 hours
Cooking time 25 minutes

2	lbs small, under-ripe, firm plum tomatoes
	lime water (see General Instructions, page 9)
2	lbs sugar
2½	cups water
2	tablespoons lemon juice
6-8	cloves
1	cinnamon stick
1/2	cup glucose (corn syrup)
	blanched almonds

Blanch the tomatoes and remove their skin. Make a few incisions at the stem end and press lightly to remove the seeds. Cover the tomatoes with lime water and let them soak for one hour. Strain and rinse them in cold water several times. Drain them thoroughly. Boil the sugar and water in a heavy-bottomed pan for about 10 minutes to make a thick syrup. Add the tomatoes, lemon juice, cloves and cinnamon. Cook, uncovered, over medium heat for about 10 minutes, removing any scum that comes to the surface. Let the tomatoes stand in the syrup overnight. The next day, pour off the syrup and boil until it is quite thick. Add the corn syrup and tomatoes. Insert one blanched almond in each tomato, before putting them back into the syrup. Cook a little longer to re-set the syrup. While still hot, put the tomatoes into sterilized jars and cover with the syrup. Seal and store in a dark, cool place or preferably in the refrigerator.

Vanilla or Mastic Fondant
(Vanilia i Masticha Gliko)

Yields 1½ lbs Vanilla Fondant
Preparation time 2 hours

2	lbs sugar
1	cup water
2	tablespoons glucose (corn syrup)
2	teaspoons vanilla or
1/2	teaspoon ground mastic

Snowy-white Vanilla or Mastic Fondant, prepared by Greek women and served in all cafes throughout Greece, is offered with a lovely and attractive presentation. It is served to the guest with the serving spoon plunged in a glass of cool water. That's why in most regions of Greece it is called "Submarine". Before the second world war "Vanilla Submarine" was the only sweet served in almost all the country cafe shops.

Put the sugar, water and glucose into a heavy-bottomed pan and stir them over low heat until the sugar is dissolved completely. Put the lid on the pan for a minute to allow the steam from the syrup to wash down the sides of the pan, dissolving any sugar crystal splashed on.

Raise the heat and bring the syrup to a boil. Continue to boil until a small amount of the syrup (½ teaspoon) dropped in iced water forms a small, soft ball, which flattens easily when pressed between your fingers. If using a candy thermometer, it should register 234°-240°F. Take the pan off the heat and quickly dip in cold water to stop the cooking. Moisten a marble slab or a baking sheet with a wet towel and pour the hot syrup on it. Let it cool for a few minutes. Using a wet, metal spatula, work the syrup by repeatedly scooping it up from the edges and folding it into the middle. Add the vanilla or mastic and continue working the syrup in a figure of eight motion for about 10 minutes or until it becomes opaque, thick and too firm to work with the spatula. Wet your hands and knead it until it is smooth, white and elastic, about 10 minutes. Wrapped and stored in a tightly sealed jar in the refrigerator, vanilla fondant will keep almost indefinitely. To serve, place a small amount on a teaspoon and plunge it in a glass of cool water. Vanilla fondant also makes a very good icing for cakes, pastries, cookies, biscuits, etc. To make it spreadable, heat it in a double boiler until soft, gradually adding a little water until the desired consistency is reached. Vanilla fondant may be colored by adding a few drops of food coloring.

Rose Petal Preserve
(Triantafillo Gliko)

Yields 2 lbs jam
Preparation time 3 hours
Cooking time 15-20 minutes

1/2	lb rose petals
2	lbs sugar
1	cup water
2	tablespoons lemon juice or
1/2	teaspoon citric acid
1	tablespoon glycerine

This preserve can be made only with one special variety of roses. The early pink roses of May which bloom at the end of April and the beginning of May. Remove the petals and with a pair of scissors cut off the white bottom part. Rinse the petals in cold water several times and drain them thoroughly. Weigh the petals and use 2 lbs sugar for every ½ lb trimmed petals. Rub the petals with the sugar between your palms until they look wilted. Let them stand for 2-3 hours. Put the petals, in a heavy-bottomed pan, add the water and cook over low heat, carefully stirring, to prevent burning. Cook until the syrup is almost set. To test for setting, a small amount of the syrup dropped in a cold surface must hold its shape for a while and then spread slightly. Add lemon juice, or citric acid and glycerine, a few minutes before setting. The glycerine makes the preserve glossy. Put in jars, cover and seal. Store in a dark, cool place or preferably in the refrigerator.

Apricots or Plums in Syrup
(Verikoko i Damaskino Gliko)

Yields 20-25 pieces
Preparation time 24 hours
Cooking time 35 minutes

2   lbs large apricots
       lime water (see General Instructions, page 9)
2   lbs sugar
2½   cups water
2   tablespoons lemon juice
1/2   cup glucose (corn syrup)
1/4   teaspoon almond extract

Use an under-ripe and easily stoned variety of apricots. Press a large metal nail through the stem end of each apricot, pushing to remove the stone from the other end, carefully, so that the fruit is not damaged. Peel the fruit and soak the apricots submerged in lime water for 3-4 hours. Strain and rinse them in cold water several times (about six). Drain them thoroughly. Put the sugar and water in a heavy-bottomed pan and boil the syrup for 5 minutes, skimming off the froth from the surface. Let the apricots stand in the syrup overnight. The next day, add the glucose and simmer gently, uncovered, until the apricots are quite soft and the syrup is completely set. If the apricots get soft before the setting point is reached, remove them from the syrup with a slotted spoon and thicken the syrup by boiling it a little longer. Replace the apricots, add the flavoring and simmer, stirring until the syrup re-sets. While still hot, put the apricots into sterilized jars and pour the syrup over them. Seal and store in a dark, cool place or preferably in the refrigerator. Follow the same procedure to preserve raw plums.

Apricots in Syrup, page 13

Green Baby Walnuts in Syrup
(Karidaki Gliko)

Yields 2 lbs
Preparation time 24 hours
Cooking time 45 minutes

2   lbs very young and tender,
     small, green walnuts
3   tablespoons lemon juice
     the peel of one orange
     whole cloves
2   lbs sugar
$2^1/_2$ cups water
1/2   teaspoon citric acid

Peel each walnut and pierce in several places with a needle. Immediately plunge them into water, mixed with the lemon juice. Bring a large pan of water to a boil, drop in the orange peel and the drained walnuts; boil them for 5 minutes and drain. Repeat the procedure twice more to soften the fruit and eliminate the bitterness. Drain and cool. Lightly squeeze each walnut between your fingers to remove part of the absorbed water, and stick a clove in it. Meanwhile, boil the sugar and water in a heavy-bottomed pan to make a thick syrup and drop in the walnuts. Add the citric acid and cook over low heat until the walnuts are soft and the syrup has reached the setting point, about 15 minutes. While warm, transfer to jars, seal and store in a dark, cool place or preferably in the refrigerator.

Orange Pieces in Syrup
(Portokali Gliko)

Yields 32 pieces
Preparation time 24 hours
Cooking time 45 minutes

4   large, thick skinned oranges ($2^1/_2$ lbs)
2   lbs sugar
$2^1/_2$ cups water
1   tablespoon lemon juice
1/2   cup glucose (corn syrup)

Rub the oranges lightly with a fine grater. Prick all over with a needle and eliminate the bitterness by boiling in water 3 times, according to the General Instructions (page 9). Rinse with cold water, strain and let them cool. Lightly squeeze each orange and cut into 4-6 wedges, depending on the size. Cut wedges in half. With a pair of scissors remove tough center and pips. Boil the sugar and water for 5 minutes to make a thick syrup. Add the orange pieces and cook, uncovered, over medium heat for 15 minutes, skimming well. Let the oranges stand in the syrup overnight. The next day, cook over medium heat, stirring frequently, for about 30 minutes or until the fruit is translucent and the syrup is set. Add the lemon juice and glucose a few minutes before the syrup is completely set. Put in sterilized jars, cover and seal. Store in a dark, cool place or preferably in the refrigerator.

Tiny Mandarins in Syrup
Seville Oranges or Kumquats

(Mandarini Gliko, Nerantzi i Koumkouat)

Yields 25-30 pieces
Preparation time 24 hours
Cooking time 45 minutes

2   lbs very young small mandarins,
     clementines, tangerines, Seville oranges
     kumquats or any young, tiny citrus fruit
3   lbs sugar
5   cups water
2   tablespoons lemon juice
1/2   cup glucose (corn syrup)

Wash the mandarins thoroughly and prick all over in several places with a needle. Eliminate the bitterness by boiling in water 3 times, according to the general instructions (page 9). Strain and cool slightly. Carefully squeeze the fruits one by one to remove part of the absorbed water and place them on paper towels. Boil the sugar and water for about 10 minutes to make a lightly thick syrup. Add the mandarins and cook, uncovered, over medium heat for about 15 minutes, removing any scum that comes to the surface. Let the mandarins stand in the syrup overnight. The next day add the glucose and simmer gently, uncovered, until the fruit is soft and translucent and the syrup is completely set. While still hot, put the mandarins, into sterilized jars and cover with the syrup. Seal and store in a dark, cool place or preferably in the refrigerator. Follow the same procedure to preserve very young green Seville oranges, or kumquats. As these fruits are quite bitter, it may be necessary to boil them more than 3 times to eliminate the bitterness. Test before putting in the syrup.

Orange Rind Rolls, page 15
Seville Oranges in Syrup, page 14
Pears in Syrup, page 15
Tiny Mandarins in Syrup, page 14

Pumpkin or Watermelon Rinds in Syrup
(Kolokithi i Karpouzi Retseli)

Yields 3 lbs
Preparation time 2-3 hours
Cooking time 20 minutes

2	lbs peeled pumpkin or watermelon rind
3	lbs sugar
	lime water (see General Instructions, page 9)
2	cups water
1/2	cup glucose (corn syrup)
1/2	teaspoon citric acid
1	teaspoon vanilla

Cut the pumpkin into cubes, or use tiny biscuit cutters to cut out various fancy shapes. Cover with lime water and let them soak for two hours. Rinse the fruit pieces in cold water several times. Bring a large pan of water to a boil, drop in the pumpkin pieces and bring to a boil again. Drain and repeat this procedure twice more to soften them. Drain and cool in a colander. Squeeze the pieces between your palms to drain off the excess water. Boil the sugar and water in a heavy-bottomed pan for 5 minutes, add the glucose and pumpkin pieces, and cook over a moderately high heat until the syrup thickens. Add the citric acid and vanilla and cook for a few more minutes until completely set. Cool slightly, spoon into jars and seal. If using watermelon rind, peel off the green skin, and continue as for the pumpkin.

Apples or Pears in Syrup
(Milo i Achladi Gliko)

Yields 20-25 pieces
Preparation time 24 hours
Cooking time 45 minutes

2	lbs under-ripe small apples or pears
4	tablespoons lemon juice
2	lbs sugar
3	cups water
25	blanched and roasted almonds (optional)
1/2	cup glucose (corn syrup)
1	teaspoon vanilla

Wash, peel and core the apples. Immediately plunge them into water, mixed with lemon juice, to avoid discoloration. Set aside. Tie the cores in a muslin bag and put them in a pan with the water. Simmer for about 10 minutes. Drain well and discard the bag with the cores. Dissolve the sugar in the liquid and boil for 5 minutes without stirring. Drain the apples and drop them into the syrup. Cook over medium heat, skimming occasionally, until the apples are soft, about 10 minutes. Let the apples stand in the syrup overnight. The next day, transfer the apples to a colander, set over a bowl, with a slotted spoon. Continue to cook the syrup until the setting point is reached, adding also the syrup that has drained off the apples. Add the glucose, vanilla and the apples. Insert one blanched, roasted almond in each fruit, before putting them back into the syrup. Cook a few more minutes to re-set the syrup. Put in sterilized jars, cover and seal. Store in a dark, cool place or preferably in the refrigerator. Pears may be preserved in the same way.

Orange Rind Rolls
(Rola apo Flouda Portokaliou)

Yields 3 lbs
Preparation time 24 hours
Cooking time 45 minutes

2$^1/_2$	lbs thick skinned oranges
2	lbs sugar
2$^1/_2$	cups water
2	tablespoons lemon juice
1/2	cup glucose (corn syrup)

Rub the oranges lightly with a fine grater. Score the peel in 4, 6 or 8 segments, according to the size of the fruit, and remove it carefully. Roll each piece tightly, thread on a cotton string, as a necklace like, using a large eyed needle. Bring a large pan of water to a boil, drop in the rind, and bring to a boil again. Drain the rind in a colander. Repeat this procedure twice more to soften the rind and eliminate any bitterness. Boil the sugar and water together for 10 minutes to make a thick syrup. Slide the rind rolls off the thread into the syrup and simmer for 15 minutes. Let them stand in the syrup overnight. The next day, add the lemon juice and glucose and cook until the setting point is reached. While still hot, put the rind rolls into sterilized jars and pour the syrup over them. Seal and store in a dark, cool place or preferably in the refrigerator. Follow the same procedure to preserve lemon, Seville orange, bergamot or grapefruit rind rolls.

Strawberries or Grapes in Syrup
(Fraoules i Staphili Gliko)

Yields 2 lbs
Preparation time 3 hours
Cooking time 45 minutes

2	lbs large, under-ripe strawberries
1/2	cup lemon juice
2	lbs sugar
2	cups water

Wash and hull the strawberries, carefully, so that the fruit is not damaged. Arrange the strawberries in a large, shallow dish and sprinkle with the lemon juice. Let them stand for 2-3 hours. Put the sugar and water into a wide heavy-bottomed pan over medium heat. Stir until the sugar is dissolved and cook the syrup for 5 minutes until it reaches the setting point. Add half the stawberries and simmer over low heat for 10 minutes, skimming often. Take the pan off the heat. With a slotted spoon carefully transfer the strawberries to a large sieve placed over a bowl. Re-set the syrup and repeat the procedure with the remaining strawberries. Add the juice that has drained off the strawberries to the syrup and cook until it again reaches the setting point. Add the strawberries and continue to cook for 5 minutes or until the syrup coats the fruits and the setting point is reached. While cooling, shake the pan several times to help the strawberries absorb syrup and plump up. Transfer to wide shallow jars, distributing the strawberries and syrup equally. Cover the jars when the preserve is completely cool. Follow the same procedures to preserve large grapes, picked over, seeded and peeled.

Grated Quince in Syrup
(Kidoni Trifto)

Yields 2 lbs
Preparation time 24 hours
Cooking time 30 minutes

2   lbs quinces
2   tablespoons lemon juice
3   cups water
1¹/₂ lbs sugar
2   geranium or lemon tree leaves
1/2   cup glucose (corn syrup)

Peel the quinces and grate them coarsely to the core, over a pan holding the water and lemon juice, so that the fruit can be dropped immediately into the acid water, avoiding discoloration. Put the pan over medium heat. Cover and cook until the fruit is soft and the water has almost been evaporated. Add the sugar and let them stand overnight. The next day, cook over low heat, stirring frequently for about 15 minutes or until the fruit is translucent and the syrup is set. Add glucose and geranium leaves 5 minutes before setting. Quinces preserved this way will have a deep, pink color. For a lighter color, boil the sugar and water in a heavy-bottomed pan for about 5 minutes to make a light syrup. Remove it from the heat, add the lemon juice and grate the quinces over it, so that the fruit can immediately drop into the syrup. Cook over medium heat, stirring frequently for about 30 minutes or until the fruit is soft and translucent and the setting point is reached. Add glucose and flavoring 5 minutes before setting. Put in jars, cover and seal. Store in a dark, cool place or preferably in the refrigerator.

Cherries or Sour Cherries in Syrup
(Visino i Kerasi Gliko)

Yields 2 lbs
Preparation time 24 hours
Cooking time 45 minutes

2   lbs sour cherries
1/2   cup water
2   lbs sugar

1/2   teaspoon citric acid or
2   tablespoons lemon juice

Wash and drain well the sour cherries. Using a special gadget, remove the stones working over a pan to catch the juice. Drop the stones into the water, stir and drain over the cherries. Put the cherries in a heavy-bottomed pan in layers, sprinkling each layer with sugar. Pour over the juice, cover and let them stand overnight. The next day, heat gently and bring to a boil. Then increase the heat and boil for 35 minutes, stirring often and removing any scum that comes to the surface. Reduce the heat, add the citric acid or lemon juice, and simmer, stirring occasionally, until the setting point is reached. Remove from the heat. While cooling, shake the pan several times to help the fruit to absorb syrup and plump up. Using ordinary cherries, reduce the sugar to 1¹/₂ lbs, and omit the water. To help the cherries keep their shape and crispness, soak them in lime water for one hour. Follow the same procedure to preserve seedless grapes. Because of their sweetness, reduce the sugar to 1 lb. Add vanilla flavoring.

Cherries in Syrup, page 17

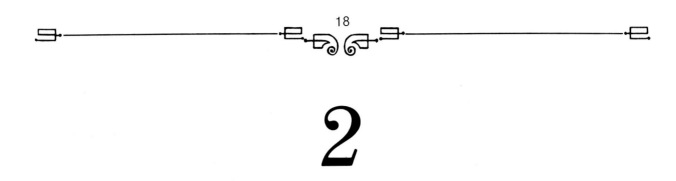

2

Breads and Doughs
(Psomia ke Zimes)

The large earthenware kneading basin, the round wooden board, "plastiri", the molder "plasti" and the "pinakoti" (the bread-carrying board with 4-5 partitions to hold the bread loaves), were my mother's basic equipment in the bread-making process. Like most Greek housewives, during my childhood (which is not all that long ago), my mother used to knead bread for the whole family once a week. The procedure was enveloped with mysticism and my mother performed it so ritualistically that it used to fill me with curiosity and stimulate my childish desire for learning. I remember every little detail from the preparation until the final result, an aromatic, heavy brown bread with a thick, golden brown, crisp crust. My mother would reactivate the starter the evening before. She worked a piece of dough, reserved in the ice box from the previous week's bread, adding water and flour. She covered it with a woolen blanket and left it overnight. The next day, early in the morning, she used this sourdough starter to prepare and knead the bread. She covered it once more with the blanket and left it to rise. Then she would keep a piece of dough for next week's bread (starter) shaping the remaining dough into 4-5 large loaves, or as many as the partitions in the carrying board. She placed one loaf in each partition, which had been lined with a well-floured woven towel. She folded the towels over each loaf and covered them all with the blanket. When the dough had risen, my mother would put the board on her shoulder and carry it to the neighborhood professional bakers' to have it baked.

Sometimes my mother used to keep more dough than was necessary for the starter and would make us "lalagites", small pancakes fried one by one in hot oil, then covered with honey and sprinkled with cinnamon. At other times she made savoury "giouzlemedes" filled with feta cheese or sweet ones with sugar and cinnamon. She made the Flat Breads for Ash Monday, the Sweet Plaited Breads for Easter and Vassilopita Bread for New Year's Eve. As far as I can remember my mother was always there, in our kitchen, being ready to satisfy every desire we had for food. I'll never forget those lovely years, full of family warmth. Whenever I think back to those days, I am filled with sweet nostalgia.

General Instructions:

Until the first decades of the 20th century in Greece, whole-grain flour was used for bread. The flour was made from wheat, rye, barley or corn which were ground between heavy millstones moved by windmills or water mills. The stones crushed the whole grain. Therefore, the flour contained all the grain's ingredients. Then the flour was sifted through a series of progressively finer sieves to obtain a better texture and color. However, with the sifting, some of the valuable vitamins from the husk of the grains were removed and discarded with the bran. Today's roller milling, unlike millstones, has the capacity of separating the various ingredients of the grains and mixing them into various proportions, thus making several varieties of flour. There are many commercial varieties of wheat flour today; soft or strong, white, semi-white, brown and yellow. All enriched with vitamins and with some chemical additives, like citric and tartaric salts to improve the nutritional value,

Assortment of Greek Breads

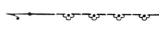

texture and taste.

Wheat flours are divided into categories, according to the gluten or bran content. High-gluten flour containing over 30% gluten, is milled from wheats with a high gluten potential and is called "strong" or "bread flour". Medium-gluten flour, containing about 28% gluten is usually labelled as "all purpose flour", and low-gluten flour, containing less than 28% gluten, is made from low-gluten wheat, labelled as "soft" or "cake and pastry flour" and produces a more tender texture than strong flour. According to the bran content, flour categories are determined by the percentage of the grain has been ground (grinding degree). Wholemeal is a whole-grain ground flour (100% type), with the highest bran content. White flour is a 55%-grain ground flour (55% type), with the lowest bran content. Many excellent flours lie between the extremes of wholemeal and white. The higher the grinding degree, the higher the bran content of the flour.

Some recipes in this book call for "strong or bread flour". This is a high-gluten flour (55% type), suitable for bread, sweet bread and choux pastry. Other recipes call for "soft or cake and pastry flour". This is a low-gluten flour, (70% type), suitable for kourabiedes, tarts, cakes, biscuits and pies. Finally, there are recipes which require "all-purpose flour". This is a medium-gluten flour, (55% type), which can be used successfully for all pastries and cakes as well as breads. Other flours mentioned in the recipes of this book are "country or yellow flour", which is a medium-gluten flour containing 30% to 50% finely ground semolina, and wholemeal flour, which as mentioned above, is a whole-grain ground flour. "Self-raising flour" is a soft flour containing baking powder especially made for cakes.

The main ingredients for bread making, is flour, salt, yeast and water. The proportion of salt is 2% for all types of flours. (Special standardized flours, which already contain salt, are excepted). The proportion of yeast varies and it comes up to 2% for the white flour and up to 3% for the brown, yellow and wholemeal flours. The proportion of the water also varies, coming up to 55% for the white flour and about 60%-65% for the yellow, brown and whole-wheat flours, according to the type. Soft flour absorbs less water than the two other categories. Start adding the largest part of the amount specified in the recipe. Then add as much as it is necessary to form an elastic and easy to handle dough. Both commercially and home prepared yeast are mixed with tepid water and flour to form a thick paste. Then it is covered and left to rise. Good yeast is ready to be used 20 minutes after being mixed with water and flour. It should be used before large bubbles are formed, since the dough tends to deflate and it would be necessary to add more flour and water to reactivate it.

Bread is mostly made from a simple mixture of flour, yeast, salt and water. Other ingredients, such as sugar, milk, oil or butter and eggs can be added to enrich the bread and improve the texture and the taste. Mix the ingredients and knead the dough with a regular, rythmic motion, stretching and folding it for 10-15 minutes to develop the gluten, the substance that gives dough its elasticity. At first the dough will be sticky and tear easily. As you continue kneading, it looses its stickiness and becomes soft and elastic. Cover it and let it stand in a warm, humid place. The yeast produces bubbles of carbon dioxide gas, which stretches the gluten and raises the dough. To test that the dough has risen, press a finger into it; if the indentation remains, filling in very slowly, the dough is ready. At a temperature of approximately 65°F the dough will be ready in $1^1/_2$ to 2 hours. To speed up the procedure, place the dough in a warmer place (85°F). However, the results will not be as good as those from slower rising. Placing the dough in a cool place, or refrigerating it overnight, gives bread a better texture and aroma. After the first rising, knead the dough once more for 3-5 minutes and shape it. Cover and let it rise once more. To increase the surface of the crust, also to give a decorative and attractive appearance to the bread, make long, shallow slashes across the top of the loaves with a sharp knife or a razor blade, tracing various patterns, if desired. The bread placed in a pre-heated oven (470°F), continues to rise, during the first 20 minutes, until the yeast dies and a crust is formed. A humid oven delays the formation of the crust and thereby allows the loaves to swell even more. To produce steam, place a wide bowl filled with hot water, on the bottom of the oven while it is being pre-heated. Placing in the bread, spray fresh water into the oven, using a plant sprayer. The baking time will vary, from 30-45 minutes, according to the size of the loaves and the type of flour that has been used. Brown bread usually needs more time. After 20 minutes, remove the bowl from the oven, reduce the temperature to 400°F and continue baking until completely done. To test for doneness, tap the bottom of each loaf with your knuckle. The bread should sound hollow. Remove it from the oven and cool it on a wire rack, to preserve the crispness of the crust.

The length of time bread will stay fresh depends on its size and ingredients used. Kept in a dry, well-ventilated bread box, plain bread will stay in good condition for at least a week. Enriched bread keeps a few days longer. In the refrigerator you may keep the bread for a couple of weeks. Bread freezes well if wrapped in tightly sealed plastic bags. Frozen bread will keep for several months. Allow it to thaw for 3-4 hours or heat it, wrapped in foil in a 400°F oven, for about 50 minutes before serving.

Traditional Sourdough Bread
in a Carrying Board, page 24

Easter Bread Rings, page 155
Easter Bread Rolls, page 32

Traditional Sourdough Starter
(Prozimi)

Yields enough starter to leaven 2$^{1}/_{2}$ lbs of dough
Preparation time 24-72 hours

1/2   oz fresh yeast or 2 teaspoons dry yeast
2   cups tepid water (100°F)
1/2   lb strong flour

Pour a little tepid water into a bowl and add the fresh yeast. With a fork, mash the yeast in the water forming a smooth, thoroughly blended paste. If using dry yeast, sprinkle the yeast granules into the water and leave it for 15-20 minutes to absorb water. Whisk it until it forms a smooth thin paste. In a large bowl, mix the yeast with the remaining tepid water and whisk in the flour to form a thick, pourable mixture. The mixture need not be absolutely smooth; any lumps will be broken down by the yeast's action. Cover the bowl with plastic wrap and leave the mixture to ferment in a warm place for at least 24 hours, at which time it should be frothy. At this stage, the starter can be used to leaven bread dough. However, you will have better results and a richer sourdough flavored bread if you let the starter stand for another 2-3 days. After this time, if the sourdough starter has not been used, it must be replenished. Simply whisk half the mixture with one cup of flour and enough water to restore it to a thick batter. Discard the other half. Cover and leave the mixture to ferment again at room temperature for a day, after which it will again be ready for use. The starter can be refrigerated for up to one week; refrigeration will inhibit fermentation and prevent the sourdough flavor from becoming too strong. The starter must be reactivated by adding flour and water and leaving it overnight in a warm place before use. When making bread with a sourdough starter, use four parts flour to one part starter. Sourdough starters can last indefinitely if replenished with flour and water once a week.
Alternate: You may substitute the rye flour for the strong wheat flour, to prepare Rye Sourdough Starter.

Wholemeal Bread
(Psomi Mavro)

Prepare the bread as in the recipe for the Village Greek Yellow Bread, substituting wholemeal flour for the country flour. Use the commercial yeast or a sourdough leaven. After the first rising, knead the dough 5 minutes and divide into 3 equal parts. Shape them into cylindrical or round loaves, cover and let them rise for about 50 minutes. Sprinkle the surface of the loaves with white flour, spreading it evenly with your palm. With a razor blade held vertically, make four parallel cuts about $^{1}/_{2}$ inch deep across the top of the loaves to give them extra crust and a decorative appearance. Bake the loaves and cool on a rack before you slice and freeze them.

Village Greek Yellow Bread
(Psomi Horiatiko)

Yields 3 small loaves
Preparation time 12 hours
Baking time 40-45 minutes

1   recipe, Traditional Sourdough Starter (page 23)
         or
1   oz fresh yeast or 1 tablespoon dry yeast
2$^{1}/_{2}$ lbs country or yellow flour
1   tablespoon salt
2$^{1}/_{2}$-3 cups tepid water (100°F)
2   tablespoons vegetable oil
2   tablespoons honey
2   tablespoons milk

To make this traditional Greek village bread, you must use country flour, or yellow flour as also it is called, which is a white wheat flour enriched with approximately 30-35 finely ground semolina. If you are not using the traditional sourdough starter that the recipe calls for, it is advisable to prepare the yeast the evening before, and let it stand in a warm place overnight. To prepare the yeast, work it with a fork into a bowl with 1 cup tepid water and mix in enough flour, to form a thick paste. If a refrigerated sourdough starter is used, it also must be reactivated the evening before. The next day, sift the flour and salt into a basin and make a well in the center. Pour in the yeast mixture, oil, honey, milk, and the remaining water. Gradually incorporate the flour from the sides of the well into the liquid, until a soft, sticky dough is formed. Turn the dough out on a cool working surface and knead it thoroughly, until it is elastic and glossy, about 15 minutes. Return it to the basin. Cover the basin with plastic wrap and leave the dough to rise in a warm place until doubled in bulk, 1$^{1}/_{2}$-2 hours, depending on temperature and humidity. The dough is ready when a finger pressed into it leaves a dent that will very slowly rise itself out. Punch the dough down, knead for a few minutes, and divide into 3 equal parts. Shape each part into a tapered cylindrical loaf and place them in an ungreased baking sheet, slightly apart, to allow space for rising. Cover the loaves with a damp cloth and let them rise again until doubled in bulk, about 45 minutes to 1 hour. With a razor blade or a sharp knife, make several $^{1}/_{2}$ inch deep slashes across the top of the loaves to give them extra crust. Bake in a 450°F oven. To help the breads rise even more when baking, place a wide bowl with hot water on the oven bottom so that steam is released into the oven as the water heats. After 20 minutes baking, remove the bowl, reduce the oven temperature to 400°F, and bake the loaves for an additional 20-25 minutes until golden brown. Remove the loaves from the oven, brush the tops with water using a pastry brush, and cool on a wire rack. You may wrap the loaves when cold, and store them in the freezer. They will keep well for several months. Slicing the loaves before freezing helps to defrost them easily. Also, you may defrost as much bread as needed each time.

Traditional Sourdough Bread
(Psomi Paradosiako)

Yields 3 small loaves
Preparation time 2-3 hours
Baking time 45 minutes

2$\frac{1}{2}$ lbs strong, plain flour
1   recipe, Sourdough Starter (page 23)
1   tablespoon salt
3   tablespoons honey
2   cups tepid water (100°F)

To reactivate the starter, which has been kept in the refrigerator, mix it into a bowl with 1 cup of the tepid water and 2 cups of the strong, plain flour. Cover the bowl and leave it in a warm place for at least 24 hours. Stir down the yeast dough and keep half of it in the refrigerator for your next baking. Sift the flour with the salt into a basin and make a well in the center. Pour in the yeast dough, honey, and the remaining water. Gradually incorporate flour from the sides of the well into the liquid until a cohesive mass is formed. Turn the mass out onto a floured work surface and knead hard for about 15 minutes, until it feels smooth and elastic to the touch. Put the dough back in the basin, cover with plastic wrap, and let it rise in a warm place until doubled in bulk, 1$\frac{1}{2}$-2 hours. To test if the dough has risen enough, press a finger into it; if the indentation remains, filling in very slowly, the dough is ready. Divide the dough into 3 equal parts. Knead each part into a ball, cover with a damp cloth, and let them rest for 10 minutes. Then shape them into 3 small loaves. Lay the loaves on a working surface covered with baking paper and cover them with two kitchen towels (the top one moistened). Leave in a warm place to rise until doubled in bulk, 45 minutes to 1 hour. With a razor blade, make 1-3 long, shallow slashes across the top of each loaf to increase the crust. Pre-heat the oven to 450°F and place an ungreased baking sheet in the center of the oven. Place a wide bowl with hot water on the bottom of the oven, while it preheats, to produce steam. A humid oven delays the crust 's formation and thereby promotes the loaves ' expansion during the first 15-20 minutes. Bake the loaves, two at a time if there is enough room in the oven, for approximately 45 minutes. After the first 20 minutes remove the bowl and reduce the oven temperature to 400°F for the rest of the baking time. The bread is done when the surface is golden brown and it sounds hollow when tapped on the bottom with the knuckles. Remove from the oven and brush the tops with a little water, using a pastry brush. Cool the bread on wire racks before slicing or storing. Wrapped after slicing in tightly sealed plastic bags, the Sourdough Bread keeps well for several months in the freezer.

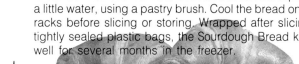

White Bread   (Psomi Lefko)

Prepare the White Bread as in the recipe for the Village Greek Yellow Bread (page 23), substituting strong white flour for the country flour. Use the commercial yeast leaven. After the first rising, knead the dough for 5 minutes. Then divide the dough into small, orange sized pieces and shape them into rounds, rotating your cupped hand on top of each piece of dough until it gathers up into a ball. Put 6 balls in a circle on a greased baking sheet, placing them about $\frac{1}{2}$ inch apart to make a daisy shaped bread. Or place the rounds, spaced well apart, on a greased baking sheet to make individual, small breads. The dough can be shaped also into plaited loaves or small individual spiral shaped rolls. Whatever the shape you have given the dough, cover and let it rise, until doubled in bulk. Brush the tops with a little milk or water and sprinkle with sesame or poppy seeds. Bake in a 440°F oven for about 20 minutes until the rolls are well browned. Cool on a wire rack before serving or storing.

Brown Bread
(Psomi Imilefko)

Yields 3 small loaves
Preparation time 2-3 hours
Baking time 25-30 minutes

1   oz fresh yeast or 1 tablespoon dry yeast
2   lbs strong flour
1/2   lb wholemeal flour
1   tablespoon salt
3   cups tepid water (100°F)
4   tablespoons vegetable oil
4   tablespoons evaporated milk
3   tablespoons honey

Mix the yeast with half cup of the tepid water and 3-4 tablespoons of the flour. Let it stand 10 minutes to rise. Sift both kinds of flour with the salt into a basin and make a well in the center. Pour in the yeast mixture, oil, milk, honey, and the remaining water. Gradually incorporate flour from the sides of the well into the liquid until all the flour is moist, and the mixture forms a stiff, sticky dough. Turn the dough out on a floured board and knead it thoroughly until it is elastic and glossy, about 15 minutes. Cover with plastic wrap and let the dough rise in a warm place until doubled in bulk, 1$\frac{1}{2}$-2 hours. Knead the dough once more for 5 minutes, and shape it into two large loaves or three smaller ones. Cover the loaves with two kitchen towels (the top one moistened) and let them rise until doubled in bulk. The loaves surface may be slashed or scored in decorative patterns or simply brushed with a little milk and sprinkled with sesame or onion seeds. Bake the loaves in a 400°F oven for 25-30 minutes. Remove them from the oven and cool on a rack before serving or storing. Stored in the freezer, the brown bread keeps well for several months.

Fluffy White Bread, page 26
Traditional Sourdough Bread, page 24
Village Greek Yellow Bread, page 23
Feta Cheese Croissants, page 35

Nut Bread
(Psomi me Karidia i Fistikia)

Yields one long loaf
Preparation time 2-3 hours
Baking time 35 minutes

1/3	recipe, White or Brown Bread Dough (page 24)
1	cup coarsely chopped walnuts or pistachio nuts, a little milk, sesame seeds

Mix and knead a White or Brown Bread Dough. Let it rise and knead it into a round. Cover with a damp cloth and let it rest for 10 minutes. On a lightly floured, wooden board, use a rolling pin to flatten the dough into an oblong 14 inches wide and less than 1 inch thick. Sprinkle the nuts on the surface and roll up the dough tightly, widthwise, to form a cylindrical loaf. Place the loaf on a greased baking sheet, cover with two kitchen towels (the top one dampened), and let it rise until doubled in bulk. Brush the top with a little milk and sprinkle with sesame seeds. Bake the bread in a 400°F oven for about 35 minutes. Remove the bread from the oven and cool on a rack. Sliced and wrapped in a tightly sealed plastic bag, the bread freezes well for several months.

Flatbread
(Lagana)

Yields 6 Flatbreads
Preparation time 12 hours
Baking time 20 minutes

1	oz fresh yeast or
1	tablespoon dry yeast
2¹/₂	cups tepid water (100°F)
2¹/₂	lbs country flour or soft flour
1	tablespoon salt
4	tablespoons olive oil
2	tablespoons sugar
	sesame seeds

Mix the yeast with 1 cup of the tepid water into a bowl. Add enough of the flour to form a thick paste. Cover with plastic wrap and leave it in a warm place overnight. Sift the flour and salt into a basin and make a well in the center. Pour in the raised yeast, oil, sugar, and the remaining tepid water. Gradually incorporate flour from the sides into the liquid until all the flour is moist. Knead the dough hard until it becomes, soft, elastic and easy to handle. Divide the dough into 6 balls, cover with a damp cloth and let them rise until doubled in bulk. With a rolling pin, flatten each ball on a floured, wooden board, shaping it into ¹/₂ inch thick oval or round bread. If the dough is too elastic and will not roll out easily, cover and let it relax 5-10 minutes. Place the flatbreads 2-3 together on greased baking sheets, cover with a damp cloth and let

Fluffy White Bread
(Psomi Politelias)

Yields 3-4 small loaves
Preparation time 2-3 hours
Baking time 30 minutes

1	oz fresh yeast or 1 tablespoon dry yeast
2¹/₂	lbs strong flour
1	cup tepid water (100°F)
1	tablespoon salt
4	tablespoons sugar
3	eggs, slightly beaten
1/2	cup tepid milk (100°F)
1/3	cup melted, unsalted butter
1	egg yolk beaten with 1 teaspoon water sesame or onion seeds

Mix the yeast with half cup of the tepid water and 3-4 tablespoons of the flour. Let it stand for 10 minutes to rise. Put the flour, sugar and salt into a basin and make a well in the center. Pour in the yeast mixture, milk, eggs, butter, and the remaining water. Mix all the ingredients together, gradually pulling the flour from the sides of the well, until a sticky dough is formed. Knead the dough thoroughly, on a floured working surface, until it loses its stickiness and becomes smooth and elastic, about 10 minutes. Cover and let the dough rise in a warm, humid place until it is three to four times its previous bulk, 1¹/₂-2 hours. Punch down the dough and divide into 3-4 parts. You may shape each part into a long cylindrical loaf or coil elongated dough cylinders into spirals. You may also braid together 2-3 elongated strands of dough to make decorative, plaited loaves. Place the loaves on greased baking sheets, cover and let them rise until they have nearly doubled in bulk. Brush the tops with a little egg yolk mixture and sprinkle with sesame or onion seeds. Bake the loaves in a 400°F oven for 25-30 minutes. Remove them from the oven and cool on wire racks. Wrapped and sealed tightly in plastic bags, they keep well in the freezer for several months.

them rise until doubled in bulk. Dust the surface with a little flour and press two fingers straight down to make fingerprints all over the tops. Brush with a little water and sprinkle with sesame seeds. Bake the flatbreads in a 400°F oven for 15-20 minutes. Because of their thinness, the flatbreads cook and dry quickly. Serve them the day they are made, preferably within minutes of their baking. Wrapped in tightly sealed plastic bags, the flatbreads can be kept in the freezer up to 3 months.

Flavored Bread, page 28
Nut Bread, page 26

Black Olive Bread (Eliopsomo)

Yields 1 long loaf
Preparation time 2-3 hours
Baking time 35 minutes

1/3   recipe, Brown Bread Dough (page 24)
2   tablespoons olive oil
1   cup sliced black Greek pitted olives

Mix and knead a Brown Bread Dough. Let it rise and
knead it into a round. Cover with a damp cloth and let it
rest for about 10 minutes. On a lightly floured wooden
board, use a rolling pin to flatten the dough into an
oblong 14 inches wide and less than 1 inch thick. Brush
the surface with the oil and sprinkle the sliced olives on
top. Roll up the dough tightly, widthwise, to form a
cylindrical loaf. Place the loaf on a greased baking sheet,
cover with two kitchen towels (the top one dampened),
and let it rise until doubled in bulk, about 45 minutes. With
a razor blade, make 7-8 parallel, diagonal cuts about $^1/_2$
inch deep across the loaves ' top. Bake the bread in a
400°F oven for about 35 minutes. Remove it from the
oven and cool on a wire rack. You may wrap it tightly in a
plastic bag and freeze it. Slicing the loaf before freezing,
helps to defrost as many slices as needed.

Feta Cheese Bread (Tiropsomo)

Follow the same procedure as in the recipe for the Black
Olive Bread substituting the olives with $1^1/_2$ cups crumbled feta cheese. Use brown bread dough as well as
white bread dough.

Flavored Bread
(Psomi me Mirodika)

Yields 3 long loaves
Preparation time 2-3 hours
Baking time 35 minutes

1   recipe, White or Brown Bread Dough (page 24)
1   tablespoon aniseeds or onion seeds
2   teaspoons cinnamon
1/4   teaspoon nutmeg
1   teaspoon garlic powder
1   teaspoon origan
      a little milk, sesame or onion seeds

Mix and knead a White or Brown Bread Dough. Let it rise.
Punch down the dough and divide into 3 equal parts.
Knead each part into a round, cover, and let them rest for
about 15 minutes. On a lightly floured working surface,
use a rolling pin to flatten the doughs less than 1 inch
thick each. Sprinkle the aniseeds onto the first flattened
dough round, the cinnamon and nutmeg onto the
second, and garlic powder with the origan onto the third.
Roll up the doughs tightly to form 3 tapered, cylindrical
loaves. Place the loaves on greased baking sheets,
cover with two kitchen towels (the top one dampened),
and let them rise until doubled in bulk, about 45 minutes.
With a razor blade, make a few parallel, diagonal slashes
across the loaves ' top, if desired. Brush the tops with a
little milk and sprinkle with sesame or onion seeds. Bake
the breads in a 400°F oven, for about 35 minutes.
Remove from the oven and cool on wire racks before
slicing or storing. Wrapped and sealed tightly in plastic
bags, the bread keeps well for several months in the
freezer.

Cornmeal Bread (Bobota)

Yields 2 small loaves
Preparation time 10 minutes
Baking time 30 minutes

2   cups fine cornmeal
2   cups self raising flour
2   tablespoons sugar
4   tablespoons baking powder
1/2   teaspoon salt
2   eggs, slightly beaten
2   cups milk
1/4   cup vegetable oil
1   cup sultana raisins (optional)

Mix all the dry ingredients in a bowl and make a well in
the center. Add the eggs, milk and oil and stir with a
spoon, gradually incorporating the flour from the sides
into the liquid until well blended. Mix in the raisins. Divide
the mixture into two well greased and floured bread pans

(4 by 9 inches), or spread the dough in a 12 inch round baking pan. Bake in a 400°F oven for 25-30 minutes until golden brown. Serve the cornmeal bread warm, preferably on the day it is made. You may freeze the leftover bread.

Metsovo Cornmeal Pita
(Kalambokopita Metsovou)

Serves 20
Preparation time 1 hour
Baking time 1 hour

4   cups milk
2   cups fine corn meal
1½   cups grated kasseri cheese
1½   cups crumbled feta cheese
1   cup steamed, well drained spinach (optional)
1/2   cup unsalted butter or margarine
        salt and pepper
1   teaspoon baking soda dissolved in
2   tablespoons milk

6   eggs, separated
1/2   teaspoon cream of tartar or
2   tablespoons lemon juice

Heat 2 cups of the milk in a small pot and set aside. Stir the cornmeal into the remaining cold milk in a saucepan and place over medium heat. Pour in the hot milk, stirring constantly with a wire whisk and cook the mixture, until thickened. Remove the pan from the heat. Stir in the grated cheeses, butter, spinach, seasoning, and baking soda. Let the mixture cool slightly and stir in the egg yolks. Put the egg whites with the cream of tartar into the mixing bowl of an electric mixer and beat until they form soft peaks. If using lemon juice, add it gradually while the egg whites are beaten. Stir 1-2 tablespoonfuls of the whites into the cornmeal mixture to loosen, and fold in the rest gently. Pour the batter into a well greased and floured 14 inch round baking pan and bake in a 330°F oven for approximately 1 hour. In Metsovo the pita is baked under a domed earthenware pre- heated pot which is called "Gastra". Let the pita stand for 10 minutes before serving. Serve at once.

Flavored Bread, page 28

Natural Sourdough Bread (Psomi Eptazimo)

Yields two loaves
Preparation time 15 hours
Baking time 30 minutes

2/3	cup chick peas (from the health food store)
1 1/2	tablespoons salt
4	tablespoons olive oil
1 1/2	cups tepid water (100°F)
3	lbs strong flour
7	tablespoons sugar
1	egg yolk beaten with 1 teaspoon water

My mother, as most housewives all around Greece, prepared the "Eptazimo" using a natural yeast that she cultivated, combining chick peas and water. "Eptazimo" was a white, aromatic bread, with a golden brown crust. Everytime my mother brought it home, fresh from the oven, its flavor filled the house, and its fine texture was fully appreciated by all. To cultivate the yeast from chick peas was not always successful. Therefore, my mother would mix chick peas and water into 3 jars, so that she could use the frothiest ones, having the most pleasant, sour flavor of chick peas. Some housewives used only the froth with a little of the liquid to make the starter. Others added the chick peas also, after liquidizing them. The yeast and the dough should be kept warm. Therefore, the kitchen door remained closed from the moment my mother started kneading the bread, until it was baked. As the cultivation of the natural yeast out of the chick peas was not always successful, each failure was superstitiously attributed to the "Evil Eye" that was given to the bread by a friend or neighbor. Even today, some Greek village women will not tell anyone that they are baking "Eptazimo". They bake the bread secretly, late at night, to prevent their efforts being wasted by someone giving the bread the "Evil Eye".

To cultivate the yeast, crush the chick peas into coarse pieces. Put them with 1/4 teaspoon of the salt in a tall, sterilized jar, and pour over 3 cups boiling water. Stir the mixture well, cover the jar and fold in a blanket. Leave it in a very warm place for 24-48 hours, until the chick peas puff up and the froth on top of the liquid measures approximately 1 1/2 inches. If there is no froth, and the liquid has turned orange in color, throw it away and make a new batch. To speed up the procedure, place the jar in an oven which has been heated to 100°F, for 6-7 hours. Strain and discard the peas. Add 1 tablespoon sugar and enough flour, into the liquid, to form a light paste. Cover and let it stand in a warm place overnight. The mixture is ready when it is spongy and has a pleasant, sour smell. Sift the flour with the remaining salt into a large basin and make a well in the center. Drop in the remaining sugar, the oil, yeast sponge mixture and tepid water (100°F). In Florina, a northern Macedonian Village, a sprig of dried basil and 1 small hot pepper are boiled in the water, for flavoring, before it is used. In other Macedonian villages, bay leaves or aniseeds are used. Mix the flour with the liquid, pulling it gradually from the sides, and kneading the dough until it is elastic and easy to handle, about 15 minutes. Divide and shape the dough into 2 cylindrical or round loaves. Place the loaves into two well-greased bread baking pans twice as large as the unrisen dough. Cover, with a greaseproof paper and a blanket, and let them stand in a warm place for approximately 2 hours, until the loaves are doubled in volume. Brush the tops with the egg yolk mixture and sprinkle with a little sugar. Bake the bread in a 450°F oven for 10 minutes. Reduce the heat to 400°F and bake 20 minutes longer. Unmold and cool the loaves on a rack. "Eptazimo" keeps fresh longer than ordinary bread and does not get moldy. You may store it in the bread box or freezer as desired.

Raisin Bread Rolls (Stafidopsoma)

Yields 26 small rolls or 2 loaves
Preparation time 3 hours
Baking time 20 minutes

1	cup milk
1/4	cup melted, unsalted butter or margarine
1/2	cup sugar
2	tablespoons grated lemon rind (optional)
1	teaspoon salt
1/2	teaspoon baking soda
1	oz fresh yeast or 1 tablespoon dry yeast
1	cup tepid water (100°F)
6-7	cups strong flour
2	cups black currants, washed and dried
1	egg yolk beaten with 1 tablespoon water

Boil the milk and stir in the butter, sugar, peel, salt and soda. Set aside to cool until lukewarm. Dissolve the yeast in the tepid water and add enough of the flour to make a thick, pourable paste. Cover and leave it in a warm place to rise until doubled in bulk, about 10 minutes. Sift the remaining flour into a large basin and make a well in the center. Pour in the yeast mixture and the milk mixture. Gradually incorporate the flour from the sides of the well into the liquid and knead the dough thoroughly, until it is smooth and elastic, about 10 minutes. Place the dough in a greased bowl and brush the surface with a little butter. Cover the bowl and let the dough rise in a warm place until doubled in bulk, 1 1/2-2 hours depending on temperature and humidity. Punch down the dough and divide it in half. With a rolling pin, flatten each half on a floured, wooden board, into 1/2 inch thick rounds. Sprinkle with the raisins and roll the rounds up tightly. Place into two greased bread pans or divide into 26 equal portions. Form each portion into a broad cigar shape, rolling the dough backwards and forwards under your fingers. Place the rolls well apart on greased or lined baking sheets. Cover with a damp cloth and let them rise until they are doubled in bulk, about 30 minutes. Brush the rolls with the egg yolk mixture and sprinkle with sesame seeds. Bake in a 400°F oven for about 20 minutes or until they are lightly browned. Transfer them to a wire rack to cool before serving or storing. Wrapped and sealed tightly in plastic bags, the rolls can keep well for several months in the freezer.

Alternate: Use the same dough to make jam filled croissants.

Easter Sweet Bread (Tsoureki)

Yields 8 plaited loaves
Preparation time 2 hours
Baking time 20 minutes

7	oz fresh yeast or
6	tablespoons dry yeast
1	cup tepid water (100°F)
5	lbs strong flour
3$\frac{1}{3}$	cups sugar
2	teaspoons salt
2	tablespoons vegetable oil
1	tablespoon ground muhlep
1	teaspoon ground cardamom
1	cup scalded milk
10	eggs, at room temperature
1$\frac{3}{4}$	cups warm, melted, unsalted butter
2	egg yolks beaten with 2 teaspoons water

Mix the yeast with the tepid water in a bowl. Add enough of the flour to form a thick paste. Cover the bowl and leave the mixture in a warm, humid place, until doubled in bulk, about 30 minutes. Put the sugar, salt, oil, and flavoring into a large kneading basin. Pour in the scalded milk and stir with a spoon. Break in the eggs; with your fingers, crush the yolks and combine the eggs with the other ingredients. Add and mix in the yeast mixture. Then add the flour in 2-3 stages, working the mixture with your hands until all the flour is moistened, and a warm, soft and sticky dough is formed. Using both hands, take handfuls of the warm, melted butter, pour it over the dough, folding and kneading it until all the butter has been incorporated into the dough. Avoid overworking the dough. Traces of butter remaining in the dough will be absorbed during the rising. The dough, must be warm, light and buttery. Cover the basin with a grease proof paper, then wrap it into a blanket. Let the dough rise, until it is three to four times its previous bulk, 1-2$\frac{1}{2}$ hours. Divide the dough into 24 equal portions. Cover with a kitchen towel. On a floured work surface, shape 3 pieces into long strands and braid them together. Continue shaping and braiding the remaining dough portions, until all of them are used and 8 plaited loaves are made. Place the loaves well apart on greased or lined baking sheets, cover and leave them in a warm place until doubled in bulk, about 45 minutes. Brush the surface of each loaf with the egg yolk mixture and sprinkle with thinly sliced blanched almonds, if desired. Bake the loaves in a 400°F oven for about 20 minutes. Avoid overbaking as they dry quickly. Cool the loaves on wire racks before slicing or storing.

Alternate: Substitute the flavoring with 1$\frac{1}{2}$ teaspoons vanilla or ground mastic or with 4 tablespoons grated citrus rind.

Easter Sweet Bread, page 31
Greek Easter Cookies, page 135
Croissants, page 32
Raisin Bread Rolls, page 30

Easter Bread Rolls
(Paschalina Tsourekakia)

Yields 30-40 rolls, depending on the size
Preparation time 2-3 hours
Baking time 10-12 minutes

1/2	recipe, Easter Sweet Bread Dough (page 30)
2	egg yolks, beaten with 2 teaspoons of water
	a few blanched almonds, halved
10	small crystallized Seville oranges
2/3	cup mixed chopped nuts and raisins

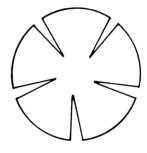

Prepare an Easter Sweet Bread Dough, let it rise, and divide it into four equal parts.

To make the daisies: Divide the dough into small, equal portions, about the size of a large egg. Roll the dough pieces on a floured board, beneath your cupped palm to shape small balls. Flatten each ball lightly with a rolling pin or by hand. Then make five cuts around, at five equal intervals to form the daisy's petal, as shown in the diagram. Put the flower on a greased or lined baking sheet. Holding each petal with your fingers, twist it to make it more pronounced. Roll and shape the rest of dough pieces in the same way. Cover and let them rise until doubled in volume, about 30 minutes. Brush the tops with the egg yolk mixture and place half almond on each petal. Bake in a 400°F oven 10-12 minutes. Cool on a rack.

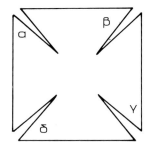

To make the windmills: Roll out the dough, on a floured board, into a square sheet $1/2$ inch thick. With a dough scraper, divide the sheet into 4 inch squares. Make a diagonal cut in each corner to about $1/2$ inch from the center of the square as shown in the diagram. Brush the surface with a little egg yolk mixture and place a small crystallized Seville orange in the center. Folding in one direction, turn one halved corner of each angle (marked a,b,c,d) over the tiny Seville orange. Leave the other half unfolded. Lightly press the folded corners to seal, and secure by inserting a toothpick. Place the windmills, well apart, on a greased or lined baking sheet. Cover and let them rise, until doubled in volume, about 30 minutes. Brush the tops with the egg yolk mixture and bake in a 400°F oven, 10-12 minutes. Cool on a rack and remove the toothpicks.

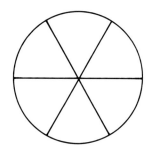

To make the croissants: Roll out the dough, on a floured board with a rolling pin, into a round, about $1/2$ inch thick. Cut it into 6-8 wedges as shown in the diagram. Place a tablespoonful of the nut and raisin mixture on the broad part of each wedge. Starting from this point, roll up towards the apex. Arrange the rolls on a greased or lined baking sheet with the folded edge just under the roll and bend the ends slightly inwards to form a crescent. Cover and let them rise until doubled in volume, about 30 minutes. Brush the tops with the egg yolk mixture and bake in a 400°F oven for 10-12 minutes. Cool on a rack.

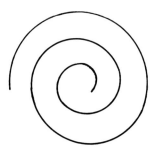

To make the spirals: Divide the dough into small, equal portions about the size of a mandarin. On a floured

board, roll and shape the dough pieces into long strands. Coil each dough strand into a spiral, tapering the free end and folding it just under the roll. Arrange the rolls on a greased or lined baking sheet, cover, and let them rise until doubled in bulk, about 30 minutes. Brush with the egg yolk mixture and bake in a 400°F oven for 10-12 minutes. Cool on a rack.

Whatever the shape, all the rolls can be wrapped, sealed tightly in plastic bags, and stored in the freezer. They keep well several months.

Easter Bread Rolls, page 32

Yeast Pancakes
(Tiganites me Mayia - Lalagites)

Yields 20-30 pancakes
Preparation time 2 hours
Frying time 5-7 minutes each

1/2   oz fresh yeast or 1/2 tablespoon dry yeast
1/2   cup tepid milk (100°F)
1   lb strong flour
1/2   teaspoon baking soda
1/2   teaspoon salt
2   tablespoons sugar
1   cup yogurt
2   eggs, lightly beaten
        vegetable oil or margarine for frying
        honey, jam or sugar and cinnamon

Dissolve the yeast in the tepid milk and leave it until the mixture is frothy. Sift the flour, soda, and salt into a large mixing bowl and make a well in the center. Put in the sugar, yogurt, eggs and the yeast mixture. Gradually incorporate flour from the sides of the well into the liquid until all the flour is moist. Knead the dough until it is soft and easy to handle. It must be softer than the bread dough. Grease the interior of a large, plastic bag and seal the dough inside, leaving enough room for expansion. Put the bag in the refrigerator. After 1$\frac{1}{2}$-2 hours, the dough will be ready to make the pancakes. On a floured kneading cloth, flatten small pieces of dough, the size of a small tangerine, into $\frac{1}{2}$ inch thick rounds. Heat a little oil or margarine in a heavy bottomed fry pan and fry the pancakes on both sides until golden. Fry as many as needed and serve them immediately covered either with honey, or jam, or sprinkled with sugar and cinnamon. Put the remaining dough in the refrigerator to use the next day. It keeps well for 3-4 days.

Phyllo Dough
(Zimi gia Fillo)

Yields about 1 lb
Preparation time 2-3 hours

1   lb all purpose flour
2   teaspoons salt
2   teaspoons baking powder (optional)
2   tablespoons olive oil
1   tablespoon vinegar
1   cup warm water

Sift the flour, salt and baking powder into a large mixing bowl. Make a well in the center and pour in the oil, vinegar, and water. Gradually incorporate flour from the sides of the well into the liquid until all the flour is moist. Knead the mixture adding more water, if necessary, to make a soft and elastic dough. Divide it into small balls, according to the number of phyllo sheets you desire and according to the size of the pan utilized. Place the balls in a floured pan, one next to the other, cover with a damp cloth, and let the dough rest for 1-2 hours. Using a special, very long and thin rolling pin called "plasti," flatten each ball first, on a floured board, called "plastiri", into a small, thick, round phyllo. Rolling repeatedly this phyllo around the rolling pin, press lightly and roll backwards and forwards, working in all directions until it is stretched to an extremely thin, transluscent sheet. To prevent sticking, spread a little flour on the surface of the sheet frequently. To make pita phyllo sheets more easily, you can roll out 3 small rounds at a time, stacked one on top of the other, and brushed generously with oil or melted butter in between. The 3 layers of phyllo will separate when baking. Therefore, the dough becomes flaky and crisp.

Leavened Puff Pastry
(Zimi Sfoliata me Mayia)

Yields about 1lb
Preparation time 3-5 hours

1   oz fresh yeast or one tablespoon dry yeast
2   tablespoons sugar
1   cup tepid milk (100°F)
4   cups strong flour
1   teaspoon salt
2   tablespoons vegetable oil
2   eggs
2/3   cup soft, cold, unsalted butter

Dissolve the yeast with the sugar in the tepid milk and let it stand until it becomes frothy. Sift the flour with the salt into a large bowl and make a well in the center. Pour in the oil, eggs and yeast mixture. With your fingers, break the yolks and combine the eggs with the liquid. Stir the ingredients together by hand, gradually pulling in the flour from the sides of the well to make a loose dough. Knead the dough until it is soft and easy to handle. It may be necessary to add more flour. Cover and let the dough rise until doubled in volume, 1$\frac{1}{2}$-2 hours. Punch the dough down and knead it for 5 minutes. On a floured board, roll out the dough into a rectangle about $\frac{1}{3}$ inch thick. With a spatula spread $\frac{1}{3}$ of the soft butter on the dough over half its length, leaving a $\frac{2}{3}$ inch wide margin around the edges. Moisten the margin with a little water and fold the dough in half, enclosing the butter. Lightly press the edges around with your fingertips to seal in the butter and prevent it from escaping. Rolling lightly, flatten the dough once more and spread half the remaining butter over half the surface of dough. Fold and seal the dough, as previously, enclosing the butter. Repeat the procedure once more using the left over butter. Sprinkle the surface of the dough with flour, brushing the excess carefully before each rolling, to prevent sticking. Prick the dough in the center with a wooden skewer to release any trapped air. Enclose it in a large, plastic bag, leaving enough room for expansion, and put it in the refrigerator. After one hour, the dough is ready for shaping, rising and baking.

Walnut and Honey Croissants
(Krouasan me Karidia ke Meli)

Serves 16
Preparation time 3-5 hours
Baking time 20 minutes

1	recipe, Leavened Puff Pastry (page 34)
1¹/₂	cups coarsely chopped walnuts
1	teaspoon cinnamon
1/2	teaspoon cloves
4-5	tablespoons honey
1	egg yolk beaten with 1 teaspoon water

The Glaze

1	cup confectioners ' sugar
1	teaspoon vanilla
1	egg white, slightly beaten

Prepare the Leavened Puff Pastry according to the recipe. Divide it into two equal parts and flatten each part, rolling with a pin on a floured surface, into a ¹/₃ inch thick round. Cut each round into 6-8 wedges as shown in the diagram. Mix the walnuts and spices into a bowl and add enough honey to make a stiff mixture. Put one tablespoonful of the mixture on the wide part of each wedge and roll it up loosely towards the apex, enclosing the walnuts. Place the croissants spaced well apart, folded edge down, on greased or lined baking sheets. Form croissants by bending the ends slightly inwards. Cover them and leave in a warm, humid place until doubled in bulk. Brush the tops with the egg yolk mixture and put them in a 450°F oven. After 5 minutes, reduce the temperature to 350°F and bake for 15-20 minutes until golden brown. Serve the croissants warm, accompanied by additional honey, or cover them with a little glaze, if desired.

The Glaze: Sift the sugar into a small bowl, add the vanilla and as much egg white as necessary to form a stiff mixture, stirring constantly with a spoon. Put the croissants on a rack and glaze the tops while they are still warm. The glaze will melt and cover the whole surface. You may freeze the croissants, unglazed, after they cool. They keep well several months.

Feta Cheese Croissants
Prepare the Feta Cheese Croissants according to the previous recipe, substituting the walnut and honey mixture with 2 cups crumbled Feta cheese. Serve them warm, preferably in minutes after their baking.

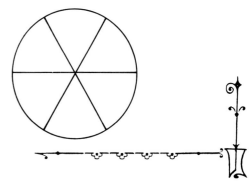

Walnut and Honey Croissants, page 35

Salonika's Sesame Bread Rings
(Koulouria Thessalonikis)

Yields 40-50 bread rings
Preparation time 24 hours
Baking time 15 minutes

1/2	oz fresh yeast or
1 1/2	teaspoons dry yeast
2 1/2	cups tepid water (100°F)
2	lbs all purpose flour
2	teaspoons salt
1/4	cup vegetable oil
1/3	cup sugar
1/2	lb sesame seeds

All over Salonika, these are sold at street stands. They used to be sold by hawkers, but now it is more common for the vendors to leave the supply of koulouria unattended with only a sign announcing the price and they trust in the honor system-customers helping themselves and leaving money in the box provided.

Dissolve half the yeast in 1/2 cup tepid water, stir in 3-4 tablespoons flour and leave the mixture covered in a warm place for 24 hours. When you are ready to knead the dough, dissolve the remaining yeast in 1/2 cup tepid water, mix in 3-4 tablespoons flour and let it rise about 15 minutes. Sift the flour with the salt into a kneading bowl and make a well in the center. Pour in both yeast mixtures, oil and remaining water. Add also the sugar. Gradually, incorporate flour from the sides of the well into the liquid until all the flour is moist and the mixture is a soft, sticky dough. Knead the dough thoroughly, until it is elastic and glossy, about 15 minutes. Cover it with plastic wrap and leave in a warm place until doubled in bulk. Punch the dough down to expel the bubbles of air. Divide the dough in half. On a lightly floured working surface, use a rolling pin to flatten each dough into an oblong shape about 10 inches long and 2/3 inch thick. With a sharp floured knife, cut the dough along its length into 2/3 inch strips. Roll each strip back and forth beneath your fingers, moving them along its length to keep the shape even, until a strip about 1/2 inch thick and 14 inches long is obtained. Brush the strips all around with tap water and roll in sesame seeds. Press the two ends together to join and shape a ring. Place the rings on a greased baking sheet, cover with a cloth and let them rise, about 20 minutes. Bake the bread rings in a 440°F oven for 10-15 minutes, until crisp and golden brown outside, but soft inside. Transfer the baked rings to a wire rack and serve them preferably warm, or fresh on the day they are made. You may wrap and freeze the leftovers.

Crispy Bread Sticks   (Kritsinia)

Yields 30 sticks
Preparation time 24 hours
Baking time 20-25 minutes

1/2	oz fresh yeast or
1 1/2	teaspoons dry yeast
1 1/3	cups tepid water (100°F)
1	lb flour
1	teaspoon salt
1	teaspoon baking powder
1/3	cup sugar
1/3	cup melted, unsalted butter
1/3	cup vegetable oil
1/2	lb sesame seeds

Prepare the dough as in the recipe for Salonica 's Sesame Bread Rings . Sift the baking powder with the flour and salt. Shape the dough into 1/2 inch thick and 8 inch long sticks. Brush them all around with tap water and roll in sesame seeds. Place them on a buttered baking sheet, cover with a cloth and let them rise briefly, about 10 minutes. Bake the sticks in a 400°F oven for 10-15 minutes. Reduce the temperature to 300°F and let them dry for about 10 minutes or until golden-brown and crispy. Transfer the baked breadsticks to a wire rack to cool. Keep in a biscuit tin.

Basic Shortcrust Pastry Dough
(Zimi Tartas 1)

Yields one 11 inch crust
Preparation time 15 minutes
Baking time 15 minutes

1 1/3	cups all purpose flour
1/8	teaspoon salt
2	tablespoons sugar
1	teaspoon vanilla or grated lemon rind
1/2	cup shortening or unsalted butter, chilled and cubed

Crispy Bread Sticks, page 36
Salonica's Sesame Bread Rings, page 36

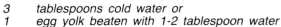

3　　　tablespoons cold water or
1　　　egg yolk beaten with 1-2 tablespoon water

Sift the flour, salt, and sugar into a bowl. Add the shortening or butter and rub it with the flour using your fingertips and thumbs, until the mixture resembles very coarse bread crumbs. Sprinkle the water or the beaten egg yolk over the dough, add the flavoring, and mix lightly until it just begins to cohere. The dough should feel crumbly. Do not knead. Just gather all the crumbs from the sides of the bowl into a ball, pressing them together with your hands. Roll out the dough on a floured surface to form an 11 inch round crust. It is better to roll it out on a lightly floured pastry cloth (canvas) to prevent sticking. Lifting up the cloth, you can easily turn the crust over on a 9 inch ungreased pie dish and line it with the dough. Cut a long strip of aluminum foil and cover the rim of the pie dish together with the dough, fasten it by folding half the strip outside, to prevent shrinking. Pierce the pastry all over with a fork, to create holes through which steam can escape, and bake in a 400°F oven for about 15-20 minutes until crisp and golden. Five minutes before the pastry is done, remove the foil strip, to allow the edge of the shortcrust to become crisp and golden, too. The dough also can be kept unbaked in a plastic bag for 3 days in the refrigerator or 3 months in the freezer. Shortcrust pastry pre-baked or unbaked, depending on the filling you use, is a perfect casing for various pies and tarts.

Rich Shortcrust Pastry Dough
(Zimi Tartas 2)

Yields two 11 inch crusts
Preparation time 30 minutes

3　　　cups all purpose flour
1　　　teaspoon baking powder
1　　　cup unsalted butter or margarine
1/3　　cup sugar
2　　　egg yolks
2　　　tablespoons brandy
1　　　tablespoon grated lemon rind or
1　　　teaspoon vanilla or any flavor desired

Sift together the flour and the baking powder into a bowl. Cream the butter with an electric mixer. Add the sugar and beat them together until the mixture is pale and fluffy. To ensure that all the sugar is blended in, scrape the sides of the bowl with a rubber spatula from time to time. Add the egg yolks one by one. Then add the brandy and the flavoring. Stop beating, and fold in the flour a little at a time, with a wooden spoon, blending it evenly into the mixture. When the dough becomes too stiff to stir, mix the flour by hand until the dough is light and smooth. Avoid overworking the dough. This would strengthen the gluten, making the dough tough when baked. The Rich Shortcrust Dough can be shaped as casings for various tarts with jam and dried fruits or it can be rolled out in many ways to crunchy, mouth melting biscuits.

Pancakes (Tiganites)

Serves 4-6
Preparation time 10 minutes
Baking time 5-7 minutes for each pancake

3　　　eggs
2　　　tablespoons sugar
1　　　cup milk or yogurt
2　　　cups self raising flour, sifted
　　　　vegetable oil for frying
　　　　honey and cinnamon

Beat the eggs with the sugar lightly, add one third of the milk and stir well. Add a little flour alternately and some more milk, stirring continuously. Add more flour and milk until all are incorporated into a thick batter having the consistency of heavy cream. Heat a little oil or margarine in a heavy-bottomed, large skillet and drop in several spoonfuls of the batter. Leave about 2 inches between them to allow room for expansion. Fry the pancakes on both sides until golden. Remove with a slotted spoon and drain on paper toweling. Serve warm, spread with honey, and sprinkled with cinnamon.

Crepe Batter (Krepes)

Yields 22-26 crepes
Preparation time 30 minutes
Frying time 1 minute for each crepe

1 1/2　cups flour
1/4　　teaspoon salt
1　　　teaspoon sugar
3　　　eggs, lightly beaten
1　　　tablespoon brandy
1 1/2　cups milk
2　　　tablespoons melted, unsalted butter

Sift the flour and salt into the mixing bowl. Add the sugar, eggs, brandy and 4 tablespoons milk. Beat the mixture at a low speed as long as it takes to produce a smooth, thick batter. Avoid overbeating. Add the remaining milk and melted butter. Whisk the mixture only until smooth and thin. The crepe batter should have the consistency of a light cream. If necessary, add a little more milk. Cover the bowl and chill for 30 minutes. If you have a crepe maker, use it. Otherwise use a non-stick pan. Wipe the pan with an oiled cloth and place over medium heat. When a light haze forms above the pan, ladle in just enough batter to cover the bottom and tilt the pan with a rolling motion to spread the batter as thinly as possible. When the crepe 's upper surface looks dry and lacy, and the edges begin to curl, turn the crepe over. The second side will cook even faster than the first. Avoid overfrying. The crepes should remain soft. Stir the batter before ladling another crepe. Stack the crepes on top of each other in a shallow dish. Covered with plastic wrap, they will keep well one week in the refrigerator, and several months in the freezer.

Butter Sponge Cake (Pandespani Voutirou)

Yields one 2 by 10 inch round cake
Preparation time 10 minutes
Baking time 30 minutes

4	eggs, separated
1/2	cup castor sugar
1	teaspoon vanilla or other flavoring
1	cup self raising flour
1	teaspoon baking powder
1/4	cup melted, unsalted butter

Beat the egg whites at high speed with an electric mixer. When the whites begin to form soft peaks, gradually add the castor sugar. Continue to whisk until the meringue forms stiff peaks and becomes smooth and glossy. Then add the egg yolks, one by one, and the flavoring. Stop the mixer. Sift the remaining dry ingredients together first. Then sift them into the beaten eggs, in two or three stages, and fold in gently. With a slow motion, starting from the center of the mixture, draw the spoon along the bottom of the bowl, and bring it up around the sides. Continue folding in the butter, a tablespoonful at a time, until it is well blended. If you are not using a mixer, beat the egg yolks with half the sugar by hand until light and lemon colored. Add the butter gradually. Then add the flour, sifted with the baking powder, in two stages alternately with the egg whites, whisked into a firm meringue with the remaining sugar. Pour the batter into a 10 inch round cake pan or into two smaller pans, lined with greased baking paper. Bake the cake in a 350°F oven for 20-30 minutes until it begins to shrink from the sides of the pan. Let it cool on a wire rack. You may store the cake wrapped, in the refrigerator or freezer. It will keep for one week in the refrigerator and several months in the freezer. Alternatively, you may flavor the cake with almond extract or grated citrus rind depending on the occasion. To make a chocolate flavored sponge cake, simply replace a quarter or half of the flour with unsweetened cocoa powder. Sift the flour and cocoa together first, to combine them thoroughly, before folding into the batter. Butter Sponge Cake cut in layers, filled with flavored cream, decorated with garlands of icing or fruits provides a variety of fancy, delicious layer cakes and log cakes.

Whole Egg Sponge Cake
(Pandespani Aplo 1)

Yields one 2 by 10 inch round cake
Preparation time 30 minutes
Baking time 30 minutes

4	eggs
2/3	cup castor sugar
1	cup self raising flour
1	teaspoon vanilla

Put the eggs and the sugar into the mixing bowl of an electric mixer. Beat them togehter at high speed, about 15 minutes, until thick and fluffy. Add the flavoring and stop beating. Sift the flour into the egg mixture, a little at a

time, and fold it gently. If the flour were added all at once or the mixture folded too strenuously at this stage, much of the air beaten into the eggs would be lost and the cake would not rise when baked. Pour the batter into a 10 inch lined spring-form tin to help unmold the cake easily. Do not grease the sides of the tin. Bake the cake in a 350°F oven for approximately 30 minutes, until the top is golden and feels springy. Before removing from the oven, test the cake with a wooden pick. If it comes out clean, the cake is done. Let the cake cool 5 minutes in the tin. Then run a knife around the inner edge of the tin to loosen the cake. Unlock the spring and gently lift off the ring. Turn the cake onto a wire rack. Lift off the base of the spring-form tin and peel away the greaseproof lining paper. Cool the cake completely, then cut it into two or three layers. Wrapped in plastic film, it will keep 3-4 days in the refrigerator and 6 months in the freezer.
Alternatively, you may flavor the cake with grated citrus rind, almond extract or brandy depending on the occasion. To make a chocolate flavored sponge cake, simply replace a quarter of the flour with unsweetened cocoa powder. Sift the flour and cocoa together first, to combine them thoroughly, before folding into the batter. Sponge cake can be cut and decorated in many ways, to provide various layer cakes.

Cocoa Sponge Cake
(Pandespani Sokolatenio)

Yields one 12 by 16 inch rectangular sheet
Preparation time 20 minutes
Baking time 20 minutes

2	tablespoons flour
1	cup unsweetened cocoa powder
1	tablespoon baking powder
8	eggs
1 1/2	cups sugar
1/4	teaspoon almond extract or
1	teaspoon vanilla

Sift together the flour, cocoa and baking powder into a bowl. Set aside. Put the eggs with the sugar into the mixing bowl of an electric mixer. Beat them at high speed for approximately 15 minutes, until the mixture is thick and pale. Add the flavoring and stop beating. Gradually sift in the previously sifted ingredients. Use a metal spoon or a whisk to fold in the ingredients gently. Starting from the center of the mixture, draw the spoon along the bottom of the bowl and bring it up around the sides. Continue until the ingredients are blended. Pour the mixture, spreading it evenly, into a lined 12 by 16 inch shallow, Swiss roll tin or into two 10 inch round baking pans, depending on the occasion. Bake the cake in a 375°F oven 20-25 minutes until it feels springy and begins to shrink from the sides of the tin. Remove from the oven and turn the cake out onto a marble surface. Peel off the paper and cover the cake with a cloth to keep moist. Let it cool. Cocoa Sponge Cake filled and decorated with cream and fruits, provides marvelous log cakes as illustrated on page 78.

Choux Pastry Dough (Zimi Sou)

Yields 20 to 40 puffs, depending on the size
Preparation time 20 minutes
Baking time 35-40 minutes

1	cup water
1/2	cup unsalted butter
1/2	teaspoon salt
1	cup strong flour
4	eggs

Put the water, butter and salt in a small deep saucepan over high heat and bring to a boil, stirring constantly until the butter is melted. Turn off the heat and add all the flour at once, stirring vigorously with a wooden spoon for about 1 minute, until the mixture forms a solid mass that comes away cleanly from the sides of the pan. Remove the pan from the heat and empty the batter into the mixer bowl. Let it cool for 2-3 minutes. Then beat the batter with the dough hook, adding the eggs one by one, beating well after each addition to incorporate each egg thoroughly. Continue beating until all eggs are added and the ingredients are smoothly blended to a satiny mass that will drop very slowly from the spoon. Grease your hands with butter, shape the dough into small balls and arrange them on a baking sheet lined with baking paper. Or spoon the batter into a piping bag fitted with a $^1/_2$ inch plain nozzle, and pipe the dough into rosettes, or 2 to 3 inch long strips or any other shapes desired. Leave about $1^1/_2$ inches between them to allow room for expansion. Bake at 425°F for 15 minutes, then reduce the heat to 300°F and bake 15-20 minutes more, to complete the baking and to dry out the inside of the pastries. Cool on a wire rack. You may place them in plastic bags and store in the freezer. They will keep for several months. Filled with flavored pastry cream and topped with chocolate glaze or caramel, the baked choux strips or balls can be used to make various pastries as eclairs and choux a la creme. Also deliciously crunchy pastries, like the honey choux puffs and puffed honey choux strips (page 108) can be made by deep frying the choux pastry dough.

Separated Egg Sponge Cake
(Pandespani Aplo 2)

Yields one 2 by 10 inch round cake
Preparation time 30 minutes
Baking time 30 minutes

4	eggs, separated
1/4	teaspoon cream of tartar
1	cup castor sugar
1	teaspoon vanilla or other flavoring
1/4	cup warm water
1	cup self raising flour

Put the egg whites and cream of tartar into the mixing bowl of an electric mixer. Beat them at high speed until they form soft peaks. Add half the sugar gradually and continue to whisk until the mixture becomes firm and glossy. Beat the egg yolks separately with the remaining sugar and vanilla until thick and lemon colored. Turn the speed down to slow and sift in half the flour in stages alternately with tepid water. Stop beating and fold in the remaining flour in two stages alternately with the beaten egg whites. Fold gently, combining the ingredients with a spoon to prevent the mixture from deflating. Pour the batter into a 10 inch round cake pan lined with greased baking paper. Smooth the surface with a metal spatula. Continue as in the recipe for Whole Egg Sponge Cake (page 38). This cake as well as all other sponge cakes, could be the base for most sponge, decorated layer or log cakes.

All in One Butter Sponge Cake
(Pandespani Voutirou 2)

Yields one 2 by 10 inch round cake
Preparation time 10 minutes
Baking time 40 minutes

1	cup self raising flour
1	teaspoon baking powder
2	eggs
1/2	cup soft unsalted margarine
1/2	cup castor sugar
1	teaspoon vanilla or grated lemon or orange rind

Sift together the flour and baking powder into the mixing bowl of an electric mixer. Add the remaining ingredients and mix lightly with a spoon. Then beat at high speed for 3-4 minutes. Pour the batter into a 10 inch round cake pan, or into two smaller pans lined with greased baking paper. Bake in a 350°F oven for 35-40 minutes, until the surface is golden and firm to the touch. Remove the pan from the oven and place it on a wire rack for 5 minutes. Then unmold the cake on to the rack to cool completely. You may wrap and store the cake in the refrigerator or freezer. It keeps well one week in the refrigerator and several months in the freezer. It can be served plain or decorated as illustrated on page 72.

3

Creams and Ice Creams
(Kremes ke Pagota)

Often I long for the simple way of life which fascinated me during my childhood. Disappeared forever are the picturesque vendors who roamed our streets. Most beloved by the children were the ice cream sellers pushing their carts with loud calls: "vanilla, chocolate ice cream, ice cream cones". How well I remember the picturesque carts, with multicolored awnings ending in scalloped edges, the bronze containers with their gleaming lids and the eager children flocking around the good man with a coin in their hand shouting: "one for me, for me too Mr. Yiannis, Nicholas or Pandelis". Whatever the man was called, children knew them all. Now that the ice cream cart, an oasis in the drab street, has been replaced by commercial, colorless refrigerators, the charm of a blissful era has gone forever.

Nowadays there are numerous kinds of ice cream, all with fancy names, flavors and wrappings. But none of them contains the wonderful taste of the simple ice cream we knew in the old days. During the winter, the same vendors used to set up stands selling chick-peas, peanuts, hazelnuts and "Passatebo" (pumpkin seeds), which as they were roasted on charcoal send out a billowing smoke. Most of these stands are also gone. The only ones left are vendors of roasted chestnuts and corn. However, ice cream is still the best, beloved delicacy for young and old, readily available everywhere today. Not so in the old days when refrigerators and mixers were unknown. Today, everyone owning a freezer and a mixer can enjoy the cool delight and wonderful texture of homemade ice cream all year round.

General Instructions

Most classic ice creams are based on a custard enriched with eggs, especially egg yolks. Whipping cream and a good amount of sugar are usually added to the custard. These two ingredients, as well as the air trapped inside the frozen mass while it is being beaten, give the ice cream a rich, smooth texture. Parfait ice creams, consisting of whipped cream beaten with egg yolks and sugar, are very rich in fat. Accordingly, parfait ice creams do not crystallize as they freeze. In contrast the ice cream based on a thin custard with less whipped cream and eggs requires continuous beating in an electric-powered ice cream churn or has to be frozen and beaten repeatedly until a uniform grainy texture has been attained. Fruit ice creams are based on a fruit puree. Fruit puree, on its own, freezes to a solid mass when left in the freezer undisturbed. Occasional beating during the freezing process breaks up the ice crystals and helps the mixture to attain a uniform grainy texture. Other ingredients, such as sugar, whipping cream, eggs, gelatine or

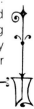

alcohol added to the fruit puree impede the forming of large ice crystals. Ice cream can be flavored with various liqueurs, coffee or chocolate. Ground nuts as almonds, hazelnuts or pistachios may be added. As parfait ice creams do not require a lot of beating, they can be placed in molds to provide attractively shaped cold desserts. When making ice cream, bear in mind that freezing reduces the flavor and aroma. Therefore, when making custard for ice cream, use slightly larger amounts of flavoring. For the same reason, ice cream should not be served straight from the freezer. Let it soften for 20-30 minutes in the refrigerator, before serving. This will improve both its texture and aroma. Ice cream served in ice cream glasses or bowls, garnished with whipped cream, various syrups or sauces and thin wafers is not only a summer pleasure but a delightful treat for all seasons.

   Granitas are the simplest of frozen desserts. They are made of frozen juices or fruit purees to which a light syrup of sugar and often liqueurs are added. By beating the mixture repeatedly in a blender or mixer, air is trapped inside, preventing the formation of large ice crystals. For a more delicate and snowy texture, whisk 1-2 egg whites until they form soft peaks and blend with the fruit mixture. Granitas can be made more easily in an electric ice cream churn. Choose fresh, unblemished and tasty fruit for a better result. Always add lemon juice to preserve the bright color of the fruit. Most granitas can be stored in the freezer in tightly sealed plastic containers. It is best to serve granitas within a few days, since their fresh fruit aroma diminishes with time. Serve garnished with whipped cream or liqueur, in tall glasses with a straw.

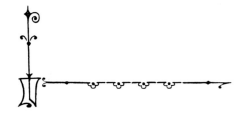

Traditional Yogurt

Since Greece is a mountainous country, its people have been always raising animals mainly sheep and goats. In all households milk was always plentiful. Cheese and yogurt were made from leftover milk. Even today in Greek villages, yogurt is made in large, earthenware basins or wooden kegs called "Kardari" or "Vidouri", specially constructed for yogurt making. If such a pot is to be used, it should be filled with warm water and left overnight to tighten the joints. Yogurt made in the region of Roumeli, in wooden kegs, has a delicious rich taste not easily forgotten. Today there is a lot of commercially prepared yogurt on the market. However, homemade yogurt cannot be compared with any of these commercial brands.

To make yogurt, boil 1 quart fresh milk and cool until lukewarm (120°F). Dissolve 2-3 tablespoons commercially prepared yogurt in a small amount of the lukewarm milk to make a starter. Add to the remaining milk and stir well. Pour the mixture into a large heavy bowl or into custard or dessert cups. Cover with a piece of baking paper, then with 4 kitchen towels or a warm cloth. Leave the yogurt in a warm place (77°F) for about 4-6 hours, until set. Keep yogurt refrigerated until served. It will keep about a week. Save some of it as a starter for a new batch. The culture eventually looses its potency. To keep the culture going, yogurt should be made every couple of days. Yogurt is served plain, with honey or fruit or mixed in sauces, salad dressings and dips. It is used as an ingredient in various sweet and savory dishes or as a topping for pilaf and stuffed vine leave dishes. Yogurt is of high nutritional value, yet low in calories. The art of yogurt making has been a tradition throughout the centuries and neighbors often used to exchange yogurt starters.

Traditional Roumelis' Yogurt in "Vidouri"

Peach Ice Cream
(Pagoto Rodakino)

Serves 10
Preparation time 8-10 hours

5	large, ripe peaches, peeled and stoned (1 $^1/_2$ lb)
2	tablespoons lemon juice
4	egg yolks
1/2	cup sugar
2	tablespoons apricot brandy (optional)
2	teaspoons gelatine
2	cups whipping cream

Cut the peaches into small pieces and puree them together with the lemon juice in a food processor. Put the egg yolks, sugar, brandy, gelatine and $^1/_2$ cup peach puree in the top pan of a double boiler over gently simmering water and heat, beating constantly, until the gelatine dissolves and the mixture thickens slightly. Remove from the heat, let it cool to lukewarm and mix in the remaining peach puree. Whip the cream until it forms soft peaks. Then fold it into the mixture. Transfer it to a freezer container and freeze for about 2 hours. Empty the slightly frozen mixture into a large mixing bowl of an electric mixer and beat at high speed until light and frothy. Repeat the procedure after another couple of hours and allow the mixture to freeze. The ice cream can be kept in the freezer up to 6 months. Serve in individual ice cream glasses, garnished with whipped cream and decorative chocolate leaves. Follow the same procedure to make apricot or melon ice cream.

Dondourma Ice Cream
(Pagoto Dondourma)

Serves 16
Preparation time 8-10 hours

3	cups milk (preferably goat milk)
1	tablespoon ground salep
1	cup sugar
4	eggs, separated plus 4 egg yolks
2	cups whipping cream

Dissolve the salep in a little milk and add half the sugar and egg yolks. Beat the mixture with a whisk until creamy in texture and lemon-colored. Boil the remaining milk and pour it on to the yolk and sugar mixture, whisking constantly. Stir the mixture over medium heat until it thickens slightly and coats the spoon. Take the pan off the heat and set in a bowl of iced water to stop the cooking process. To avoid skin forming, place a sheet of plastic wrap on the surface of the custard and let it cool. Whip the cream lightly and fold it into the cold custard. Pour the mixture into a large, metal freezer container and freeze 2-3 hours until it is barely frozen. Beat the egg whites until they hold soft peaks. Add the remaining sugar in 3 stages, beating until the mixture is thick and glossy. Take the custard out of the freezer and beat it until light and smooth. Gradually add the beaten egg

Vanilla Ice Cream
(Pagoto Vanilia)

Serves 16
Preparation time 8-10 hours

1	tablespoon cornstarch
1	cup sugar
1/4	teaspoon salt
9	egg yolks
1/2	cup evaporated milk
3	cups milk, scalded
2	cups whipping cream
3	teaspoons vanilla
3	egg whites

Mix the cornstarch, sugar and salt in the top pan of a double boiler. Add the egg yolks and beat with a whisk or a hand operated mixer until the mixture is thick and lemon-colored. Gradually add the evaporated milk, then the hot scalded milk, stirring constantly, over the simmering water bath or over direct very low heat and cook the custard without allowing it to boil. When a coating consistency is reached, remove the custard from the heat and chill it stirring over iced water to stop cooking. Place a sheet of plastic wrap on the surface to avoid skin forming and let the custard cool completely. Meanwhile, lightly whip the cream with the vanilla flavoring and fold it into the custard. Pour the mixture into a metal freezer container and chill until frozen, but not solid, about 2-3 hours. Beat the egg whites to a soft meringue. Remove the custard from the freezer, transfer to a large mixing bowl and beat at the highest speed until light and smooth. Gradually incorporate the meringue into the mixture, beating constantly, until it is smooth and fluffy again. Return to the freezer. It can be kept up to 6 months. To serve, scoop the ice cream into individual bowls, garnish with whipped cream, chopped nuts, little biscuits or fresh fruit. Pour over fruit or chocolate sauce.

Praline Ice Cream: Substitute $^1/_2$ teaspoon almond extract for the vanilla flavoring and fold 1 $^1/_2$ cups chopped praline (page 132) into the mixture after folding the meringue.

Moca Ice Cream: Substitute 4-5 tablespoons instant coffee for the vanilla flavoring or serve Vanilla Ice Cream sprinkled with 1 teaspoon instant coffee (on each individual bowl) and garnished with whipped cream and chopped roasted almonds.

whites, beating constantly until all the meringue is incorporated and the mixture is smooth and fluffy. Return to the freezer container and freeze. To serve, scoop into ice cream bowls. Garnish with whipped cream and roasted almonds. Pour over sour cherry syrup.

Ice Cream Torte with Strawberry Sauce
(Tourta Pagoto me Saltsa Fraoula)

Serves 10
Preparation time 24 hours
Baking time 2 hours

1/2	recipe, Meringue (page 145)
1	recipe, Vanilla Ice Cream (page 44)
1	recipe, Strawberry Sauce (page 90)
1	cup whipping cream
2	tablespoons confectioners ' sugar
1	teaspoon vanilla

Prepare the meringue mixture. Trace about a 10 inch circle on a non-stick paper placed on a baking tray. To ensure that the meringue is the right size, trace the outline of the spring form base which will be used to mold the ice cream torte. Using a piping bag fitted with a plain 1/2 inch nozzle, pipe the meringue starting from the pencil mark and working inwards until the entire round surface is covered. Bake the meringue in a 210°F oven for 1 hour and 30 minutes. Turn off the oven and leave the meringue inside to cool. Place the meringue into the spring-form pan. Prepare the vanilla ice cream. After folding in the beaten whites, pour the mixture into the pan over the meringue and place in the freezer. Prepare the Strawberry Sauce and whip the cream together with the sugar and flavoring until it forms soft peaks. Refrigerate. To serve, unlock the spring, run the tip of a knife around and between the rim of the mold and ice cream to loosen edges, and gently lift off the ring. Then slide a wide spatula under the meringue and transfer the Ice Cream Torte to a serving dish. Just before serving, garnish the ice cream with whipped cream and a little strawberry sauce. Serve the remaining sauce separately in a bowl.

Ice Cream Torte with Strawberry Sauce, page 45

Strawberry Ice Cream
(Pagoto Fraoula)

Serves 10
Preparation time 8-10 hours

2	lbs good quality ripe strawberries
4	egg yolks
1	cup sugar
2	tablespoons lemon juice
2	teaspoons gelatine
2	cups whipping cream

Wash, hull and drain the strawberries. Puree them in a food processor. Put the egg yolks, sugar, lemon juice, gelatine and one cup of the strawberry puree in the top pan of a double boiler over gently simmering water and heat, beating constantly, until the gelatine dissolves and the mixture thickens slightly. Remove from the heat and let the mixture cool until lukewarm. Mix in the remaining strawberry puree. Whip the cream lightly and fold it into the mixture. Pour the mixture into a metal container and freeze for about 2 hours until frozen but not solid. Transfer to a large mixing bowl of an electric mixer and beat it at high speed until smooth and light. Return to the freezer. After another couple of hours beat the mixture once more. Beated repeatedly, the mixture becomes light and airy, thus preventing ice granules from forming, which would spoil the rich, smooth texture of the ice cream. It keeps in the freezer up to 6 months. Serve in individual ice cream bowls, garnished with whipped cream and fresh strawberries.

Lemon Granita
(Granita Lemoni)

Serves 10
Preparation time 8 hours

	the peel of two lemons
1	cup sugar
1	cup water
1/4	cup orange liqueur
2	cups orange juice
1	cup lemon juice
2	egg whites (optional)

Put the lemon peel, sugar and water in a heavy saucepan. Stir over low heat until the sugar is dissolved, pressing the lemon peel with a wooden spoon to extract the aromatic oils. Skim off any froth that comes on the surface. Boil the syrup for 5 minutes without stirring. Take the pan off the heat, cover and let the syrup cool. Remove and discard the lemon peel. Then stir in the liqueur and fruit juices. Pour the mixture into a shallow ice tray and set in the freezer. Chill 2-3 hours, stirring occasionally during the freezing process to break up the ice crystals and help the mixture to attain a uniform, grainy texture. Whisk the whites until they stand in peaks. Transfer the quite frozen mixture to a food processor, add the whites, and whisk until it is light and airy. Return

Chocolate Ice Cream
(Pagoto Sokolata)

Serves 16
Preparation time 8-10 hours

3	cups milk, scalded
1	tablespoon cornstarch
1	cup sugar
1/4	teaspoon salt
9	egg yolks
1/2	cup evaporated milk
10	oz baking chocolate, cut in small pieces
2	cups whipping cream
2	teaspoons vanilla
3	egg whites (optional)

On the top pan of a double boiler, mix the cornstarch, sugar and salt. Add the egg yolks and beat with a whisk until the mixture is thick and lemon-colored. Gradually add the evaporated milk, then the hot scalded milk, stirring constantly over the simmering water bath, and cook the custard without allowing it to boil. When a coating consistency is reached, remove the custard from the heat and stir in the chocolate pieces until they are melted and blended with the custard to a smooth mixture. Let the mixture cool completely. Meanwhile, lightly whip the cream with the flavoring and fold it into the chocolate mixture. Pour it into a large, metal container and set it in the freezer. Chill until barely frozen, about 2-3 hours. Beat the egg whites until they form soft peaks. Remove the cream from the freezer, transfer to a large mixer bowl and beat at highest speed until the mixture is smooth and light. Gradually incorporate the meringue into the mixture, beating constantly until it is smooth and fluffy again. Return to the freezer. It can be kept up to 6 months. To serve, scoop the chocolate ice cream into tall champagne glasses, sprinkle with roasted almonds and top with hot chocolate sauce. Decorate with two chocolate wafers and a tiny paper umbrella.

the mixture to the freezer and after another couple of hours, whisk it again, 1-2 minutes. To have the best airy texture, whisk the granita once more just before serving. Pour into tall sorbet glasses, decorate with a lemon slice, and serve with a straw. Frozen granitas should be served within a few days as their fresh fruit flavors fade rapidly.

Fresh Apple Mousse
(Mous Milo)

Serves 8-10
Preparation time 1 hour

2	lbs apples, peeled and coarsely grated
2	tablespoons lemon juice
1/2	cup sugar
2	cups whipping cream
2	tablespoons confectioners ' sugar
2	teaspoons vanilla
1/4	cup chopped walnuts

Put the grated apples together with the lemon juice and sugar into a heavy saucepan and stir over low heat until all the liquid has been evaporated. Allow to cool; then puree the apple mixture in a blender or a food processor. Put the puree in a metal bowl and cover with plastic wrap. Place the bowl in a larger bowl or pan containing crushed ice and refrigerate for at least 1 hour. Remove the bowls from the refrigerator and beat a little cream into the apple mixture. Return the bowls to the refrigerator for 15 minutes. Continue beating in small quantities of cream, refrigerating for 15 minutes between each addition, until half the cream has been added. Whip the remaining cream with the confectioners ' sugar and vanilla until stiff peaks are formed, and fold into the apple mixture. Pour into 8 champagne glasses or a crystal bowl and sprinkle the chopped walnuts on top. Chill for at least 2 hours before serving.

Fresh Kiwi Mousse
(Mous me Aktinidia)

Serves 4-5
Preparation time 15 minutes
Freezing time 4 hours

6	large kiwis, peeled and sliced
2	tablespoons lemon juice
2	tablespoons cointreau liqueur
1½	cups whipping cream
1/2	cup confectioners ' sugar

Sprinkle the kiwis with the lemon juice and liqueur. Puree the fruit into a food processor or a blender. Set aside. Whip the cream with the sugar until thick and light. Reserve some cream for garnishing and fold the remainder into the pureed fruit. Pour the mixture into 4-5 glasses or ice cream bowls and chill for at least 4 hours before serving. Garnish with the reserved cream and decorate with sliced kiwis.

Kiwi Granita, page 47

Kiwi Granita
(Granita me Aktinidia)

Serves 4-5
Preparation time 15 minutes
Freezing time 6 hours

6	kiwis, peeled
1	cup sugar
1	cup water
1/4	cup lemon juice
3	tablespoons gin or cointreau liqueur

Puree the kiwis in a food processor. Put the sugar with the water in a saucepan and stir over low heat until it is dissolved. Increase the heat and boil the syrup for 5 minutes. Cool thoroughly and stir in the fruit puree, lemon juice and gin or liqueur. Pour the mixture into a metal container and set it in the freezer. Freeze until it is loosely frozen, 2-3 hours. Transfer the mixture to a food processor and whisk until it is light and snowy. Return to the freezer and for a better uniform grainy texture, whisk once again after it has been frozen for a couple of hours. You may whisk the granita once more just before serving in tall sorbet glasses. Garnish with a little whipped cream and top with a slice of fresh kiwi. Serve with a straw.

Praline Parfait Torte
(Pagoto Armenonville)

Serves 10
Preparation time 1 hour
Baking time 2 hours

1/2   recipe, Meringue (page 145)
2   cups whipping cream
4   egg yolks
1/2   teaspoon almond extract
1   cup coarsely chopped Praline (page 132)

Prepare the meringue mixture. Spoon it into a piping bag fitted with a plain $1/2$ inch nozzle and pipe 10 small rosettes on a non-stick baking paper placed on a rack. Pipe the remaining meringue into a large spiral. Bake the meringue in a 210°F oven for about 2 hours or until dry and slightly brown. Turn off the heat and leave the meringue inside to cool. Meanwhile, put the cream together with the egg yolks into a mixing bowl of an electric mixer and whip until the mixture is thick and fluffy. Avoid overbeating as the cream tends to curdle. Break the large meringue into uneven, coarse pieces and fold them into the whipped mixture together with the praline and flavoring. Pour the mixture into a loaf-shaped pan, 12 inches long and set it in the freezer. Chill the ice cream at least 24 hours before serving. To unmold the torte, wrap the mold in a towel soaked in warm water. The light heat will melt the surface of the dessert and loosen it from the pan 's sides. Invert it on to a serving dish and carefully lift the mold away. Return the ice cream to the freezer for about 15 minutes. Meanwhile, prepare the chocolate sauce and pour it over the ice cream. Garnish with meringue rosettes and serve. The torte can be kept in the freezer for up to 6 months.

Praline Parfait Torte, page 48

Chocolate Sauce
(Glasso Sokolatas)

Preparation time 5 minutes

10   oz baking semi-sweet chocolate
1   cup whipping cream

Cut the chocolate into small pieces and put them together with the cream into a heavy-bottomed saucepan. Stir over low heat until the chocolate is melted and well blended with the cream. Cool to lukewarm and pour the sauce over the ice cream. You may flavor the sauce by adding vanilla, almond extract or various liqueurs. The sauce can be used as an icing for cakes and cookies. If a thick consistency is required, let the sauce cool. It thickens as it cools. Beaten with a whisk or in the mixer the sauce becomes light and fluffy and can be used as a filling or frosting in various cases.

Whipped Cream
(Krema Santigi)

Yields $^1/_2$ lb
Preparation time 2-3 minutes

1   cup whipping cream, refrigerated
2-4   tablespoons confectioners ' sugar
1-2   teaspoons vanilla

Put the whipping cream together with the sugar and flavoring into the mixing bowl of an electric mixer. Beat the mixture at medium speed until it is light and fluffy and has been almost tripled in volume. Avoid overbeating as the cream tends to curdle. To prevent curdling, also keep the cream refrigerated until used. If the cream curdles, do not discard. Mixed with hot milk, it may be used in making a rich and very tasty pastry cream or heated with melted baking chocolate, in making chocolate sauce. Whipped cream can be stored 4-5 days in the refrigerator and up to 6 months in the freezer. To thaw, refrigerate it for 12 hours before using. Almond extract, grated citrus rind or liqueurs may be substituted for the vanilla flavoring. To make a chocolate flavored whipped cream, sift 2 tablespoons cocoa powder into the remaining ingredients before beating. Whipped cream may be lightened by mixing in a small amount of meringue.

Chocolate Flavored Pastry Cream

Prepare the Pastry Cream according to the recipe. When ready, remove from the heat, add 4 oz semi-sweet baking chocolate, cut into pieces, along with the butter. Stir well until the chocolate is melted and well blended. Use the Chocolate pastry cream on its own, or mixed with whipped cream to fill chocolate cakes, eclairs or profiteroles.

Pastry Cream
(Krema Zacharoplastikis)

Yields 2 cups
Preparation time 10 minutes
Cooking time 10 minutes

3   tablespoons all purpose flour
2   tablespoons cornstarch
1/2   cup sugar
4   egg yolks
2   cups milk
1   teaspoon vanilla
2   tablespoons unsalted butter, cubed
1   cup whipped cream (optional)

Mix the flour, cornstarch and sugar in a heavy-bottomed, preferably non-stick saucepan. Lightly beat the egg yolks with $^1/_4$ cup milk and pour into the saucepan. Mix well. Heat the remaining milk to a boiling point and pour it into the egg and flour mixture, stirring vigorously. Stir the mixture over medium heat until it comes to a boiling point. Reduce the heat and continue to cook, stirring constantly for about 15 minutes until the cream is thick and smooth, and any flour smell has been eliminated. Remove from the heat and stir in the cubed butter and flavoring until well blended. (If the cream is too stiff, gradually stir in a little milk until the desired consistency is attained. If cream is too thin, mix a little additional cornstarch with two tablespoons milk, add to the mixture and continue boiling until it is thickened. If the cream is lumpy, strain it through a fine sieve or blend in a blender). To cool, press a piece of plastic wrap against its surface to prevent it from forming a skin. When the cream is completely cold, fold in the whipped cream. Pastry Cream keeps for up to 2 days in the refrigerator. It should not be frozen. Pastry cream can also be prepared as follows:
Mix the sugar, flour, and cornstarch with a little cold milk into a saucepan. Stirring vigorously, pour in the boiling milk all at once and cook the cream, stirring constantly over low heat until thickened. Lightly beat the egg yolks with the vanilla, mix in a small amount of the hot cream, then pour the mixture back into the remaining cream. Stirring continuously, cook the cream for 3-4 minutes longer. When cold, fold in the whipped cream. You may substitute vanilla with other flavorings. To make coffee pastry cream, dissolve one tablespoon instant coffee into the hot milk, or add 2 teaspoons grated lemon or any other citrus rind to the cream for a zest fruit flavor. Pastry cream is a perfect filling for cakes, triangles, horns or choux.

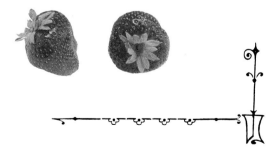

Vanilla Souffle
(Krema Vanilia sto Fourno)

Serves 6
Preparation time 30 minutes
Baking time 20-25 minutes

3	tablespoons butter
4	tablespoons all purpose flour
1	cup milk, scalded
4	eggs, separated
4	tablespoons sugar
1	teaspoon vanilla

In a heavy saucepan, melt the butter. Stir in the flour and saute 2-3 minutes (as for bechamel sauce). Pour in the hot milk stirring vigorously with a wire whisk and cook slowly for about 2 minutes. Remove from the heat and cool slightly. Beat the egg yolks lightly, add the flavoring and mix thoroughly with the custard. Whisk the egg whites until they form soft peaks. Add the sugar, a tablespoon at a time, and continue to whisk until the mixture becomes firm and glossy. Carefully fold the beaten egg whites into the custard. Divide the mixture into 6 lightly greased, small, ovenproof pyrex dishes and bake in a 350°F oven for 20- 25 minutes or until the souffles are well risen. Serve immediately.

Chocolate Souffle
(Krema Sokolata sto Fourno)

Follow the Vanilla Souffle recipe, decreasing the flour to 3 tablespoons and adding 2 oz melted baking chocolate to the warm milk.

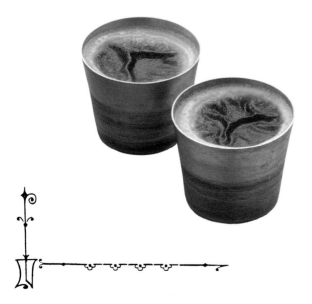

Rice Pudding (Rizogalo)

Serves 6
Preparation time 10 minutes
Cooking time 30 minutes

1/2	cup short grain rice
1¹/₂	cups water
1/8	teaspoon salt
4	cups milk
2	tablespoons cornstarch
2	teaspoons vanilla
1/2	cup sugar
	a little cinnamon

Thoroughly wash the rice and drain. In a heavy-bottomed pan, bring the water to a boil. Add the rice and a pinch of salt. Stir well, cover and simmer until the rice is very soft and the water has been evaporated. Dissolve the cornstarch in ¹/₄ cup of the milk and scald the remaining milk. Pour scalded milk into the pan over the rice, add the sugar and stir over low heat until the sugar is dissolved. Cover the pan and simmer for about 20 minutes. Add the cornstarch mixture together with the flavoring and cook, stirring constantly, until the mixture is slightly thickened, about 5-8 minutes. Remove from the heat and pour the rice pudding into 6 glass bowls. Cool slightly and dust the surface with cinnamon. Serve warm or cold. Covered with plastic wrap, it keeps in the refrigerator 3-4 days.

Custard Buttercream
(Krema Voutirou me Kastard)

Yields about 1 lb
Preparation time 30 minutes

1	cup unsalted butter, softened
1	cup confectioners ' sugar
1¹/₂	cups milk
1/4	cup custard powder
2	egg yolks

Cream the butter and sugar with an electric mixer until light and fluffy. Set aside. In a heavy saucepan, mix the custard powder, egg yolks and 2 tablespoons of the milk. Heat the remaining milk to a boiling point and pour it into the custard mixture, stirring vigorously. Slowly bring the mixture to a full boil stirring constantly over medium heat. Remove from the heat and cool. Press a piece of plastic wrap against its surface to prevent a skin from forming. Gradually add the creamed butter into the cold custard, blending it gently and evenly. Light handling is important at this stage, as the mixture tends to curdle. Custard buttercream may be used like ordinary buttercream. It should be flavored with vanilla, coffee or grated citrus rind. Various liqueurs, praline or cold melted baking chocolate can also be added, depending on the occasion. Put the cream in an airtight container and refrigerate for 24 hours or store in the freezer for up to 3 months.

Caramel Custard
(Krema Karamele)

Serves 10-12
Preparation time 30 minutes
Baking time approximately 1 hour

The Caramel

1	cup sugar
1/2	cup water
2	teaspoons lemon juice

The Custard

8	whole eggs
8	egg yolks (optional)
2/3	cup sugar
2	teaspoons vanilla
1/8	teaspoon salt
4	cups milk

Cook the caramel ingredients in a heavy saucepan over low heat until the mixture is light brown colored. Stop the cooking by dipping the pan in a bowl of iced water, thus preventing the caramel from turning too dark. Divide the caramel into 10-12 individual warmed metal molds and rotate them so that the caramel runs around the insides of the molds, coating them evenly. Lightly blend the eggs and egg yolks with the sugar, salt and flavoring. Heat the milk, and pour it gradually into the egg mixture, stirring constantly with a wooden spoon. Strain the mixture through a fine sieve, then skim off any foam from the surface. Fill the prepared molds up to $^3/_4$ with the custard and place in a deep baking pan. Pour warm water into the pan to immerse the molds up to $^2/_3$ of their depth, and bake in a 350°F oven for approximately 1 hour. Test for doneness inserting the blade of a sharp knife into the custard. It should come out clean, when the custard is ready. If not, continue baking for another 10 minutes and test again. Remove the pan from the oven and the molds out of hot water. Let the custards cool before turning them out. To serve, loosen edges with a sharp knife and invert each mold onto a serving dish. Shake the tin sharply to release vacuum and lift off. The custard will stay on the dish topped with the caramel. Serve warm or cold.

Caramel Custard, page 51

Grape Must Pudding
(Moustalevria)

Serves 8
Preparation time 12 hours
Cooking time 15 minutes

6   cups grape must
9   tablespoons charcoal ashes
2/3 cup flour or preferably cornstarch
2/3 cup coarsely chopped walnuts
     a little cinnamon

Grape Must Pudding is made in September when the grapes are trodden to produce wine. Must is unfermented wine. You may produce your own must, by crushing grapes in a wooden mortar and draining off the juice. Boil the juice and skim the froth from the surface. The more condensed the grape must, the sweeter the moustalevria. Must should be clarified before used. Pour into a non reacting pan (stainless steel or enamel). Tie the ashes into a muslin bag and drop it into the must. Boil for about 10 minutes. Then let it stand for 12 hours. Strain the liquid through a fine sieve which has been lined with a double thickened muslin and measure the liquid. Add 2 tablespoons of flour to each one cup must. In a heavy-bottomed pan, stir the flour over low heat until lightly browned. Mix the flour with a little must into a heavy saucepan. Heat the remaining must to a boiling point and pour it into the flour mixture, stirring vigorously to avoid lumps forming. Then cook the mixture, stirring constantly until it is thick and clear. Pour it into individual glass bowls and sprinkle with nuts and cinnamon. If using cornstarch, it is not necessary to brown it. Semolina may be used instead. However, traditional moustalevria is made with flour from which it gets its name. Alevri means flour in Greek.

Fruit Cream
(Krema Froutou)

Yields 2 cups
Preparation time 15 minutes
Cooking time 15 minutes

1/2 cup sugar
5-6 tablespoons cornstarch
1/8 teaspoon salt
4   egg yolks, slightly beaten
2   cups fruit juice (orange, tangerine or pineapple)
2   teaspoons grated rind of the fruit used
2-3 tablespoons unsalted butter (optional)
2   cups whipped cream (optional)

Mix the sugar, cornstarch and salt in a heavy-bottomed saucepan. Lightly beat the egg yolks with 2 tablespoons fruit juice and pour into the saucepan. Mix well. Heat the remaining fruit juice to a boiling point and pour it into the mixture, stirring vigorously. Simmer the custard over low heat or on top of a double boiler, stirring constantly until thickened. Remove from the heat and add the grated rind. Butter, stirred into the hot custard, enriches the taste and adds a shiny appearance. Press a piece of plastic wrap against its surface to prevent forming a skin and let the cream cool completely. The cream may be lightened by adding whipped cream. Fold in gently as the cream tends to curdle. Fruit cream can be kept in the refrigerator for 2 days. It should not be frozen. Fruit Cream makes a light, tasty filling for cakes, fruit pies, choux or cones. It is advisable to taste the fruit juice before using it. If it is too sweet, add less sugar. If it is sour, increase the amount of sugar. To prepare lemon fruit cream, use water in making the custard and add 5-6 tablespoons lemon juice along with the rind after removing it from the heat. The amount of the cornstarch needed may vary depending on its thickening capability. If the custard is too thick, stir in a little more juice. If it is thin, dissolve a little more additional cornstarch in 1-2 tablespoons juice, add to the custard and cook until thickened. Commercially prepared fruit juice may also be used. Test the sweetness of the juice and decrease the proportion of sugar as the custard tends to turn out too sweet.

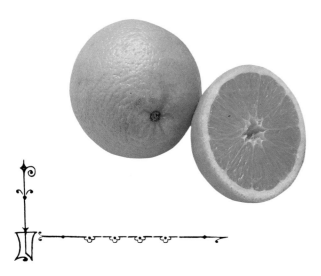

Yogurt and Sour Cherry Parfait
(Yiaourti Parfe Visino)

Serves 18
Preparation time 24 hours

1	can sour cherry compote (1$^{1}/_{2}$ lbs)
1	package (3 oz) sour cherry gelatine
1	tablespoon powdered gelatine
2	eggs, separated
1/4	cup sugar
1	cup strained yogurt ($^{1}/_{2}$ lb)
1/2	teaspoon almond extract
1/2	recipe, Whipped Cream (page 49)

Strain the compote and keep the cherries and the juice separated. Measure the juice and if it is less, add water to make 3 cups. Use 2 cups of the liquid to make the sour cherry jelly as directed on the package and chill until slightly thickened. Meanwhile, stir the gelatine into the remaining liquid and let it soften. Place the mixture over simmering water until the gelatine is completely dissolved. Add half the amount of sugar and the egg yolks. Whip the mixture until thick and light. Remove from the heat and cool it until slightly warm. Add the flavoring and beat in the yogurt. Chill until it begins to thicken. Whisk the egg whites with the remaining sugar to form soft peaks and gradually fold into the yogurt mixture. Pour it into a large, turban mold and chill until set but not firm. Remove the thickened cherry jelly from the refrigerator and stir in the strained cherries. Pour it over the yogurt jelly. Refrigerate overnight. To unmold, see Apple Jelly recipe (page 53). Garnish with the whipped cream. Keep in the refrigerator.

Apple Jelly (Zele me Mila)

Serves 8-10
Preparation time 30 minutes
Setting time 4 hours

4	apples, coarsely grated
1/2	cup sugar
1	tablespoon lemon juice
2	packages (3 oz each) pineapple or banana gelatine
1/2	cup coarsely chopped walnuts

Put the grated apples together with the sugar and lemon juice in a heavy saucepan. Stir over low heat until all the water has been evaporated. Prepare the jelly as directed on the package. Chill until slightly thickened. Fold in the apples. Pour the mixture into a jelly mold and chill until set, about 4 hours. To unmold, run the tip of a knife around and between the rim of the mold and gelatine to loosen edges. Then dip the entire mold briefly in warm water to loosen the jelly. Invert a serving plate over the mold. Holding the mold firmly against the plate, turn over mold and plate together. Shake to release vacuum and lift the mold away from the jelly. Serve sprinkled with walnuts.

Buttercream
(Krema Voutirou)

Yields about 1 lb
Preparation time 30 minutes

1	cup unsalted butter, softened
4	eggs, separated
1$^{1}/_{2}$	teaspoons vanilla
1/2	teaspoon lemon juice
1	cup confectioners' sugar

Cream the butter with an electric mixer until it is light and fluffy. Beating continuously, add the egg yolks one at a time; then add the vanilla. Whisk separately the egg whites until light and foamy. Add the lemon juice, then gradually add the sugar, beating continously, until a stiff and glossy meringue is formed. Gently fold the meringue into the creamed mixture. Light handling is important at this stage since overworking tends to deflate or curdle the mixture. The finished buttercream should be smooth, light in texture and shiny. Buttercream may be used as a filling in various cakes, pies and biscuits.
Alternate: Vanilla can be substituted by other flavorings as almond extract, grated citrus rind, coffee or liqueurs. One cup crushed praline, pistachio nuts, hazel nuts or small pieces of candied fruit may be added also, depending on the occasion. For chocolate buttercream, mix $^{1}/_{3}$ cup cocoa with 3-4 tablespoons confectioners' sugar and beat into the creamed butter before folding in the meringue. Four ounces cold melted chocolate could be added instead. Sealed in airtight containers, Butter Cream can be kept for 2-3 days in the refrigerator and up to 3 months in the freezer.

Yogurt and Sour Cherry Parfait, page 53

Peach Granita
(Granita Rodakino)

Serves 10
Preparation time 8 hours

1 1/2	lbs peaches, peeled and cut into small pieces
2/3	cup sugar
1	cup orange juice
1/2	cup lemon juice
2	egg whites (optional)

Choose ripe, tasty and aromatic peaches. Puree them in a food processor together with the sugar. Add the fruit juices and blend for a few seconds more. Pour the mixture into a metal freezer tray and freeze until it is about set (not solid). Whisk the egg whites until they stay in soft peaks. Beat the almost frozen fruit mixture in a food processor for about 1-2 minutes; then add and beat in the whites. Return the granita to the freezer and freeze for about 2 hours. Then transfer to the food processor again and whisk for 1-2 minutes until it looks snowy. For a more delicate texture, beat the mixture once more after freezing it for another couple of hours. Store in the freezer. It keeps up to 3 months. To serve, scoop and stack the granita into tall glasses. Garnish with a little whipped cream and top with a fresh cherry. Serve with a straw.
Alternate: Substitute 1 1/2 cups grapefruit juice for the orange and lemon juices. Follow the same recipe to make apricot, melon, pineapple or mango granitas.

Fruit Granitas
(Granites apo Fruta)

To make fruit granitas, cut fresh or canned fruit (apples, apricots, peaches, bananas, melon or pineapple) into small pieces and puree them in a food processor or blender. Various fruits may be combined. Add the juice of 2-3 oranges and 1-2 lemons. If using fresh fruit it may be neccessary to add a little sugar. Taste the mixture to estimate how much sugar is required. Grapefruit, other citrus fruit or pineapple juice may be substituted for the orange and lemon juices. Pour the mixture into a shallow ice tray and set it in the freezer for 1-3 hours, until it is loosely frozen. Then whisk it in a food processor for 2-3 minutes until snowy textured. To have the best snowy texture, whisk the granita up to 2 or 3 times, freezing slightly in between. A little gin, rum or liqueur may be added but not only for flavor. Alcohol also impedes the formation of large ice crystals, thus contributing to the uniform grainy texture of the granita. For a more delicate texture, beat in 1-2 lightly whipped egg whites. Store in the freezer. You should not keep granitas more than 3 months as the fresh fruit flavors fade as time passes. Fruit granitas can be served either in tall glasses with a straw or in ice cream bowls with a spoon.

Strawberry Granita
(Granita Fraoula)

Serves 6-10
Preparation time 8 hours

1	lb ripe strawberries (washed, hulled and sliced)
2/3	cup sugar
1	cup orange juice
1/2	cup lemon juice
1-2	egg whites (optional)

Puree the strawberries with the sugar in a food processor. Add the fruit juices and blend for one minute longer. Pour the mixture into a large, shallow freezing tray and freeze until most of the mixture close by on all sides of the tray is frozen, about 3 hours. Remove and whisk the mixture in the food processor or in a blender, for 1-2 minutes, until mushy. Return the mixture to the freezer. Beat the mixture up twice, freezing slightly in between, until a fluffy, snowy texture is reached. For a more delicate and snowy granita, whisk 1-2 egg whites until they form soft peaks and blend with the fruit mixture. Store in the freezer. You should not keep the Strawberry Granita more than 3 months as the fresh fruit flavor fades as time passes. To serve, scoop and stack in tall glasses. Garnish with a little whipped cream and top with a fresh strawberry.

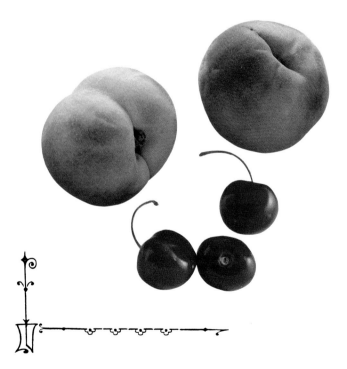

Peach Granita, page 54
Strawberry Granita, page 54

4

Cakes and Tortes
(Keik ke Tourtes)

In Greece Cakes and particulary Tortes are attributed to the younger generation. There are quite a few desserts of this category I remember from my mother (Yogurt Cake, Syrupy Walnut or Almond Cake, Marmalade Tart, Cream Horns and Cream Filled Round Sponge Biscuits). Having the basic knowledge of the old traditional desserts, the housewives of the new generation, being inspired by special events (a birth, a wedding, a graduation), experimented and they opened up a new chapter in Greek Pastries. Pastries presented in this chapter, mostly assembled with fruits and nuts, are recipes of contemporary Greece. Cakes and tortes are the sweets which are mostly linked with the best moments of our lives. An inseparable part of every celebration, the beautifully decorated birthday or wedding cake is of great interest to all guests. The art of decorating a cake requires talent and fantasy. It is a skill that expresses our artistic sensitivities. It fills us with the joy of creativity. No commercially prepared cake, however beautiful, can grant us the satisfaction we feel when presenting our own creation and seeing the admiration in the eyes of our loved ones or hearing our friends approval.

General Instructions

The chapter addresses three fields in the same category. Cakes, Tortes and Tarts. For successfull results all ingredients should be carefully measured, always using standard measuring cups and measuring spoons.

Cakes that contain eggs, are best mixed using an electric mixer. The ingredients are either beaten together at medium speed or in stages. In other words, the butter is beaten first with the sugar to a creamy consistency. Then the eggs are added one at a time. Lastly, after reducing the speed to a minimum, the flour is folded in stages alternated with the liquid. Cake batter should be smooth, thick and fluffy. Whichever method you use, the secret is to whisk as much air as possible into the batter. The air trying to escape during baking expands and causes the cake to rise. In cakes that do not contain eggs, like lenten cakes, all the ingredients are lightly mixed together by rubbing. For best results, rubbing must be quick and with a light touch. Overworking the batter would make the cake tough.

To bake a cake, pour the batter into the specified size cake pan, filling it up to $2/3$ of its depth. Baking time varies according to the size of the pan. The same amount of batter concentrated in a deep, high pan, requires a longer baking time than if it were spread in a wide, shallow pan. The oven temperature must be approximately 350°F, and the cake should bake for about one hour. If the

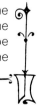

temperature is higher, the cake will bake quicker and will not rise properly. The oven always should be preheated and the heat should be evenly distributed from the top to the bottom of the oven. In circulating air ovens (convection ovens), it is best to cook cakes and pastries on the middle shelves, occasionally turning them around as necessary for even baking. The simplest of cakes is the sponge cake, which is made of eggs beaten with sugar and mixed with flour. Walnuts, almonds, hazelnuts or pistachios mixed in the batter, or lightly sprinkled on top of the cake, produce a special uneven texture and add flavor. Chocolate, crystallized or dried fruit, and spices also could be mixed into the batter to give the cake a delicious taste and aroma. Crystallized fruits and raisins should be floured well before adding to the batter, since otherwise they tend to sink to the bottom of the cake during baking.

Glazing or icing a cake not only adds flavor, but also helps to keep it moist. The simplest glaze is made with confectioners ' sugar and a little warm water. Stir the water a little at a time into the sugar until a thick mixture is formed. The glaze may be flavored by adding a little vanilla or grated orange or lemon rind. It should be spread on top of the cake while the cake is still warm.

Tortes are created by combining layered cakes, particularly sponge cakes, with one of the basic creams (whipped, pastry cream or butter cream) and other ingredients like fresh or crystallized fruit, nuts or chocolate. The ingredients can be combined in various ways according to taste. For a successful torte, always use high quality ingredients.

Tarts are made of a shortcrust pastry casing filled with various sweet fillings. Such fillings could be fresh fruit, cream, or a mixture of several ingredients like jams, nuts and dried fruit. The filling is partly covered with decorative designs of pastry strips or whipped cream rosettes. Fillings may be added either before or after the pastry is baked. However, when the pastry is covered with the filling, the moisture of the filling impedes the base to bake and be crispy. Therefore, it is better to bake the dough before filling the tart. To prevent the dough from shrinking or buckling at the center during baking, prick the entire surface with a fork or cover it with a piece of baking paper and fill up the tart with beans or lentils. To produce a crisp pastry, the dough should not be kneaded too much. Work it as lightly as possible with your fingertips or a pastry blender until it forms a ball and leaves the sides of the mixing bowl clean. The dough should feel crumbly. Cover the dough and chill it 10 minutes in the refrigerator. To prevent sticking, roll the dough out with a rolling pin on top of a floured pastry cloth (canvas). For best results, use special pastry blenders for mixing and pastry cloths for rolling out the dough. For a decorative top, place dough strips in a lattice pattern over the filling and brush with egg white or egg yolk beaten with a little water before baking.

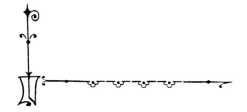

Cream and Chocolate Torte
(Tourta Sokolatas me Krema)

Serves 12
Preparation time 1 hour
Baking time 30 minutes

The Cake

3	tablespoons self raising flour
4	tablespoons cocoa
2	teaspoons baking powder
5	eggs, separated
5	tablespoons sugar

The Filling

2	cups Pastry Cream (page 49)
1	cup whipping cream
2	tablespoons confectioners' sugar
1	teaspoon vanilla

The Icing

4	oz baking chocolate
4	tablespoons confectioners' sugar
2	tablespoons milk
1	tablespoon brandy
3	oz unsalted butter, cubed

Sift the flour, cocoa, and baking powder together, set aside. Whisk the egg whites at high speed with an electric mixer. When the whites begin to form soft peaks, sprinkle over the sugar, a tablespoon at a time, beating well after each addition. Then add the egg yolks, one by one. Lower the speed and gradually fold in the dry ingredients, taking care not to break down the air bubbles. Spread the batter on a 10 inch round cake pan lined with greased baking paper, and bake in a 350°F oven for 25-30 minutes. Turn the cake out on a dish and leave to cool. Meanwhile, prepare the pastry cream, and let it cool. Beat the whipping cream with the sugar and vanilla, until thick and light. Reserve some for the decoration and fold the remaining into the cold pastry cream. Spread the mixture over the cake and refrigerate until firm.

Prepare the Chocolate Icing: Stir the chocolate in the top pan of a double boiler until it melts to a smooth liquid. Add the sugar, milk, and brandy at once, stirring constantly until well blended. Then stir in the butter, a few cubes at a time, until the butter melts and the mixture is smooth and glossy. Remove from the heat, cool to lukewarm and spread the icing over the cake to cover it completely. Garnish the torte with the reserved whipped cream and refrigerate. Serve it preferably on the day it is made. The cake must not be frozen.

Yogurt Cake (Yiaourtopita)

Yields 20 pieces
Preparation time 15 minutes
Baking time 1 hour

1	cup unsalted butter
1¹/₂	cups sugar
4	large eggs
3¹/₂	cups self raising flour
1/2	teaspoon baking soda
1	cup yogurt
1	teaspoon vanilla

The Filling

1/2	cup brown or ordinary sugar
1	teaspoon cinnamon
1	cup finely chopped walnuts or almonds
	confectioners ' sugar for dusting

Put the first seven ingredients in the large mixing bowl of an electric mixer and mix lightly with a spoon. Then beat for 4 minutes at medium speed until light and doubled in bulk. Mix the filling ingredients in a small bowl. Spread half the batter in a 10 by 14 inch greased cake pan and sprinkle the walnut mixture on the surface. Spread the remaining batter on top. Bake the yogurt cake in a 350°F oven for approximately one hour. Test the cake with a toothpick before removing it from the oven. If the toothpick comes out clean, the cake is done. Allow it to cool 5 minutes in the pan. Then turn it out on a rack, and allow to cool completely before cutting it into diamond-shaped pieces. Trace hearts, circles or other patterns on a heavy piece of paper and cut them out. Lay the patterns on top of each piece of cake, and secure them with pins. Let the pins protrude. Spoon icing sugar into a small sieve and shake it gently to sprinkle a layer of sugar over the surface of each piece of cake. Carefully lift up the pins and papers to leave clear patterns on top of cake pieces. To keep the cake fresh, cover it with plastic wrap. It can be kept 3-4 days at room temperature, a week in the refrigerator, and several months in the freezer. Serve at room temperature.

Hazelnut Torte
(Tourta Foundoukiou)

Serves 16
Preparation time 30 minutes
Baking time 30 minutes

The Cake

8	egg whites (1 cup)
1/2	teaspoon cream of tartar or
1	tablespoon lemon juice
1	cup sugar
1/4	teaspoon almond extract
2¹/₂	cups coarsely ground hazelnuts (10 oz)
3	tablespoons rusk crumbs

The Filling

2	cups Chocolate Pastry Cream (page 49)

The Garnish

1	recipe, whipped Cream (page 49)
3	oz whole hazelnuts
	a little Chocolate Icing (page 59)

Put the egg whites and cream of tartar into the mixing bowl of an electric mixer. Beat them at high speed until they form soft peaks. If cream of tartar is not available, add the lemon juice gradually while beating the egg whites constantly. Then add the sugar, a tablespoon at a time, and the almond extract. Continue to whisk until the mixture becomes firm and glossy. Stop beating. Gently fold in the ground hazelnuts and crumbs, taking care not to break down the air bubbles. Spread the batter on a 12 by 16 inch baking sheet lined with greased baking paper and bake in a 400°F oven for about 30 minutes. Meanwhile prepare the chocolate pastry cream. Turn the cake out on a rack and let it cool. Cut the cake vertically into four equal parts and sandwich two and two together, spreading the chocolate filling in between. Using a piping bag, pipe whipped cream rosettes on the tops and decorate with whole hazelnuts. Spoon the chocolate icing into a piping bag fitted with a fine, plain nozzle and decorate each hazelnut. Serve the tortes preferably on the day they are made as the moisture from the cream will soak into the sponge and make it soggy. You may freeze the leftovers.

Yogurt Cake, page 60

Hazelnut Torte, page 60

Hamburg Cake
(Keik Amvourgou)

Serves 20
Preparation time 30 minutes
Baking time 40 minutes

2½   cups all purpose flour
3   teaspoons baking powder
1   cup butter
2/3   cup sugar
4   eggs
2   teaspoons vanilla
4   oz baking chocolate, cut into small squares
1   cup blanched almonds, coarsely chopped

   The Syrup
2   cups sugar
1½   cups water
1   tablespoon lemon juice

Sift the flour with the baking powder. Set aside. Cream the butter and sugar with an electric mixer. Beating continuously, add the eggs one by one alternated with a tablespoon of flour to prevent the mixture from curdling. Lower the speed and gradually add the remaining flour

until all is incorporated and the mixture is smooth and fluffy. Pour the batter into a 12 inch round cake pan lined with a greased baking paper. Sprinkle the chocolate pieces on the surface and press them lightly into the batter. Then sprinkle the chopped almonds on top and bake the cake in a 350°F oven for about 40 minutes. Remove from the oven and cool. Meanwhile, boil the sugar, water, and lemon juice for 5 minutes and pour the syrup over the cake. Cover and let it stand overnight. Cut into diamond shaped pieces, arrange on a serving dish and dust with confectioners' sugar. Wrap any leftover with plastic foil and keep refrigerated.

Heart Shaped Chestnut Torte
(Tourta Kardia me Kastano)

Serves 16-18
Preparation time 1 hour and 30 minutes
Baking time 30 minutes

   The Cake
   recipe for Walnut and Cream Torte (page 64)

   The Filling
12   oz unsweetened chestnut puree
2   egg yolks
2/3   cup confectioners' sugar
2   tablespoons brandy
1   cup whipping cream

Prepare the cake according to the recipe, substituting 1 teaspoon vanilla for the almond extract. Line two 14 inch round cake pans with baking paper and trace two equal hearts, one on each. Divide the batter into two equal parts and spread them inside the hearts, covering the shapes completely. Bake the cakes in a 400°F oven for approximately 30 minutes. Remove from the oven and cool. Meanwhile, prepare the filling: If chestnut puree is not available, it can be made from fresh boiled or canned chestnuts, pureed in a blender. Press the chestnut puree through a fine sieve to smoothen. Mix in the brandy. Whip the cream together with the egg yolks and sugar until light and fluffy. Gradually add it to the chestnut puree, folding in gently until the mixture is smooth and light. Assemble the torte on a serving dish, using a spatula to spread each layer and the top with chestnut cream, reserving some cream for piping. Swirl the cream on the surface with a metal spatula to create an attractively rough finish. Fit a piping bag with a star nozzle and pipe rosettes all around the sides of the cake. Garnish with crystallized figs and cherries. Serve the torte preferably on the day it is made. It keeps 2 days in the refrigerator and 3 months in the freezer.

Hamburg Cake, page 62
Jam Filled Cookies, page 138
Salted Cookies, page 131

Walnut and Chocolate Torte
(Tourta Sokolata me Karidia)

Serves 16
Preparation time 1 hour
Baking time 40 minutes

The Cake

1/2	cup fine rusk crumbs
1	teaspoon cinnamon
1	teaspoon baking powder
1	teaspoon vanilla
6	eggs, separated
1½	cups sugar
1½	cups coarsely chopped walnuts

The Frosting

6	oz baking chocolate
2	tablespoons milk
2	tablespoons brandy
2	cups whipping cream
1/2	cup confectioners' sugar
1	teaspoon vanilla

Mix the crumbs, cinnamon and baking powder in a bowl. Set aside. Beat the egg yolks with half the amount of sugar and flavoring until thick and lemon colored. Whisk the egg whites, separately, with the remaining sugar until stiff and glossy Mix the crumb mixture with the egg yolks. Gradually fold in the egg whites, taking care not to deflate them. Add the walnuts in 3-4 stages and mix gently. Pour the batter, spreading it evenly, into a lined 12 inch round baking pan and bake in a 350°F oven for 35-40 minutes. Cool and slice in half. Cut the cake by using a serrated knife to score a guide-line round the sides, then cut through with a strong thread.

Prepare the Frosting: Melt the chocolate over a water bath or over direct, very low heat. Remove from the heat and stir in the milk and brandy. Let it cool. Meanwhile, whip the cream with the vanilla and confectioners' sugar until light and fluffy. (Ready made whipped cream can be bought from a pastry shop, if preferred. You should buy 18 oz). Reserve ⅓ of the whipped cream and fold the remaining into the cold, melted chocolate. Spread some of the chocolate mixture between the two slices. Fit a piping bag with a star nozzle and decorate the top of the cake with the remaining chocolate frosting and reserved cream. Cover the cake with plastic wrap and refrigerate to keep fresh. It keeps 2 days in the refrigerator and up to 3 months in the freezer.

Heart Shaped Chestnut Torte, page 62
Walnut and Chocolate Torte, page 63

Walnut and Cream Torte
(Tourta Aspri me Karidia)

Serves 20
Preparation time 30 minutes
Baking time 30 minutes

The Cake

8	egg whites (1 cup)
1	cup sugar
1	tablespoon lemon juice
1/4	teaspoon almond extract
2¹/₂	cups ground walnuts
3	tablespoons fine rusk crumbs

The Filling

2	recipes, Whipped Cream (page 49)
3	oz almonds, blanched, chopped and roasted

Whisk the egg whites with an electric mixer at high speed until they form soft peaks. Gradually add the lemon juice and flavoring. Then add the sugar a tablespoon at a time and continue to whisk until the mixture is firm and glossy. Gently fold in the crumbs and the walnuts. Pour the mixture, spreading it evenly, into a lined 12 by 16 inch baking sheet and bake in a 400°F oven for about 30 minutes. Remove from the oven and turn it out on a rack to cool. When cold, cut it vertically into four equal parts. Sandwich two and two together, spreading whipped cream in between. Fit a piping bag with a star nozzle and cover the tops with piped, whipped cream rosettes. Sprinkle generously with the almonds. They keep 3-4 days in the refrigerator and several months in the freezer. **Alternate:** Pistachio nuts may be substituted for both the walnuts and almonds. The torte will be just as delicious.

Almond Cake
(Keik Amigdalou)

Serves 20
Preparation time 1 hour
Baking time 1 hour

1	cup unsalted butter or margarine
1	cup sugar
6	eggs, separated
1/2	teaspoon almond extract or
2	teaspoons vanilla
1¹/₂	cups self raising flour
1¹/₂	cups blanched, ground almonds

The Syrup

2	cups sugar
1¹/₂	cups water
1	tablespoon lemon juice

Cream the butter with half the amount of the sugar in high speed until light and fluffy. Beating continuously, add the flavoring and the egg yolks one at a time, alternated with a tablespoon of flour to prevent the mixture from curdling. Then lower the speed and gradually mix in the remaining flour and the almonds. Whisk the egg whites and gradually beat in the remaining sugar. Stir a few spoonfuls of the whites into the batter to loosen it and then gently fold in the remaining meringue. The batter should be light and smooth. Pour it into a large, greased turban cake mold, filling it up to ²/₃ of its depth, and bake in a 350°F oven for about 1 hour. Combine the ingredients of the syrup in a saucepan and boil for 5 minutes. Ladle the syrup over the lukewarm cake. Cool the cake completely, before cutting. Place it in an airtight container to keep moist. It keeps 3-4 days out of the refrigerator and freezes well for several months.

Almond and Cream Torte
(Nougatina)

Serves 16
Preparation time 30 minutes
Baking time 30 minutes

The Cake

8	egg whites (1 cup)
1/2	teaspoon cream of tartar or
1	tablespoon lemon juice
1/4	teaspoon almond extract
1	cup sugar
2¹/₂	cups ground almonds
3	tablespoons fine rusk crumbs

The Filling

2	cups Pastry Cream (page 49)

The Garnish

1	recipe, Whipped Cream (page 49)
3	oz almonds, blanched, chopped and roasted

Whisk the egg whites with the cream of tartar at high speed. If cream of tartar is not available, gradually add the lemon juice while the whites are beaten. Add the flavoring, then add the sugar a spoonful at a time and continue to whisk until the mixture is firm and glossy. Gently fold in the almonds and crumbs. Spread the batter into a lined 12 by 16 inch baking sheet and bake in a 400°F oven for about 30 minutes. Remove from the oven and turn it out on a rack to cool. Meanwhile, prepare the pastry cream. Cut the cake vertically into 4 equal pieces and sandwich two and two together, spreading the pastry cream in between. Fit a piping bag with a star nozzle and cover the tops with piped, whipped cream rosettes. Sprinkle with the almonds. It should be served preferably on the day it is made. Keep refrigerated.

Almond and Cream Torte, page 64

Peach Tart
(Tarta me Rodakina)

Serves 10
Preparation time 30 minutes
Baking time 50 minutes

1 1/2 recipe, Basic Shortcrust Pastry Dough (page 37)
1   recipe, Peach Sauce (page 90)
     a few blanched almonds

Prepare the dough according to the recipe. Reserve 1/3 of the dough and roll out the remaining into 1/8 inch thick round, large enough to line an ungreased 12 inch pie dish. Pierce the pastry all over with a fork and pre-bake in a 400°F oven for 10 minutes. Prepare the peach sauce and pour it into the pie. Roll out the reserved dough to a thickness of 1/8 inch and cut it into strips 1/2 inches wide. Lay them across the filling in lattice pattern. Decorate with the almonds and bake the tart in a 400°F oven for about 40 minutes or until the top is lightly golden. Serve the tart lukewarm, accompanied by whipped cream or one scoop vanilla ice cream. Follow the same procedure to make cherry, apple or strawberry tart.

Cream Horns (Korne me Krema)

Yields 12 horns
Preparation time 1-2 hours
Baking time 30 minutes

1/2   lb puff pastry
1   egg yolk beaten with 1 tablespoon water
     Pastry Cream (page 49)
1   recipe, Whipped Cream (page 49)
1/3   cup finely chopped pistachio nuts

Roll out the puff pastry to a 12 inch square on a floured surface. Cut the dough into 12 strips 1 inch wide each. Brush one edge of each strip with yolk mixture. Starting at narrow end of horn mold, roll the dough strip around so that the edge brushed with egg overlaps the unbrushed edge by about 1/4 inch. Press both edges together. Brush the horns with the remaining egg yolk and place on an ungreased baking sheet. Bake in a 400°F oven for about 20 minutes. When slightly cool, carefully loosen horns from molds and cool on a rack. Prepare the pastry cream and fill the horns 2/3 full. Pipe a whipped cream rosette on top of the cream and sprinkle with pistachio nuts. Serve on the day they are made, preferably within minutes of their completion.

Peach Tart, page 66

Puff Pastry Dough
(Zimi Sfoliata)

Yields 2 lbs
Preparation time 3-4 hours

1	lb all purpose flour (4 cups)
2	teaspoons salt
1	lb butter (2 cups)
3/4	cup cold water

Sift the flour and salt into a bowl. Cube one fourth of the butter and add it to the flour. Using two knives or a pastry blender, cut the butter into the flour following a rapid criss-cross movement until the mixture has a coarse and mealy texture. Add just enough water to bind the ingredients and work them into a ball with your fingertips. Cover the dough with plastic wrap and refrigerate for about 45 minutes, or half the time, in the freezer. Place the remaining butter between two sheets of baking paper and using a rolling pin flatten it into a 6 inch square. Chill for about 30 minutes. Roll out the dough on a lightly floured surface, preferably marble, into a 8 by 14 inch rectangle. Peel the top sheet of baking paper off the butter and invert the butter over the dough. Then peel off the second paper. Lightly moisten the edges of the dough and fold the two short sides over the butter so that they meet in the center. Press the edges together sealing the air inside and fold the dough in the middle. Roll out the folded dough into a rectangle, pressing evenly so as not to squeeze out the butter. Fold over in the middle once more, lightly moistening the edges and pressing them together. Wrap the dough in a plastic foil and refrigerate for 30 minutes. Repeat the procedure twice. Let the dough relax in the refrigerator for about 30 minutes in between. Sprinkle the surface of the dough with flour, brushing the excess carefully before each rolling to prevent sticking. The dough will keep 2-3 days in the refrigerator and 6 months in the freezer.

Puff Pastry Dough, page 67
Cream Horns, page 66

Plum Tart
(Tarta me Damaskina)

Serves 16-20
Preparation time 1 hour
Baking time 1 hour

The Dough

2/3	cup sugar
2	cups all purpose flour
1	teaspoon baking powder
1	teaspoon cinnamon
1	teaspoon vanilla
1/8	teaspoon cloves
1	cup unsalted butter or margarine, cubed
1	egg, lightly beaten with 2 tablespoons brandy
1/2	cup ground almonds

The Filling

5-6	tablespoons plum jam
1 1/2	lbs fresh plums, cut into fourths
3	tablespoons melted unsalted butter
3	tablespoons sugar

Mix the sugar with flour, baking powder and spices in a bowl. Add the butter and rub the mixture with your fingertips until it resembles coarse crumbs. You may use a pastry blender to do it easier. Add the egg mixture and almonds, mix gently, then gather the dough crumbs with your fingertips and form a ball. Avoid overworking. Roll out the dough into a round and line an ungreased 12 inch pie dish. Prick all over the surface with a fork and bake in a 350°F oven for 15 minutes. Remove the tart from the oven, cool slightly and brush with the jam. Arrange the plums, cut side up, in overlapping rows on the dough. Sprinkle with the sugar and melted butter. Replace it in the oven and bake for 30-35 minutes until golden brown. Serve it on the day it is made.

Meringue Nests with Fruit
(Folies Marengas me Frouta)

Yields 16 nests
Preparation time 2 hours
Baking time 1 hour and 30 minutes

1	recipe, Meringue (page 145)
2	recipes, Whipped Cream (page 49)
2	lbs strawberries, cherries or other fruit
3	oz pistachio nuts, chopped

Prepare the meringue as directed in the recipe. Spoon into a piping bag fitted with a star nozzle and pipe small rounds onto a greased baking paper. Pipe a ring around the edge of each round to make a nest shape. Bake in a 200°F oven for 1 hour and 30 minutes. Turn off the oven and let the meringues cool inside. Meanwhile, wash, clean, and dry the fruit thoroughly. If using cherries, remove the stones. Spoon or pipe a little whipped cream into the nests and place 3-5 fruits in each, depending on the size. Pipe whipped cream rosettes all around the fruit. Prepare the sauce: Boil the remaining fruit with 1/2 cup water, drain and thicken the juice adding 2-3 tablespoons sugar and 1 1/2 tablespoons cornstarch to 1 cup of juice. Spoon a little sauce over the fruit and sprinkle with pistachio nuts. Serve within minutes of its completion or the moisture from the fruit will soak into the meringue and make it soggy.

Lemon Cream Tart
(Tarta Lemoniou)

Serves 16-20
Preparation time 1 hour
Baking time 15 minutes

1	recipe, Rich Shortcrust Pastry Dough (page 37)
5-6	tablespoons lemon or grapefruit marmalade
1	recipe, Whipped Cream (page 49)
1/2	cup chopped, roasted almonds

The Custard

2	cups milk, scalded
5	tablespoons cornstarch
1/4	teaspoon salt
2/3	cup sugar
4	egg yolks
1	teaspoon grated lemon rind
3-4	tablespoons lemon juice

Prepare the dough according to the recipe. On a floured surface roll out the dough into a round and line an ungreased 11 inch pie dish. Pierce the dough all over with a fork and bake in a 400°F oven for 15 minutes or until golden brown. Remove from the oven and cool. Meanwhile, prepare the custard. Mix cornstarch, salt and sugar with a little cold milk into a saucepan. Stirring vigorously pour in the scalded boiling milk, all at once, and cook the cream, stirring constantly over low heat until thickened. Lightly beat the egg yolks, add a little hot custard, mix well and pour them into the remaining custard, stirring vigorously. Cook the cream 4 minutes longer stirring continuously. Remove from the heat, add the grated lemon rind then the lemon juice, one tablespoon at a time, and stir until well blended. Press a sheet of plastic wrap on the surface, to prevent a skin from forming and let the custard cool to lukewarm. Brush the tart with the marmalade, and pour in the lukewarm custard. Refrigerate until set. Fit a piping bag with a star nozzle and pipe whipped cream rosettes all over the top. Sprinkle with almonds. Serve the Lemon Cream Tart on the day it is made. Keep any leftover in the refrigerator uncovered to preserve the pastry crispness.

Walnut Tart (Tarta me Karidia)

Serves 10
Preparation time 1 hour
Baking time 30 minutes

1/2	cup unsalted butter
2	tablespoons sugar
1	egg
2	tablespoons brandy
1	teaspoon vanilla
2	cups all purpose flour
1/4	teaspoon salt

The Filling

10	oz plum jam
4	eggs
1/2	cup sugar
1	cup coarsely chopped walnuts
2	tablespoons cornstarch

Cream the butter and sugar with an electric mixer until pale and fluffy. Beating continuously at low speed, add the egg then brandy and flavoring. Sift the flour and salt and gently fold into the creamed butter a little at a time until well blended. Avoid overworking the dough as it will be tough when baked. Pat the dough and line the base of a 10 inch spring form mold and pre-bake in a 400°F oven for 10 minutes. Meanwhile, prepare the filling. Beat the eggs and sugar with the mixer at high speed until thick and light. Mix chopped walnuts with cornstarch and gradually add into beaten eggs, folding lightly to avoid deflating the eggs. Remove the tart from the oven and spread the jam over the dough. Pour in egg and walnut mixture and replace into oven. Bake for about 20 minutes longer. Cool for 5 minutes, then run a thin sharp knife around the edges to loosen, unlock the spring and gently lift off the ring. To remove the tart from the base, slide a wide spatula under the pastry, and transfer the tart to a serving dish. Let it cool completely and sprinkle with confectioners' sugar.

Alternate: Any other jam may be substituted for the plum jam. Almonds or pistachio nuts could also be used in place of walnuts. Coconut should be added along with all kinds of nuts as well as grated chocolate or dried fruit (dates, figs or prunes). One or two additional eggs may also be added, if mixture is too stiff.

Meringue Nests with Fruits, page 68

apple mixture on top. Sprinkle with cinnamon and spoon the remaining batter over the apples to cover. Smoothen the top with a spatula. Bake the cake in a 350°F oven for approximately 1 hour and 10 minutes. Let the cake stand for 5 minutes, then invert it on a serving dish. Let it cool completely. Measure the apple juice and if less than a cup, complete by adding canned apple juice. Mix the cornstarch with 2 tablespoons juice. Put the remaining juice in a small saucepan and stir in gelatine. Let it soften for 5 minutes, then stir in cornstarch mixture. Cook the mixture, stirring with a wooden spoon over low heat until clear and slightly thickened. Cool thoroughly and spread it over the cake. Let the icing set, then cut the cake into diamond shaped pieces. Top each piece with half walnut.

Apple Cake
(Keik me Mila)

Serves 20
Preparation time 1 hour
Baking time 1 hour and 10 minutes

The Filling
8	large tart apples, coarsely grated
1/2	cup sugar
1/8	teaspoon salt
2	tablespoons lemon juice
1	teaspoon cinnamon

The Cake
1	cup soft, unsalted butter or margarine
1 1/2	cups sugar
3	cups self raising flour
1/2	teaspoon vanilla
1/3	cup milk
5	eggs

The Icing
1	cup apple juice
1	tablespoon cornstarch
1	teaspoon gelatine
20	walnut halves for garnishing

Mix the apples, sugar, salt and lemon juice in a colander set over a bowl. Let them drain for about 2 hours. Press them lightly with your palms to expel all the juice. Keep the apples and juice separately. Place all the ingredients for the cake in the mixing bowl of an electric mixer. Stir them, to moisten, with a spoon. Then beat at high speed for 4 minutes until the batter is light and fluffy. Spread half the batter over the bottom of a well greased and floured, round cake pan (12 inches in diameter) and place the

Rena's Baked Halva
(Halvas tis Rinas)

Yields 20 pieces
Preparation time 30 minutes
Baking time 35 minutes

1	cup unsalted butter
3/4	cup sugar
6	eggs, separated
1/3	cup milk
1/4	teaspoon almond extract, or
1	teaspoon vanilla
1	teaspoon grated lemon rind
2	cups fine semolina
2	teaspoons baking powder
1	cup blanched and ground almonds

The Syrup
2	cups sugar
2	cups water
1	tablespoon lemon juice

Cream butter and half the sugar until light and fluffy. Beating continuously, add the egg yolks one at a time, beating well after each addition; then add milk and flavoring. Stop beating. Mix semolina with baking powder and gradually fold into creamed butter. Then fold in the ground almonds. Whisk the egg whites with the remaining sugar until they form soft peaks. Gently fold the meringue into the batter taking care not to break down the air bubbles beaten in. Pour the batter into a well greased 10 by 14 inch baking pan and bake in a 350°F oven for about 35 minutes or until the surface is golden brown. Remove from the oven, cool slightly and cut into diamonds. Boil syrup ingredients for 5 minutes and pour over the lukewarm cake. Cover and let it absorb the syrup and cool completely. Transfer to a serving dish and decorate with halved cherries and almonds, if desired.

Apple Cake, page 70

Apple Tart (Glikisma me Mila)

Serves 12
Preparation time 30 minutes
Baking time 1 hour

1/2	cup unsalted butter or margarine
1	cup sugar
2	eggs
2	cups self raising flour
1/8	teaspoon salt
6	tablespoons milk
2	teaspoons grated lemon rind
4	medium sized apples, cut into eights
1/4	cup unsalted butter, melted
2	tablespoons sugar
1	teaspoon cinnamon
	a little confectioners ' sugar and cinnamon for dusting

Cream butter and sugar at medium speed with an electric mixer. Beating continuously, add the eggs one at a time alternated with a tablespoon of flour to prevent the mixture from curdling. Sift flour and salt. Fold it into the creamed butter in 3-4 stages alternated with the milk. Mix in the lemon rind and pour the mixture into a greased 12 inch round cake pan. Arrange the apples on top of the dough in overlapping rows. Sprinkle the apples with melted butter and sugar and dust with cinnamon. Bake in a 350°F oven for 50-55 minutes. If the apples are browning too fast, cover with a piece of aluminum foil. Cool and transfer the tart to a serving dish. Dust with confectioners ' sugar and cinnamon.

Marmalade Tart (Pasta Flora)

Serves 18
Preparation time 30 minutes
Baking time 35 minutes

1	recipe, Rich Shortcrust Pastry Dough (page 37)
1	lb apricot or strawberry jam, or any other jam

Prepare the dough according to the recipe. On a floured surface, roll out $^2/_3$ of the dough into a round and line a greased 10 inch pie dish. Spread the jam over the dough. Roll the remaining dough into strips and lay them on top of the jam in a lattice pattern. Bake the tart in a 350°F oven for 30-35 minutes until slightly golden. Store the tart, uncovered, in a dry, cool place to prevent it from getting soggy too fast. It can be kept one week at room temperature.

Marmalade Tart, page 71
Apple Tart, page 71
Rena's Baked Halva, page 70

Sponge Cake with Jam
(Glikisma me Marmelada)

Serves 20
Preparation time 30 minutes
Baking time 40 minutes

2   recipes, All in One Butter Sponge Cake (page 39)
1   lb apricot jam, or any other jam
3-4 tablespoons confectioners ' sugar, or Chocolate Icing (page 49)

Prepare the sponge cake according to the recipe. Pour the batter into two 11 inch round cake pans, lined with greased baking paper, and bake in a 350°F oven for 40 minutes. Remove the cakes from the oven and turn out on a rack to cool completely. Spread the jam on the surface of one cake and set the second cake on top. Sift a little confectioners ' sugar over the second cake or spread it with chocolate icing, if preferred. Store in a cake container to keep it fresh. Serve it on the day it is made. You may wrap and freeze, if desired.

Strawberry Jelly Roll
(Rolo me Marmelada)

Serves 10
Preparation time 30 minutes
Baking time 20 minutes

1   recipe, Butter Sponge Cake (page 38)
2-3 tablespoons confectioners ' sugar
1   lb strawberry jam or any other jam

Prepare the sponge cake according to the recipe. Pour the batter into a 12 by 16 inch baking sheet, lined with greased baking paper, smoothing the top with a spatula. Bake in a 350°F oven for 15-20 minutes until golden. Remove the cake from the oven and turn it out on a kitchen towel, generously sprinkled with confectioners ' sugar. Trim the crusty edges with a knife. Carefully peel off the paper and roll the sponge along with the towel, starting at the long end. Cover the rolled sponge with plastic wrap to keep it moist until cold. Unroll it carefully, spread over the jam, and re-roll. Dust the top with additional confectioners ' sugar. Serve the roll the day it is made. You may wrap and freeze, if desired.

Sponge Cake with Jam, page 72
Strawberry Jelly Roll, page 72

Lenten Cake
(Keik Nistissimo)

Serves 15-20
Preparation time 15 minutes
Baking time 1 hour

The Cake

1/2	cup vegetable oil
1	cup sugar
1	tablespoon grated orange rind
3/4	cup orange juice
1/4	cup brandy
3	cups self raising flour
1	teaspoon baking soda
1 1/2	teaspoons cinnamon
1	teaspoon cloves
1/2	cup blackcurrant raisins
1/2	cup sultana raisins
1/2	cup coarsely ground walnuts

The Icing

1	cup confectioners' sugar
1	teaspoon grated orange rind
2	tablespoons orange juice

Put the first 5 ingredients in a blender and blend for 3-4 minutes until the mixture is thickened and light colored. Sift together into a large bowl the flour, soda, cinnamon, and cloves. Make a well in the center. Pour in the oil mixture and gradually fold in the flour, working by hand or with a mixer at low speed until the ingredients are well blended. Avoid overworking. Stir in the raisins and walnuts. Pour the batter into two small or one large cake pan, well greased and floured, filling them up to $^2/_3$ of their depth. Bake in a 350°F oven for about 1 hour. When ready, the cake should be brown and a toothpick should come out clean when inserted into the cake. Let the cake stand for 5 minutes before inverting it on a serving dish. Mix all icing ingredients into a small bowl and pour it over the cake while still warm. The icing will spread and cover the cake all over, forming a thin, translucent crust that keeps the cake moist and fresh.

Fruit Cake
(Keik Froutou)

Serves 20
Preparation time 30 minutes
Baking time 1 hour

2$^3/_4$	cups self raising flour
1/4	teaspoon salt
1/2	teaspoon baking soda
1	cup soft unsalted butter or margarine
1$^1/_4$	cups sugar

4	eggs
1/2	cup milk
1	tablespoon grated orange or lemon rind
1	cup chopped dried apricots
1/2	cup coarsely chopped walnuts

The Icing

2	tablespoons unsalted butter
1/2	cup apricot jam
2	tablespoons water
5	apricot preserves for garnishing

Sift the flour, salt, and soda. Set aside. Cream the butter and sugar until light and fluffy. Beating continuously, add the eggs one by one alternated with a tablespoon of flour to prevent the mixture from curdling. Then lower the speed and add the remaining flour in 2-3 stages, alternated with the milk. Fold in grated rind, apricots, and walnuts. Pour the batter into a deep 10 inch round cake pan, well greased, filling it up to $^2/_3$ of its depth. Bake the cake in a 350°F oven for about 1 hour. Test for doneness before removing from the oven. Insert a toothpick in the center of the cake. It should come out clean when the cake is ready. Invert the cake on a rack to cool. Meanwhile, prepare the icing. Melt the butter in a saucepan, add jam and water and stir over low heat for 1-2 minutes. Strain through a fine sieve. Decorate the cake with the apricot preserves and pour over the glaze while still warm.

Alternate: Prunes or 1 cup finely cut crystallized orange rind may be substituted for the apricots.

Walnut Dessert (Glikisma me Karidia)

Serves 16
Preparation time 45 minutes
Baking time 45 minutes

1¼   cups all purpose flour
2   teaspoons baking powder
2/3   cup unsalted butter or margarine, softened
1   cup sugar
1   teaspoon vanilla
5   egg whites
1¼   cups coarsely chopped walnuts
5   egg yolks
2/3   cup sugar
1   teaspoon vanilla
3   tablespoons self raising flour

The Icing

1/3   cup sugar
3   tablespoons cocoa
1/2   cup milk
3/4   cup finely chopped walnuts

1/3   cup unsalted butter, cubed
1   tablespoon brandy

Sift the flour with the baking powder. Set aside. Beat the butter and half the sugar together to a pale cream. Add the flavoring. Whisk separately the egg whites with the remaining sugar to form a soft and glossy meringue. Gradually fold the sieved flour a little at a time into the creamed butter. If the mixture becomes too stiff, add a little meringue to loosen. Gently fold in the remaining meringue. Then fold in the walnuts sprinkling them on the mixture lightly as you fold. Spread the batter into a greased and lightly floured 12 inch spring form mold and bake in a 350°F oven for about 30 minutes. Beat the egg yolks with the sugar at high speed until thick and lemon colored. Add vanilla and fold in the flour. Remove the cake from the oven and spread the egg yolk mixture on top. Continue baking it for about 15 minutes until done. Cool the cake 5 minutes in the mold then unlock the spring and using a wide spatula transfer it to a serving dish to cool completely. Meanwhile, prepare the icing:

Walnut Dessert, page 74

Mix sugar and cocoa in a heavy saucepan. Add milk and walnuts and stir the mixture over low heat until smooth. Off the heat, stir in the butter, a few cubes at a time, until the butter melts and the mixture is glossy. Stir in brandy. Cool and spread it on the cake. Let the icing set before you cut the cake into wedges and serve. You may garnish the wedges with dots of vanilla fondant stucked with halved walnuts.

Sweet Cheese Tart
(Glikisma me Anthotiro)

Serves 18
Preparation time 1 hour
Baking time 10 minutes

The Cake

1	cup Graham Cracker Crumbs
1	tablespoon flour
1	tablespoon sugar
1/4	teaspon salt
1/2	cup ground walnuts
1/3	cup melted unsalted butter
1/4	teaspoon almond extract
2	tablespoons cold water

The Custard

1/2	lb soft Anthotiro cheese (Cottage cheese)
1/4	teaspoon salt
1/2	cup confectioners ' sugar
1	teaspoon vanilla
3	egg yolks
1	cup whipping cream

The Garnish

5	pineapple slices
	little whipped cream
8	maraschino cherries
	crystallized figs, cut into leaf shapes

Mix crumbs, flour, sugar, salt and walnuts together into a bowl. Add the butter, almond extract and water working by hand until well blended. Pat the mixture into a well greased 10 inch spring form mold and cover the base. Bake in a 400°F oven for about 10 minutes. Remove from the oven and cool the tart thoroughly. Meanwhile, blend the cheese with salt and sugar in a food processor for 1-2 minutes, until smooth. Add the egg yolks, vanilla and 2-3 tablespoons cream. Blend for 1 minute longer. Whip separately the remaining cream with 3 tablespoons confectioners ' sugar until thick and light. Reserve a little cream for garnishing and gently fold the remaining into the cheese mixture. Pour the mixture over the baked tart, smoothing the surface with a spatula. Refrigerate until set. Run a knife around and between the rim of the mold and tart to looosen edges. Unlock the spring and lift off the ring. Using a wide spatula transfer the Cheese Tart to a serving dish. Garnish with pineapple slices, whipped cream and crystallized fruit. Keep refrigerated.

Tahini Cake   (Tachinopita)

Serves 20
Preparation time 30 minutes
Baking time 1 hour

3 1/2	cups self raising flour
1	teaspoon baking soda
1	teaspoon cream of tartar
1	teaspoon cinnamon
1/2	teaspoon cloves
1/2	cup coarsely chopped walnuts
1/2	cup sultana raisins
1/2	cup blackcurrant raisins
1	cup tahini
1	cup orange juice
1/2	cup honey
1/2	cup sugar
4	tablespoons brandy

Sift the flour, soda, cream of tartar, cinnamon and cloves together into a bowl. Mix in walnuts and raisins. Blend tahini, orange juice, honey and sugar in a blender for 2-3 minutes. Pour the mixture on the dry ingredients and mix together, working by hand, until well blended. Spread the mixture on a well greased and floured 12 inch round cake pan and bake in a 350°F oven for about 1 hour. Cool the cake 5 minutes in the pan, then turn it on to a serving dish and sprinkle with the brandy. When completely cold, cut the cake into wedges and sprinkle with confectioners ' sugar. Keep it moist, stored in a cake container. It keeps well up to one week.

Orange, Lemon or Tangerine Cake
(Keik Portokaliou, Lemoniou i Mandariniou)

Serves 15-20
Preparation time 10 minutes
Baking time 1 hour

The Cake

3¹/₂   cups self raising flour
2   cups sugar
1   cup soft margarine
2/3   cup orange juice or milk
4   large eggs
4   teaspoons grated lemon or tangerine rind

The Garnish

3-4   tablespoons confectioners ' sugar
     Orange or Chocolate Icing (page 49)

Put all the cake ingredients together into the mixing bowl of an electric mixer. Mix lightly with a spoon, then beat at medium speed for 4 minutes (scraping the sides of the bowl frequently with a spatula) until doubled in bulk, light and fluffy. Pour the batter into a large, 10 inch in diameter, turban cake mold, well greased and floured. Bake in a 350°F oven for about 1 hour, or until a wooden pick inserted into the cake comes out clean. Remove from the oven, let the cake cool for 5 minutes in the mold, then turn it out on a serving dish. Dust the top of the cake with confectioners ' sugar. To make it more appetizing, pour over the top orange or chocolate glaze, or a little of both. Placed in an airtight cake container. It keeps fresh and moist for up to one week. Stored in the freezer, it keeps for several months.
Orange Icing: In a small bowl, blend together with a spoon 2 tablespoons softened, unsalted butter, 1 cup confectioners ' sugar, 1 teaspoon finely grated orange rind and 2-3 tablespoons orange juice.

Orange Torte
(Tourta Portokaliou i Mandariniou)

Serves 16
Preparation time 1 hour and 30 minutes
Baking time 20 minutes

1   recipe, Butter Sponge Cake, or
     Whole Egg Sponge Cake (page 38)
1   recipe, Fruit Cream, Orange or
     Tangerine (page 52)
2   recipes, Whipped Cream (page 49)
16   caramel-glazed orange or tangerine segments
3   oz almonds, blanched, chopped and roasted

Prepare the sponge cake according to the recipe. Also prepare the fruit cream, cool, and fold in ¹/₃ of the whipped cream. Cut the cake into three layers, and stack them together, onto a serving dish, with fruit cream spread in between. If the sponge cake looks dry, sprinkle it with orange or tangerine juice, before covering with the cream. Spread the entire cake with the remaining whipped cream, reserving a small amount for piping rosettes. Garnish with rosettes, roasted almonds and caramel-glazed orange segments. To make the caramel-glazed oranges, separate 16 orange segments taking care not to tear the skin, and impale each one separately on a wooden skewer. Prepare caramel as in the recipe for the Caramel Custard (page 51), and dip the fruits in, one at a time. Hold over the pan until excess syrup has drained off and let them cool on a rack. Glaze the orange segments just before serving. Place them on top of the torte and serve at once.

Prunes with Whipped Cream
(Damaskina me Santigi)

Serves 16
Preparation time 30 minutes

2   lbs prunes
2   cups water
1/2   cup sugar
4-5   cinnamon sticks
10   whole cloves
1/2   lb walnuts, halved

The Syrup

1/2   cup sugar
1/4   cup water
1   tablespoon lemon juice
2   tablespoons of any liqueur (banana, cherry, orange)

The Garnish

1   cup whipping cream
1   tablespoon confectioners ' sugar
1   teaspoon vanilla
1/4   cup chopped pistachio nuts

Put the water and sugar into a heavy pan and stir over low heat until sugar dissolves completely. Add prunes and spices and bring to a boil. Lower the heat and simmer the prunes for 10 minutes. Drain well, then slit the prunes and remove the stones, replacing with halved walnuts. Boil the sugar and water in a heavy saucepan to make a thick syrup. Stir in the lemon juice and cool. Add the liqueur. Heap the prunes in the center of a serving dish and sprinkle with syrup. Whip the cream with sugar and flavoring until thick and light. Spoon it into piping bag fitted with a star nozzle and pipe whipped cream rosettes all over the surface. Sprinkle with pistachio nuts. Keep prunes refrigerated. Serve them at once.

Orange Torte, page 76

Tangerine Cream Sponge Log
(Kormos Mandariniou)

Serves 16
Preparation time 1 hour
Baking time 20 minutes

1   recipe, Butter Sponge Cake (page 38)
1/3 cup tangerine juice

The Filling

Buttercream or Custard Buttercream (page 50)
3   tablespoons tangerine liqueur
3   tablespoons grated tangerine rind
2/3 cup crystallized tangerine, or
     tangerine preserves, chopped

The Garnish

2   recipes Whipped Cream (page 49)
     green and red icing

Prepare the sponge cake according to the recipe. Pour

the batter, spreading it evenly, into a lined 12 by 16 inch shallow, Swiss roll tin. Bake in a 350°F oven for 15-20 minutes. Remove from the oven and turn the cake out on a kitchen towel, generously sprinkled with confectioners ' sugar. Carefully peel off the paper and trim the crusty edges of the sponge with a knife. Roll together with the towel, starting at the long end. Cool thoroughly, covered with plastic wrap to keep moist. Meanwhile, prepare the buttercream substituting tangerine liqueur for the vanilla flavoring. When the butter is creamed, fold in grated rind and chopped crystallized tangerine. Unroll the sponge carefully, sprinkle with tangerine juice spread on the cream and re-roll. Refrigerate until firm. Diagonally cut one slice from each end of the roll and press against two opposite sides of the log, securing with whipped cream and wooden picks, to look like short branches. Spread the whipped cream all over the roll, covering it completely, and trace a sprig of holly with red and green icing on top. Keep refrigerated.

Cream Cherry Cocoa Sponge Roll, page 79
Tangerine Cream Sponge Roll, page 78

Cream and Cherry Cocoa Sponge Log
(Kormos Kakao)

Serves 16
Preparation time 1 hour
Baking time 30 minutes

1   recipe, Cocoa Sponge Cake (page 38)

The Filling

6   oz baking chocolate
3   tablespoons milk
3   tablespoons maraschino syrup
3   egg yolks
2   recipes, Whipped Cream (page 49)
1/2   cup chopped maraschino or crystallized cherries

Prepare the Cocoa Sponge Cake according to the recipe. Pour the batter, spreading it evenly, into a lined 12 by 16 inch shallow, Swiss roll tin. Bake in a 350°F oven for approximately 30 minutes. Remove the cake from the oven and turn it out on a kitchen towel generously sprinkled with confectioners' sugar. Carefully peel off the paper. Trim the crusty edges with a knife and roll along with the towel, starting at the long end. Cover the rolled sponge with plastic wrap, until cold, to keep it moist. Meanwhile, melt the chocolate in a saucepan over low heat, add the milk, syrup and egg yolks, stirring vigorously to form a smooth paste. Gently fold chopped cherries into the whipped cream. Unroll the sponge cake, carefully, spread on the chocolate mixture, then spread cream with cherries over it, and re-roll. Refrigerate until firm. Using a sharp knife, diagonally cut off one slice from each end of the roll and press against two opposite sides of the log, securing with whipped cream and wooden picks, to look like short branches. Dust the log with confectioners' sugar to look like snow. Keep refrigerated. Keeps well for 3-4 days. To keep moist, cover with plastic wrap.

Hazelnut Cake (Keik Foundoukiou)

Serves 15-20
Preparation time 15 minutes
Baking time 1 hour

The Cake

1   cup soft margarine
2   cups sugar
3   cups self raising flour
2   teaspoons vanilla
2/3   cup milk
4   large eggs
1   cup roasted, ground hazelnuts

The Garnish

confectioners' sugar, or
Chocolate Icing (page 49)

Put all cake ingredients except for the hazelnuts into a mixing bowl of an electric mixer. Mix lightly with a spoon, then beat at high speed for 4 minutes (scraping the sides of the bowl frequently with a spatula), until doubled in

Black and White Cake
(Keik Aspromavro)

Serves 15-20
Preparation time 10 minutes
Baking time 1 hour

The Cake

1   cup soft margarine
2   cups sugar
3 1/2   cups self raising flour
4   large eggs
2/3   cup milk
2   teaspoons vanilla
4   tablespoons cocoa
4   tablespoons confectioners' sugar
1/8   teaspoon baking soda

The Garnish

3-4   tablespoons confectioners' sugar
     Chocolate Icing (page 49)

Put 6 first cake ingredients in a mixing bowl. Mix lightly with a spoon, then beat at high speed for 4 minutes (scraping the sides of the bowl frequently with a spatula) until fluffy and doubled in bulk. Pour $^2/_3$ of the batter into a greased and lightly floured 10 inch turban cake mold. Sift the cocoa, confectioners' sugar and soda and fold into the remaining batter. Spoon chocolate batter over plain batter in mold. To marble batter, swirl a spatula through batters all around. Bake in a 350°F oven for approximately 1 hour, or until a wooden pick inserted in center comes out clean. Cool for 5 minutes, then invert the cake on a serving dish. While warm, dust with confectioners' sugar or spread with chocolate icing. To keep moist, store in an airtight container. It freezes well.

bulk and fluffy. Add ground hazelnuts in handfuls, sprinkling them on the batter, lightly, as you are folding. Pour the batter into a large 10 inch in diameter turban mold, greased and lightly floured, filling it up to $^2/_3$ of its depth. Bake in a 350°F oven for 1 hour. Test with a wooden pick before removing the cake from the oven. Cool the cake 5 minutes in the mold, before turning it out on a serving dish. While warm, dust with confectioners' sugar or spread it with chocolate icing. Store in an airtight cake container or freeze it.

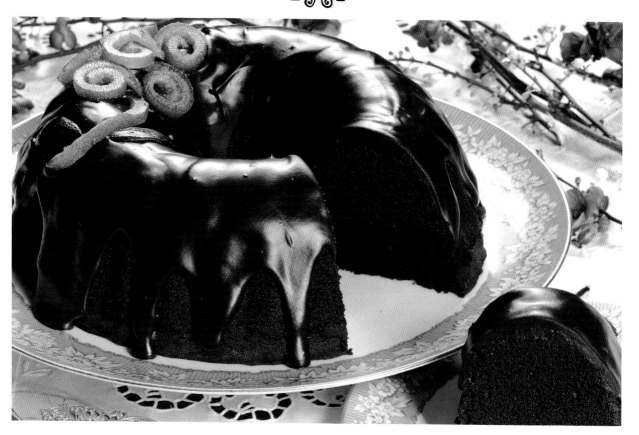

Chocolate Cake (Keik Sokolatas)

Serves 20
Preparation time 10 minutes
Baking time 1 hour

The Cake

2	cups self raising flour
3/4	cup cocoa
3/4	cup soft margarine
2	cups sugar
6	eggs
1/2	cup milk
1/4	teaspoon almond extract
1	teaspoon vanilla
1/4	teaspoon baking soda

The Icing

4	oz baking chocolate
1	cup confectioners ' sugar
2	egg yolks
2	tablespoons brandy
1	tablespoon milk
2	tablespoons butter

Place all cake ingredients in a mixing bowl. Mix lightly with a spoon, then beat for 4 minutes at high speed until double in bulk and fluffy. Pour the batter into a large, well greased turban mold, filling it up to $^2/_3$ of its depth. Bake in a 350°F oven for 1 hour. Cool the cake 5 minutes, then invert on a serving dish. Cool it thoroughly. Meanwhile, prepare the icing. Melt the chocolate in the top pan of a double boiler or over very low heat. Add the remaining ingredients all at once, stirring vigorously with a spoon. Remove from heat. Spread the icing all over the cake.

Date Lenten Cake
(Keik Nistissimo me Hourmades)

Serves 20
Preparation time 1 hour
Baking time 1 hour

$3^1/_2$	cups self raising flour
2	teaspoons cinnamon
1/2	cup olive oil or vegetable oil
1	cup sugar
1	cup orange juice
1	teaspoon baking soda, dissolved in 2 tablespoons brandy
1	cup coarsely chopped walnuts
1	cup chopped dates
	sesame seeds

Sift flour and cinnamon in a bowl and make a well in the center. Add in oil, sugar, orange juice and soda. Stir with a spoon, then mix in the flour, working by hand, until all the ingredients are well blended. Avoid overworking. Fold in nuts and dates. Spread the mixture into a well greased and floured, 12 inch round cake pan and bake in a 350°F oven for approximately 1 hour. Let the cake cool in the pan. Cut it into square or diamond shaped pieces and place on a serving dish. If desired, dust with confectioners ' sugar. Store in an airtight container. It keeps up to one week.

Chocolate Cake, page 80

Date and Whipped Cream Dessert
(Glikisma me Hourmades)

Serves 16
Preparation time 1 hour
Baking time 45 minutes

2	tablespoons flour
1	tablespoon cocoa
1/2	teaspoon cinnamon
1/8	teaspoon salt
2	cups chopped dates ($^1/_2$ lb)
2	cups coarsely ground walnuts ($^1/_2$ lb)
10	egg whites
3/4	teaspoon cream of tartar
1	cup sugar

The Garnish

1	cup whipping cream
1	teaspoon vanilla
16	dates, pitted
	crystallized fruit, or Seville orange preserve

Sift the first 4 ingredients together and mix with the dates and walnuts. Whisk the egg whites with the cream of tartar until they form soft peaks. Gradually add the sugar, beating continuously at the highest speed, until a thick and glossy meringue is formed. Gently fold the nut mixture into the meringue. Spread the mixture evenly into a 10 inch round cake pan lined with greased baking paper, and bake in a 350°F oven for 45 minutes. Cool the cake 5 minutes in the pan, then invert it on a serving dish. Let it cool completely. Meanwhile, whip the cream with vanilla until thick and fluffy, spoon it into a piping bag and garnish the top of the cake. Decorate with whole dates and crystallized fruit. Keep refrigerated.

Chocolate Torte
(Pasta Sokolatina)

Serves 20
Preparation time 1 hour and 30 minutes
Baking time 1 hour

The Cake

1$^1/_2$	cups self raising flour
1	cup cocoa
1/4	teaspoon baking soda
3/4	cup soft margarine
1$^1/_2$	cups sugar
6	eggs
1/4	cup milk
1/4	teaspoon almond extract
1	teaspoon vanilla

The Frosting

8	oz baking chocolate
3	egg yolks
3	tablespoons brandy
2	tablespoons milk
3	tablespoons butter

1$^1/_2$	cups confectioners ' sugar
2	recipes, Whipped Cream (page 49)

The Garnish

crystallized or maraschino cherries
leaves cut out from crystallized figs or Seville oranges
chocolate sprinkles

Place all cake ingredients in a mixing bowl, and mix lightly with a spoon. Then beat for 4 minutes at medium speed until doubled in bulk and fluffy. If a mixer is not available, sift the flour, cocoa and baking soda together. Set aside. Beat the butter with the sugar until light and fluffy and add the eggs one at a time, alternated with 1 tablespoon of the flour mixture to prevent curdling. Beating continuously, add the sifted ingredients in stages alternated with the milk. Pour the batter, spreading it evenly, into a greased and lightly floured 12 inch round cake pan and bake in a 350°F oven for 1 hour. Meanwhile, prepare the chocolate frosting. Melt the chocolate in the top pan of a double boiler. In a bowl, mix egg yolks, brandy and milk. Add in the cubed butter. Pour this mixture together with the confectioners ' sugar into the melted chocolate, stirring vigorously with a wooden spatula, until well blended. Cool thoroughly. Remove the cake from the oven. When it is completely cold, cut into 3 layers with a piece of string. Spread half of the chocolate frosting onto the first layer, top with the second layer, and spread with whipped cream, reserving a small amount for garnishing. Top with the third layer. Spread the entire cake with the remaining chocolate frosting. Press chocolate sprinkles into the sides of the cake and garnish the top with reserved whipped cream and crystallized fruits. Keep refrigerated. Let it stand 10 minutes at room temperature before serving.

Chocolate Torte

Egg White Cake
(Keik me Aspradia)

Serves 15-20
Preparation time 15 minutes
Baking time 1 hour

The Cake

1	cup soft margarine
2	cups sugar
$3^1/_2$	cups self raising flour
4	egg whites
3/4	cup orange juice
1	tablespoon grated orange rind
1	tablespoon grated lemon rind
1	cup coarsely chopped walnuts

The Garnish

2	tablespoons rose water
	a little confectioners ' sugar

Put all the cake ingredients, except for the walnuts, into a mixing bowl. Stir lightly with a spoon, then beat at high speed for 4 minutes until light and fluffy. Fold in the walnuts. Pour the batter into a well greased and floured turban cake mold, filling it up to $^2/_3$ of its depth. Bake in a 350°F oven for 1 hour. Before removing the cake from the oven, insert a wooden pick into the center of the cake. If it comes out clean, the cake is done. Cool it for 5 minutes in the mold, then invert the cake on a serving dish. While still warm, sprinkle it with rose water and dust the top with confectioners ' sugar. Keep it in an airtight container. You may freeze it, if desired.

Fresh Plum cake
(Keik me Freska Damaskina)

Serves 20
Preparation time 30 minutes
Baking time 1 hour and 10 minutes

5	eggs
2	cups sugar
1	cup butter or margarine, melted
1/2	cup milk
4	cups self raising flour
2	tablespoons grated lemon rind
2	lbs fresh plums, stoned and sliced

Beat eggs and sugar with a mixer at the highest speed until thick and lemon colored. Decrease the speed and beating continuously, add butter and milk in stages alternated with the flour. Fold in the lemon rind. Pour the batter, spreading it evenly, into a well greased and floured 14 inch round cake pan and arrange the plums on top. Bake in a 350°F oven for approximately 1 hour and 10 minutes. Serve the cake slightly warm, preferably on the day it is made. Keep leftovers in the freezer. Reheat before serving.

Truffles
(Troufes)

Serves 16
Preparation time 1 hour
Baking time 10 minutes

1	recipe, Sponge Biscuit Dough (page 137)
1/4	cup liqueur any flavor as preferred
	Chocolate Cream (page 49)
	Chocolate Icing (page 59)
10	oz chocolate sprinkles or
10	oz almonds, blanched,
	chopped and roasted

Prepare a sponge biscuit dough. Spoon it into a piping bag fitted with a $^1/_2$ inch wide plain nozzle. Pipe $1^1/_3$ inch wide dots of the mixture onto lined baking sheets, spaced well apart to allow room for expansion. Through a sieve, sprinkle a generous amount of confectioners ' sugar over each biscuit and bake them in a 400°F oven for about 8 minutes until lightly colored. Cool and peel off the paper. Prepare the chocolate cream and cool. Brush the bottom side of biscuits with a little liqueur and sandwich pairs of them together, spreading a thick layer of cream in between. Refrigerate until firm. Meanwhile, prepare the chocolate icing and, while lightly warm, dip in the sandwiched biscuits, one by one, then roll either in chocolate sprinkles or in chopped almonds, until covered all over. Place the truffles in candy caps and dust with confectioners ' sugar. Keep refrigerated.

Kariokes
(Kariokes)

Yields 60 pieces
Preparation time 2 hours

18   oz baking chocolate
1   lb sponge cake, dried out
10   oz vanilla fondant, softened
1/4   cup brandy
1/2   cup thick cold syrup, as for Baklava
1   lb coarsely chopped walnuts
12   oz dipping chocolate

Melt the chocolate and vanilla fondant in the top pan of a double boiler Finely grind the sponge cake in a food processor and mix with the melted chocolate, vanilla fondant and brandy. Add as much syrup as necessary. The mixture should be firm enough to be shaped by hand. Fold in walnuts. Roll the mixture into two, 4 inch wide each, cylinders. Cover them with a sheet of plastic wrap and refrigerate until firm. Using a very sharp knife cut each cylinder into $^1/_4$ inch thick slices, then cut each slice in half. Put the slices back in the refrigerator. Melt dipping chocolate over a water bath or over direct very low heat and keep it warm. Secure each Karioka on to a dipping fork, dip into the melted chocolate and lift it out. Allow the excess chocolate to drip off and place Kariokes one next to the other onto a greased sheet of baking paper placed over a tray. Chill and allow the chocolate coating to set and harden completely. Wrap each one individually in alluminum foil and keep refrigerated. They keep well up to two weeks.

Cream Filled Round Sponge Biscuits
(Kok)

Serves 12
Preparation time 1 hour
Baking time 10 minutes

1   recipe, Sponge Biscuit Dough (page 137)
2   recipes, Whipped Cream (page 49), or
1/2   recipe, Pastry Cream (page 49)
1   recipe, Chocolate Icing (page 59)

Prepare a sponge biscuit dough and spoon it into a piping bag fitted with a $^1/_2$ inch wide plain nozzle. Pipe 2 inch wide dots onto greased baking papers placed on baking sheets. Leave 1 inch space between them to allow for expansion. For your convenience and a uniform shape, trace circles on the baking paper before greasing it and pipe the dough inside them. Through a sieve, sprinkle a generous amount of confectioners ' sugar over each biscuit and bake them in a 400°F oven for about 10 minutes or until lightly browned. Remove the biscuits from the paper and cool on a rack. Sandwich pairs of biscuits together, spreading a thick layer of pastry cream or whipped cream in between. Place the cakes on a serving dish. Prepare the chocolate icing and spread over the tops. Keep refrigerated.

Kariokes, page 83
Cream Filled Round Sponge Biscuits, page 83

5

Jams and Compotes
(Marmelades ke Kobostes)

Hundreds of years ago, when refrigerators and freezers were unknown, women, around all the world, were discovering ways and means to preserve fruits for out-of-season use. Fruits always have been plentiful in Greece. Grown in their natural season out of green houses under the Greek sun, fruits are juicy and tasteful and have a superior flavor and color. Careful Greek housewives have been collecting and preserving for years the golden gifts of Greek nature, at the height of the season, preparing jams, compotes, spoonsweets, fruit jellies and sauces. These preserved treasures made in Greek kitchens with the loving care of Greek housewives are special and much tastier than commercially made products. Try the following basic recipes, then make your own combination of fruits to create your own unique preserves.

General Instructions

A large variety of preserved fruit are made by cooking the fruits with sugar. Preserved fruit as jams, marmalades, compotes, fruit sauces and syrups being prepared and stored according to the basic preserving principles, will keep for weeks, months or even years. In the presence of high concentrations of sugar, microorganisms stop growing. On the other hand sugar retains the color, texture and flavor of fruit. Sugar also helps in setting. For good keeping, the appropriate proportions of sugar may vary from $3/4$ lb to 1 lb for every 1 lb of fruit, according to the quality of the fruit and your own preference. Setting, except for sugar, depends also on the presence of two other factors, both contained to some degree in the fruit, pectin and acid. A correct balance of pectin, sugar and acid ensures a good set. The pectin and acid content varies from fruit to fruit. Even the same kind of fruit will have different levels of pectin and acid according to age. The acidity of the fruit can be judged by taste and corrected by adding lemon juice. About 2 tablespoons of lemon juice will be enough for 1 pint of low acid fruit or fruit juice. It should be added at the beginning of the cooking to help the fruit expel out its natural pectin. In low-pectin fruit, such as apricots, peaches, pineapples, cherries and kiwis, a quantity of fruit, especially rich in pectin, such as apples, quince, plums, oranges or grapes, can be combined in the preserve mixture. Commercially prepared or homemade Natural Pectin (page 93) can be added instead. One half cup of natural pectin will be enough to set 2 pints of low-pectin fruit. It should be added at the end of cooking, if necessary, after testing for setting.

Marmalades and jams can be made from almost any kind of fruit. The technique is simple and easy. The fruit should be ripe, but not over-ripe. Wash and dry the fruit, remove pits, stones, cores or any damaged part, before using. Cut into pieces and cook the fruit, slowly, until tender. Add the sugar and simmer, stirring with a wooden spoon, until the sugar is completely dissolved. Increase the heat and boil carefully, stirring to prevent burning, until the fruit is soft and the syrup is ready to set. (Simmering softens the fruit and gradually extracts its pectin. Boiling helps the pectin and sugar to gel). Then begin to test for setting. Pick up a little jam with a spoon. When you tip the spoon, two large distinct drops should form, combine and fall off the spoon cleanly. If using a candy thermometer, it should register 220°F. Once the setting point is reached, skim off the froth and ladle the jam into hot, sterilized jars leaving $1/2$ inch of headspace. Seal, when completely cold, and store in a dark, dry and cool place or, preferably, in the refrigerator. To sterilize storing jars, dip them in boiling water for five minutes and let them dry, set upside down on absorbent paper.

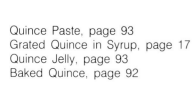

To retain the quality and aroma of the fresh fruit, for up to one year, compotes must be heat-processed into a hot bath. The fruit is packed in heat-proof glass jars fitted with rubber rings and clamp tops that fasten the lids to the jars for a tight seal. (The jars must be filled leaving a headspace of $1/2$-1 inch. Rubber rings must be renewed every time the jar is used). Then the jars are bathed in boiling water for the proper time and temperature specified in each case. If a heat-processor is not available, any large cooking pot with a tight-fitting lid can be used. The pot must be 3 inches taller than the jars. Place a metal rack on the bottom of the pot to protect the jars from direct heat and wrap each jar in a cloth to prevent cracking. Pour enough water into the pot to cover the jars. Cover the pot, bring the water to a boil, then simmer as long as required. Count the time from the moment the water begins to boil. The heat treatment kills spoilage microorganisms and drives out some of the air, sealing the jars and preventing recontamination. In this process fruit may be packed either pre-cooked in a light syrup, or raw. Raw fruit may be packed into jars with alternating layers of sugar or covered with a light syrup. The proportion of sugar varies according to your taste and the tartness of the fruit. The processing time needed will depend on the kind, size and tartness of the fruit, also on the size of the jars. Acidity is the main factor for a safe sterilization. Because the acidity of fruits can vary depending on their variety and ripeness, it is advised to add 2-3 teaspoons of lemon juice in each 1 pint jar to sweet fruits, such as figs and pears or any over-riped fruit. The sterilization time for raw packed fruit is a little longer than the time needed for the pre-cooked ones. Time indicated for apples, apricots, peaches, plums, nectarines whole or halved, cherries and sliced pineapples is about 15 minutes if the fruit is packed raw and 10 minutes if it is pre-cooked. When the fruit is sliced, required time is 5 minutes less in both cases. Whole or halved pears and sliced quinces require 30-40 minutes if packed raw and 20-25 minutes if pre-cooked. Suggested time refers to $1^1/_2$ pint jars. For larger jars add 3-4 minutes. Store the jars in a dark, cool place.

Orange Marmalade, page 87
Strawberry Jam, page 87
Apricot Jam, page 87

Orange Marmalade
(Grapefruit, Seville Orange,
 Tangerine or Lemon)

(Marmelada Portokali)

Yields 4 lbs
Preparation time 24 hours
Cooking time 2 hours

2	lbs oranges
1	lemon
2	lbs sugar
3¹/₂	pints water

Wash the oranges and lemon thoroughly. Cut each fruit into 8 wedges and remove the pips with a pair of scissors. Put the pips in a bowl and cover with part of the water. Thinly slice the fruit wedges with a knife, or a pair of scissors. Put in a heavy- bottomed pan, preferably non-stick, and cover them with the remaining water. Let the pips and oranges soak for 24 hours. The next day, place the pan over medium heat. Drain the water in which the pips were soaked, into the pan,and tie the pips in a muslin bag. Add it also to the pan. Cover and simmer the fruits for about 1 hour, then remove the bag with the pips, pressing the cloth to extract all the juice, and add the sugar. Stir over a very low heat until the sugar is dissolved. Then increase the heat to medium and cook, uncovered, stirring occasionally with a wooden spoon until the jam is translucent and set. Take the pan off the heat and skim the surface of the jam with a metal spoon. Cool it slightly, shaking the pan to distribute the orange pieces evenly, and ladle into warm, sterilized jars. Seal and store preferably in the refrigerator. The marmalade keeps well up to one year.
Alternate: Follow the same procedure for any citrus fruit, or combine 2-3 fruits, according to your preference.

Apricot or Peach Jam
(Marmelada Verikoko i Rodakino)

Yields 6 lbs
Preparation time 30 minutes
Cooking time 1 hour

5	lbs ripe apricots
4	tablespoons lemon juice
3	lbs sugar
1/2	lb glucose (corn syrup)

Wash and drain the apricots thoroughly. Stone and halve them. Sprinkle them with the lemon juice, to avoid discoloration. In a large, heavy-bottomed, preferably non-stick pan, layer the apricots with the sugar, finishing with a layer of sugar. Mash the apricots with your hand breaking them up and mixing with the sugar. Place the pan over low heat and stir until the sugar is completely dissolved. Increase the heat and adjust to maintain a steady simmer. Stir occasionally to prevent burning and cook until the jam is very thick and translucent. Add the glucose during the last 5 minutes of cooking. Remove from the heat and skim the jam carefully. Cool slightly and ladle into warm, sterilized jars. Seal and store in a dark, cool place or preferably in the refrigerator. It keeps well up to one year.
Variation: Crack 15-20 apricot stones and remove the kernels. Blanch the kernels and remove the brown skin. Add the kernels to the jam along with the glucose. Follow the same procedure for peach jam.

Strawberry Jam
(Marmelada Fraoula)

Yields 2 lbs
Preparation time 20 minutes
Cooking time 20 minutes

2	lbs strawberries
2	cups sugar
1	cup water
2	tablespoons lemon juice

Wash carefully and hull the strawberries. Drain them and cut in half. Put the sugar, water and half the lemon juice in a heavy- bottomed pan and stir over low heat until the sugar is dissolved. Increase the heat and boil the syrup for 5 minutes without stirring. Drop in half the strawberries, bring back to a boil and cook for 5 minutes, skimming well. Transfer the strawberries with a slotted spoon to a colander placed over a bowl, to catch the juice. Continue boiling the syrup until it has reduced to its original volume. Add the remaining strawberries, cook and remove to the colander as previously. Pour the juice that has been drained off the strawberries back into the pan and cook the syrup rapidly until it is set. Add the strawberries along with the remaining lemon juice and simmer stirring gently for about 10 minutes or until the setting point is reached. Take the pan off the heat and skim the froth from the surface of the jam with a metal spoon. Shake the pan to distribute the fruit evenly and cool, slightly, before ladling the jam into jars. Seal and store in the refrigerator. The jam will keep for up to a year.

Plum Jam
(Marmelada Damaskino)

Yields 4 lbs
Preparation time 30 minutes
Cooking time 55 minutes

4	lbs under ripe plums
1 1/2	cups water
2	lbs sugar
1	teaspoon almond extract
	the kernels of a few stones, for flavor

Wash, drain and halve the plums. Remove the stones and discard. If desired, keep a few stones, crack them, remove the kernels, blanch and put them together with the plums in a heavy-bottomed pan. The kernels will give a special flavor to the jam. Add the water and simmer the plums, for about 40 minutes, until very soft. Remove the pan from the heat, add the sugar and stir well, until the sugar is dissolved. Return the pan to the heat and cook rapidly for about 15 minutes, stirring carefully with a wooden spoon until the setting point is reached. Remove from heat, skim the froth off the surface. Cool the jam slightly and ladle into warm, sterilized jars. Seal and store in the refrigerator. The jam keeps well up to a year.

Apple or Pear Compote
(Milo i Achladi Komposta)

Serves 4
Preparation time 15 minutes
Cooking time 30 minutes

1 1/2	lbs firm apples or pears
2	tablespoons lemon juice
1	cup sugar
1	cup water
1	teaspoon vanilla or
1	stick cinnamon and 3-4 cloves or
	thinly pared citrus rind

Peel and core the apples or pears. Cut each fruit in half and plunge, immediately, into cold water mixed with the lemon juice to avoid discoloration. Put the sugar and the water into a pan and stir over low heat until the sugar is dissolved. Bring the syrup to a boil and cook rapidly 5 minutes. Add the flavoring of your choice, and then add the fruit draining them with a slotted spoon, and simmer until they are barely tender, 5-15 minutes. The time will vary with the quality of the fruit. Avoid overcooking. Transfer the compote with a slotted spoon to a bowl or to a jar. Boil the syrup until it is slightly thickened and ladle it over the fruit. Serve the compote warm or cold. It keeps in the refrigerator for about a week. To keep longer, once it is potted, it must be heat-processed. See General Instructions (page 85, 86).
Alternate: Add 1 cup red wine into the syrup along with the fruit.

Prune Compote
(Damaskina Xera Composta)

Serves 4
Preparation time 12 hours
Cooking time 20 minutes

1	lb prunes
1	cup orange juice
	thinly pared orange rind
1	cinnamon stick
1/2	cup sugar

Put the prunes in a pan and cover with water. Let them soak overnight. The next day put the pan over medium heat and cook the prunes for 5 minutes. Take off the heat. Remove the prunes with a slotted spoon, cool slightly, and lift out the stones. Add the orange juice, rind, cinnamon and sugar to the liquid in the pan. Cover and cook the syrup for about 10 minutes. Remove the cinnamon stick, and skim off the froth. Drop in the prunes and cook for 5 minutes or until the syrup is slightly thickened. Serve the compote warm or cold. Follow the same procedure for dried apricots, or combine prunes and dried apricots.
Alternate: During the last 5 minutes of cooking, add 1/4 cup sultana raisins and 1/4 cup chopped nuts, if desired.

Peach or Apricot Compote
(Rodakina i Verikoka Komposta)

Serves 4
Preparation time 10 minutes
Cooking time 15 minutes

4	large peaches (1 1/2 lbs) peeled and halved
2/3	cup sugar
1	cup water
4	tablespoons brandy

In a pan, dissolve the sugar in the water over low heat. Bring to a boil. When the syrup is clear, add the peaches and simmer until they are barely tender, about 8 minutes. Avoid overcooking. Transfer the fruit to a bowl with a slotted spoon and continue cooking the syrup until slightly thickened. Stir the brandy into the syrup and pour it over the peaches. Serve the compote warm or cold. Follow the same procedure for apricots. Compotes can keep up to a year if they are heat-processed after bottling.

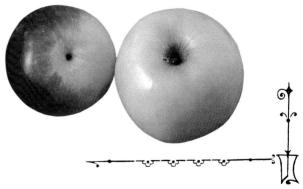

Fresh Cherry Sauce
(Saltsa me Kerasia)

Yields about 2 cups
Preparation time 10 minutes
Cooking time 25 minutes

1	lb red cherries
1/3	cup sugar
1	teaspoon grated lemon rind or
1/4	teaspoon almond extract
1	cup cherry juice
2	tablespoons cornstarch
2	tablespoons lemon juice
4	tablespoons cherry brandy

Wash, drain and stone the cherries, reserving the stones. Put the stones, sugar and lemon rind into a pan. Add the cherry juice and stir, over low heat, until the sugar is dissolved. Turn up the heat and boil for 5 minutes without stirring. Strain the syrup into a clean saucepan; discard the stones. Mix the cornstarch with a little of the syrup, and add it into the remainder along with the cherries and lemon juice. Cook slowly, for about 5 minutes, stirring occasionally until the sauce is thick and translucent. Cool slightly and stir in the cherry brandy. Serve the sauce, hot or cold, with vanilla or chocolate ice cream, or use it as a pie filling. Tightly sealed in a plastic container, the sauce keeps 1 week in the refrigerator and several months in the freezer.

Fruit Sauce
(Saltsa Froutou)

Yields about 4 cups
Preparation time 30 minutes
Cooking time 10 minutes

4	cups sliced fruit (strawberries, kiwi, peaches, apples, pineapple, washed, pared and hulled, stoned or cored, before slicing)
1-1½	cups sugar
3	tablespoons cornstarch
4	tablespoons lemon juice
4	tablespoons brandy or fruit liqueur

Put the fruit into a heavy-bottomed, preferably non-stick pan. In a small bowl, mix the cornstarch and sugar. The quantity of sugar will vary with the sweetness of the fruit and your own preference. Spread the mixture over the fruit and sprinkle with the lemon juice. Cover the pan and cook the sauce gently over low heat, stirring occasionally, until it is translucent and thick. Let it cool slightly and stir in the brandy or liqueur. Shake the pan or stir the sauce gently to distribute the fruit pieces evenly. When it is completely cool, ladle it in small plastic containers, seal tightly and store or freeze. It keeps 1 week in the refrigerator and 6 months in the freezer. Use the sauce to garnish ice cream, as illustrated on page 45, or make delicious fruit pies (page 66).

Lemonade
(Lemonada)

Yields about 3 pints
Preparation time 10 minutes
Cooking time 15-20 minutes

2	cups water
2	tablespoons grated lemon rind
2	lbs sugar
2-2½	cups lemon juice

Put the water in a saucepan together with the grated lemon rind and simmer, covered, for 10-15 minutes. Strain through a fine sieve into another saucepan. Add the sugar and cook over low heat, stirring constantly until the sugar is dissolved. Increase the heat and cook the syrup without stirring for 5-8 minutes until it reaches the hard ball stage or registers 250°F on a candy thermometer. Stir in the lemon juice and take it off the heat immediately. Remove any scum with a metal skimmer and cool slightly before bottling into hot sterilized bottles. Seal and store in the refrigerator. To serve, place 4-5 tablespoons lemonade syrup in each glass, add 3-4 ice cubes and fill up the glasses with iced water. Add more, or less syrup according to taste. Stir and serve the lemonade with a straw.

Strawberry Sauce, page 90

Sour Cherry Syrup
(Vissinada)

Yields about 3 pints
Preparation time 24 hours
Cooking time 20 minutes

4	lbs washed and stoned ripe sour cherries
4	lbs sugar
2	tablespoons lemon juice

Crush the cherries with a wooden pestle until they form an uneven puree, or process 1-2 seconds in a food processor. Transfer the crushed fruit to a large bowl, cover and refrigerate for 24 hours. The next day, put the cherries in a muslin bag and squeeze, pressing the cloth with your hands, to extract all the juice. It would be easier if an electric fruit juicer could be used. Measure the juice and add 1 lb sugar to each 1 cup (8 fl oz) juice. Transfer the juice to a large, non-reactive saucepan (stainless steel or enamelled) and stir over low heat until the sugar is dissolved. Put the lid on the pan for a minute, to allow the steam to dissolve any sugar, splashed on the sides of the pan. This prevents the syrup from crystalizing. Increase the heat, add the lemon juice and boil the syrup without stirring for 5 minutes or until set. Remove from the heat, skim off the froth and pour the juice into hot, sterilized bottles. Do not seal until the syrup is completely cold. Refrigerate the bottles. The juice will keep for about one year. To serve, place 4-5 tablespoons in a glass, add 3-4 ice cubes and fill it up with iced water. Add more, or less syrup according to taste. Stir and serve with a straw. Decorate the glass with two fresh cherries or sour cherries.

Sour Cherry Syrup, page 91

Sour Cherry Liqueur
(Kerasso, Liker me Vissina)

Yields about 2 pints
Preparation time 2 months

2   lbs sour cherries
2   lbs sugar
10   whole cloves
2   sticks cinnamon, crushed
1½   pints good quality brandy

Wash the cherries thoroughly and remove the stems. Rinse and leave them to drain in a colander. Put the cherries into a wide- mouthed bottle. Add the sugar and spices. Cover tightly, shake well and allow to macerate in a sunny place for about 2 months. Shake the bottle once or twice every day. Drain the flavorful cherry juice and mix with the brandy. Bottle and cork. Keep the bottles of liqueur in a cool place or in a wine cellar.

Carrot Jam
(Marmelada Karoto)

Yields 4 lbs
Preparation time 1 hour
Cooking time 30 minutes

3   lbs tender young carrots, peeled and grated
3   lbs sugar
6   lemons, rind grated, juice strained
6   oz coarsely chopped almonds, lightly roasted

Place the carrots in a heavy-bottomed, preferably non-stick pan and pour over enough water to cover. Cook covered, over medium heat, until the carrots are soft and the water has been evaporated. Add the sugar, grated lemon peel and lemon juice. Continue cooking over medium heat, stirring frequently, for about 30 minutes or until the setting point is reached and the jam is thick and glossy. Stir in the almonds and remove from the heat. Skim and ladle into warm, sterilized jars. Seal and store in the refrigerator. Jam will keep for up to a year.

Baked Apples (Mila Psita)

Serves 8
Preparation time 30 minutes
Baking time 1 hour and 30 minutes

8   large apples
2   tablespoons lemon juice
1/3   cup water
1   cup sugar
2/3   cup soft butter
1/2   cup coarsely chopped walnuts
1   teaspoon cinnamon
1/2   teaspoon ground cloves
1/2   cup brandy

Wash and dry the apples. Cut a horizontal slice from the top of each apple and core them. Rub the cut surface with lemon juice. Arrange the apples close together in a buttered, ovenproof dish or pan. Add just enough water to prevent burning. Mix the sugar and butter in a small bowl; add the nuts, flavoring and half the amount of the brandy. Mix well. Fill up the centers of the apples with part of this mixture. Sprinkle the remaining brandy on top. Bake in a 300°F oven for 1 hour and 30 minutes. Meanwhile, as the filling melts, use any surplus mixture to top the cavities several times until all of it is used up. Using a plastic syringe, baste the apples frequently with the juices from the pan. Serve the apples warm, garnished with whipped cream.

Baked Quinces (Kidonia Psita)

Serves 8
Preparation time 20 minutes
Baking time 1 hour and 30 minutes

4   large quinces
1½   cups sugar
1   cup water
2   tablespoons lemon juice
      few whole cloves (optional)

Wash the quinces thoroughly and wipe. Rub all around with a cloth removing the fuzz and shining the skin. Cut the fruit into 4-6 wedges, depending on the size, and remove the cores. Arrange the quince wedges, cut side up, in a buttered, ovenproof dish or pan. Sprinkle them with the sugar. Put the cores with the water in a saucepan. Cover and simmer for about 10 minutes. Strain the juice, mix in the lemon juice, and sprinkle the mixture over the quinces. Cover with aluminum foil and bake slowly in a 350°F oven for 30 minutes. Remove the foil, turn the quinces upside down in the pan and stick a clove into each one. Bake them, uncovered, until they are soft and golden. Let them cool slightly in the pan. The cooking liquid will gel as it cools. Transfer the quinces to a serving dish and pour one tablespoonful of the warm jelly over each one. If more jelly is required, use more sugar. Serve the baked quinces warm or cold, topped with whipped cream.

Natural Pectin
(Fisiki Pictini)

Yields 6 cups
Preparation time 24 hours
Cooking time 30 minutes

10   lbs under-ripe, hard apples, preferably tart apples
     about 5 pints water

Wash the apples and slice them thinly, without peeling or coring. Place them in a large heavy-bottomed pan. Add water to the level of the apples. Cover the pan and bring to a boil. Reduce the heat and simmer for 20-30 minutes or until the apples are soft. Pour the mixture into a large colander, lined with a double thickness muslin, and allow the juice to run through without stirring or pressing, as the pulp would be forced through and cloud the liquid. Let the juice strain for 24 hours. The next day, pour the strained juice into a saucepan and cook until it has reduced to about half its original volume. Pour the juice through a strainer lined with two layers of muslin and refrigerate until thickened. Divide into small portions, a half cup each, pour into small, thick plastic bags, seal and freeze; or pour pectin into small jars, cover and heat-process them for 5 minutes. Both ways it keeps well up to a year and it will be available whenever required. Add half cup of pectin to each 2 pints of low-pectin fruit juice to help setting. You may add pectin to set jams also, reducing the sugar to cut down the sweetness. However, these jams must be consumed earlier than those preserved in proper ways as they grow moldy rather quickly.

Apple or Quince Jelly
(Peltes apo Mila i Kidonia)

Yields 3 lbs
Preparation time 24 hours
Cooking time approximately 1 hour

4   lbs under-ripe apples or quinces
3   lbs sugar, approximately
2   tablespoons lemon juice
1   teaspoon vanilla or
2-3 geranium leaves

Wash the apples or the quinces and cut them into pieces, without peeling or coring. Put them in a saucepan, add enough water to cover, and simmer, covered, for about 30 minutes or until the fruit is soft. Let them stand overnight. The next day, pour the fruit into a strainer lined with a double thickness muslin, and let the juice drip into a bowl, without squeezing the apples or quinces, as the pulp would be forced through and cloud the liquid. Measure the juice (3 pints approximately) and add 1½ lbs sugar to each 2 pints. Boil the mixture rapidly for

about 10 minutes or until it gels when a drop is cooled. Add the lemon juice and flavoring towards the end of cooking. While still warm, pour the jelly into sterilized jars and seal when completely cold. Store in a cool, dark place or preferably in the refrigerator. Jelly keeps well up to one year. Follow the same procedure to make jelly from other fruit. In low-pectin fruit like strawberries, pineapples, pears, peaches, nectarines, cherries, kiwis, grapes, you may add a quantity of fruit especially rich in pectin such as apples, quinces, blackcurrants, redcurrants, cranberries, plums, and all citrus fruit, or you can add natural pectin, home or commercially prepared (page 93). Half cup of natural pectin is sufficient to thicken 2 pints of low-pectin fruit juice. As apple pectin is almost flavorless and of a dull yellow color, it will not affect flavor and color of other fruit, but will enhance its own.

Quince Paste
(Kidonopasto)

Yields 80 small diamond shaped pieces
Preparation time 3 to 4 days
Cooking time 1 hour and 30 minutes

4   lbs quinces
2   lbs sugar, approximately
2   tablespoons lemon juice
2-3 geranium leaves
1   cup blanched, chopped and roasted almonds

Wash the quinces, dry and rub them to remove the fuzz. Place the quinces in a baking pan with a little water and bake in a 350°F oven until soft. Cool and cut them into small pieces. Remove the cores and discard. Press the fruit through a sieve or process in a food processor to make a smooth pulp. Weigh the pulp and put it in a heavy-bottomed, non-stick pan, adding an equal weight of sugar. Cook over medium heat, stirring constantly with a wooden spoon until the pulp thickens and detaches itself from the sides of the pan, about 30 minutes. Add the lemon juice, flavoring and almonds during the last 5 minutes of cooking. Remove from the heat and spread the mixture on a 12 by 14 inch baking sheet lined with baking paper. Smoothen the surface with a metal spatula dipped in brandy and let the paste dry to the open air for 3-4 days. Cut it into squares, triangles or diamonds, roll them in sugar, place on grease-proof paper, and leave for another few days to dry completely. Store the paste pieces in a tightly closed container. Quince paste will keep for many months.

Alternate: The paste also can be made from quinces left over when making quince jelly. However, it will be less tasty. If chopped almonds are not added, each individual piece may be decorated with half blanched almond or half walnut.

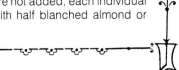

6

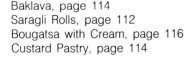

Syrup Pastries and Desserts
(Glika Siropiasta)

Pastry desserts with syrup are the most representative of the traditional Greek sweets. Since they are quite rich, they are served only occasionally as a conclusion to a dinner. The best time for enjoying these delicacies is either mid-morning or late afternoon. At those hours the Greeks usually meet at the local outdoor pastry shops for a cup of coffee. Coffee alone seems incomplete, unless accompanied by a sweet. Sitting at the tiny tables, set out in front of the shop they sip their coffee, nibble at sweets, converse with friends and watch the people go by. There are countless pastry shops throughout Greece. Their showcases are attractively arranged and the sweets are so tempting that one hardly could leave without buying some to take home.

Walnuts, hazelnuts, almonds, pistachios are plentiful in Greece and are the main ingredients in most Greek pastries, especially in syrup desserts, like baklava, kataifi, nut cakes and macaroons. Nuts also are sprinkled in smaller quantities on top as a finishing touch to many other Greek desserts or cookies.

Honey, produced in an abundance by apiarists in most regions of Greece, is used in many syrup desserts and has an exquisite taste as well as nutritional value. Phyllo dough stretched to a thin, transparent sheet is the basis for most Greek syrup desserts. It still is prepared in many households by the Greek women. However, it is difficult and time consuming to prepare. Nowadays there are many good brands of ready-made phyllo. So, if using one of them, it becomes quite simple to master a baklava. Phyllo dough can be baked either flat and layered with a filling in a baking pan or folded around the filling into various shapes. Either way a lot of imaginative and delicious pastry desserts can be created with phyllo. Greek pastry desserts contain a lot of butter and sugar and are quite fattening. Through repeated experimentation on each recipe of this chapter, I succeeded in minimizing the amount of sugar as well as the amount of butter, while retaining the pastries' luscious flavor and texture.

General Instructions

Half the success in making a dessert depends on the good quality and fresh taste of the ingredients used. Nuts often go rancid. Buy them just before using. Otherwise, tightly seal the nuts in plastic bags and keep them refrigerated or frozen until used. The phyllo pastry should be fresh and soft, so that it can be used easily without crumbling. While working with phyllo sheets cover the rest with a plastic wrap and a slightly moistened towel, to keep the phyllo from drying out. Treat kataifi pastry dough the same way. The multiple layer effect of a phyllo pastry dessert is achieved by layering or folding the phyllo sheets with a light hand so that they will barely touch each other, allowing room for the syrup to penetrate them thoroughly. Cut the phyllo dough into the right size to fit in your baking tray and layer the sheets, generously brushing each one with melted butter. Intersperse the layers with the dough trimmings, also brushed with butter. After finishing the layering, score and sprinkle the surface with some drops of warm water to prevent the phyllo from curling up while it is baking. Clarified butter is a fundamental element in most Greek pastries, such as baklava, kataifi, galaktoboureko (custard pastry dessert) or saragli and is very simple to make. Melt the butter over low heat, cool and refrigerate overnight. The next day lift off the solid butter and discard the water and impurities.

All the above are important for a successful result. But what really makes a syrup dessert perfect is the correct consistency of the syrup. However, any rules you follow, your personal experience will help you best. This may take some time to acquire. All syrup desserts do not require the same density of a syrup. For example, baklava, kataifi and custard pastry dessert do not require the consistency of syrup which is required for ravani or walnut cake. A light syrup generally is used for pouring over cakes, ravani, sponge cakes or to dip in cookies as walnut macaroons, before they are rolled in sugar. Using a candy thermometer, a light syrup consistency is attained when it registers 220°F. A medium syrup consistency, attained when the thermometer registers 223°F, generally is used for pouring over nut cakes, diples, honey cookies and finikia. A heavy syrup, attained when the thermometer registers 227°F, generally is used for pouring over phyllo pastry desserts, such as baklava, saragli rolls, galaktoboureko or kataifi. To avoid crystallization, the sugar must be completely dissolved before boiling point is reached. Stir it continuously over low heat, washing down sugar granules from the sides of the pan with a brush dipped in cold water. Otherwise, put the lid on the pan, for a minute, to allow the steam to dissolve any sugar that has splashed on the sides of the pan. When the boiling point is reached, boil the syrup for the time specified in the recipe without stirring. Add 1-2 tablespoons lemon juice or glucose to the syrup a few minutes before removing it from the heat. After pouring the syrup over a pastry dessert, do not cover so that the pastry will absorb the syrup while keeping its crispness. (Use the spices such as cinnamon, cloves, nutmeg, allspice sparingly as they are heavy to the stomach).

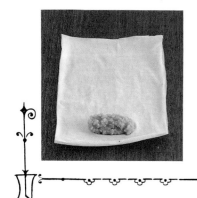   

Flute Folding Technique

Esle
Smyrna Honey Cookies
(Isli)

Yields 32 cookies
Preparation time 2 hours
Baking time 45 minutes

The Dough
6	cups all purpose flour
1/2	teaspoon salt
4	tablespoons sugar
1/2	cup water
2	cups unsalted butter, clarified

The Filling
2	cups chopped walnuts
2	tablespoons cinnamon
1	tablespoon cloves

The Syrup
2	cups sugar
2 1/2	cups water
1	tablespoon lemon juice

Sift the flour and salt into a kneading basin and make a well in the center. Put in the sugar, water, and butter. Start by stirring with a wooden spoon, folding the flour a little at a time into the other ingredients. When the mixture becomes too stiff to stir, mix in the flour by hand and knead lightly until the dough is soft and pliable. Avoid overkneading the dough as this would strengthen the gluten, making the dough tough when baked. Divide the dough into four equal portions. Then divide each portion into eight small balls. Mix all the filling ingredients in a bowl. Flatten each ball into a round, place a teaspoonful of the filling in the center and fold the dough over it to form a small triangle. Arrange the cookies onto an ungreased baking sheet, seam side down, and decorate the surface, pinching the dough with the prongs of two forks. Bake in a 350°F oven for about 45 minutes, or until golden brown. Allow the cookies to cool; then prick them with a metal skewer in two or three places, going right through the center of the filling. Put the syrup ingredients in a saucepan, stir over low heat until the sugar is dissolved, and cook the syrup for 8 minutes. Keeping the syrup hot over low heat, drop in 4-5 cookies at a time and let them soak for 3 minutes. Remove them with a slotted spoon and place on a large serving dish. They keep well at room temperature for several weeks covered with plastic wrap.

Constantinople Honey Dipped Cookies
(Melomakarona Politika)

Yields 50-60 small cookies
Preparation time 2 hours
Baking time 40 minutes

1	cup unsalted butter,
1	cup shortening

3	teaspoons vanilla
6	cups all purpose flour
1/2	cup ash water or
1/2	cup tap water and
5	teaspoons baking powder

The Filling
2	cups coarsely chopped walnuts
3	teaspoons cinnamon, 1 teaspoon cloves
1	teaspoon grated lemon rind

The Syrup
3	cups sugar or half sugar and half honey
3	cups water
1	lemon, juice and rind

Mix all the filling ingredients in a bowl. Cream the butter and shortening with an electric mixer until pale and fluffy. Stop beating. Add flavoring; then gradually add the flour (if using baking powder, sift it with the flour) in 3-4 stages, alternated with the ash or tap water, and lightly knead the dough with the kneading hook, or by hand, adding as much flour as necessary to form a smooth, easy to handle dough. Avoid overworking as the dough will be tough when baked. Divide the dough into walnut size pieces. Roll each piece between your palms into a ball. Pressing with your fingers, flatten the ball and shape a cavity in the middle. Spoon a little filling into it and press the edges together to seal over the filling. Lightly roll it between your fingers into an oval shaped cookie. Arrange the cookies on a lightly greased baking sheet. Pinch and decorate the tops. Bake in a 350°F oven for 35-40 minutes. Put the syrup ingredients in a saucepan and boil for 5 minutes. Keeping the syrup hot over low heat, drop in 4-5 cookies at a time and let them soak for a few seconds. Remove with a slotted spoon and place on a serving dish.

Walnut Cake
(Keik me Karidia)

Serves 12
Preparation time 30 minutes
Baking time 1 hour

The Cake

2	cups finely chopped walnuts
4	oz grated baking chocolate
1	cup soft margarine
1½	cups sugar
1½	cups all purpose flour
3	teaspoons baking powder
1	teaspoon cinnamon
6	eggs

The Garnish

confectioners ' sugar
cinnamon for dusting

Mix the walnuts with the grated chocolate. Put all the remaining ingredients into a mixing bowl of an electric mixer. Stir with a spoon; then beat the mixture for 4 minutes, until light and fluffy. Stop beating. Carefully fold in the walnut and chocolate mixture. Spread the batter into a 12 inch, round cake pan lined with a greased baking paper. Bake the cake in a 350°F oven for 1 hour or until a wooden pick inserted into the cake comes out clean. Remove it from the oven and sprinkle with 3-4 tablespoons brandy, or pour over a light syrup. When the cake is completely cold, sprinkle it with confectioners ' sugar and a little cinnamon.

The syrup: Stir 1½ cups sugar with 1½ cups water over medium heat until the sugar is completely dissolved. Add 1 tablespoon lemon juice. Boil the syrup for 5 minutes. Remove from the heat, let it cool slightly, and stir in 2-3 tablespoons brandy.

Walnut Semolina Cake (Melachrini)

Serves 20
Preparation time 40 minutes
Baking time 30 minutes

1/4	cup flour
1¼	cups fine semolina
2	teaspoons baking powder
1	teaspoon cinnamon
3	teaspoons cocoa
6	eggs
1	cup sugar
1/4	cup olive or vegetable oil
1	cup finely chopped walnuts

The Syrup

2	cups sugar
2	cups water
1	tablespoon lemon juice

Mix together flour, semolina, baking powder, cinnamon and cocoa in a bowl. Set aside. Beat the eggs and sugar with an electric mixer at high speed until thick and light. Gently fold in mixed ingredients, then oil and walnuts, sprinkling them on lightly as you fold. Light folding is very important at this stage as strenuous folding would break down the air bubbles beaten into the eggs, and the cake would be heavy when baked. If you are not experienced, beat separately the egg yolks with half the amount of sugar; then whisk the whites with the remaining sugar. Mix dry ingredients with the egg yolk mixture, adding a few spoonfulls of the meringue to loosen the mixture. Then gently fold in the remaining meringue. Pour the mixture, spreading it evenly into a well greased and floured, 12 inch, round cake pan and bake in a 350°F oven for about 30 minutes. Remove from the oven, cool slightly and cut into squares. Boil the syrup ingredients for 5 minutes and pour it over the cake while still warm. Let it cool completely before transferring to a serving plate. It keeps well up to a week at room temperature.

Walnut Semolina Cake,
Walnut Cake, page 98

Copenhagen (Kopenhaghi)

Yields 20-24 pieces
Preparation time 2 hours
Baking time 1 hour

The Crust
1   recipe, Rich Shortcrust Pastry (page 37)

The Filling
1   cup rusk crumbs
1   tablespoon baking powder
1/4   teaspoon ground cloves
1   teaspoon cinnamon
1   cup coarsely ground, unblanched almonds
6   large eggs
1   cup sugar
4   sheets phyllo pastry
1/4   cup melted, unsalted butter

The Syrup
3   cups sugar
2¼   cups water
2   tablespoons lemon juice

This tasty dessert bears the name of the capital city of Denmark. It was created and offered in 1863 to the Danish Prince George upon his coronation as King George I of Greece.

Prepare the shortcrust pastry dough as directed in the recipe. Roll out the dough and use it to line a 10 by 14 inch buttered baking pan. Pat evenly and smoothly. Prick all over with a fork and bake in a 400°F oven for 10-15 minutes, or until lightly golden. Remove from the oven and set the pastry aside to cool to room temperature. (Optionally, spread the surface with 3 tablespoons orange or apricot jam). To prepare the filling, mix the crumbs, baking powder, spices, and almonds in a bowl. Set aside. Beat the eggs and sugar in the large mixing bowl of an electric mixer at high speed until thick and creamy. Gently fold in the mixed, dry ingredients using a metal spoon. Work carefully to prevent breaking down the air bubbles beaten into the eggs. Pour the mixture over the cooled, baked shortcrust pastry. Cut the phyllo sheets to the size of the baking pan, and lay them on a working board, one on top of the other, brushing each one with the melted butter. Cut them lengthwise into 4 strips, without cutting through the edges, to prevent separating the strips. Lift the strips of phyllo carefully and place lightly on top of the filling. Bake in a 350°F oven for about 45 minutes or until the top of the pastry is golden brown. To make the syrup, put the ingredients in a large pan and bring them to a boil. Boil for 5 minutes and ladle the syrup over the cooled cake, slowly and evenly. Allow the cake to cool completely before cutting it.

Copenhagen, page 99

Walnut Dessert (Karidogliko)

Yields 30-35 pieces
Preparation time 30 minutes
Baking time 30-35 minutes

1	cup olive or vegetable oil
1	cup water
1	cup sugar
2	tablespoons honey
1/3	cup margarine
1	tablespoon grated orange or tangerine rind
1/4	teaspoon salt
2	tablespoons cinnamon
1	teaspoon baking soda
1	cup sultana raisins
6-7	cups all purpose flour
1	cup coarsely chopped walnuts

The Syrup

2$\frac{1}{2}$	cups sugar
2	cups water
1	tablespoon lemon juice

The Garnish

35	walnut halves
3	tablespoons confectioners ' sugar

Place the first 9 ingredients in a saucepan and bring to a boil. Remove from the heat and let the mixture cool until lukewarm. Add the raisins and walnuts and as much flour as necessary to make a soft dough (softer than the dough for Kourabiedes). Spread the dough into a well-greased 10 by 14 inch cake pan and press the surface with moistened palms to smoothen. Cut the cake into diamond shaped pieces and place half a walnut on each piece. Bake in a 400°F oven for about 35 minutes. Put the syrup ingredients in a saucepan and stir over medium heat until the sugar is dissolved. Boil the syrup for 5 minutes and pour it over the cake as soon as it is removed from the oven. Allow the cake to absorb the syrup and cool completely. Transfer the pieces to a serving dish and dust with confectioners ' sugar, if desired. It keeps well at room temperature up to one week. Keep it covered.

Haslama
(Haslamas)

Yields 16-20 pieces
Preparation time 30 minutes
Baking time 40 minutes

5	cups country flour or
4	cups all purpose flour and 1 cup fine semolina
1/3	cup fine semolina
1/2	cup sugar
1	teaspoon cinnamon
1/2	teaspoon cloves
1$\frac{1}{4}$	cups olive or vegetable oil
1	teaspoon baking soda
2	tablespoons brandy
1	cup ash water or 1 cup water plus 2 teaspoons baking powder
1	teaspoon lemon juice

The Syrup

1$\frac{1}{2}$	cups sugar
1	cup water
1	teaspoon lemon juice
2	cinnamon sticks cut into pieces
10	whole cloves

Sift together flour, semolina, sugar and spices into a kneading basin. Make a well in the center. If baking powder is used, it should be sifted with the flour. Heat the oil until a small bread cube dropped in will fry in one minute. Gradually pour the hot oil onto the flour, stirring with a wooden spoon until all the flour is greased. Dissolve the soda in brandy and sprinkle over the mixture. Then sprinkle the ash or plain water and lemon juice, and knead lightly. Avoid overkneading. The dough should be a little softer than the dough for Kourabiedes. Spread the dough into a greased, 10 inch, round cake pan. Smoothen the surface with a spatula and bake in a 350°F oven for about 40 minutes until golden brown. Meanwhile, prepare the syrup. Boil all the ingredients together for 5 minutes. Remove the spices and pour the syrup over the cake as soon as it is taken out of the oven. Allow the cake to cool completely, and cut it into squares. Transfer to a serving plate. It keeps well at room temperature for up to one week. Keep covered.

Walnut Dessert, page 100

Walnut Cake with Syrup
(Karidopita)

Serves 16
Preparation time 30 minutes
Baking time 35 minutes

6   eggs
1   cup sugar
1   cup rusk crumbs
1½   teaspoons baking powder
2   teaspoons cinnamon
1/4   teaspoon cloves
1½   cups finely chopped walnuts

The Syrup

2   cups sugar
2   cups water
1   tablespoon glucose or
1   tablespoon lemon juice
3   tablespoons brandy
      confectioners' sugar for dusting

Beat the eggs and sugar with an electric mixer at high speed until they triple in bulk and fall from the whisk in a thick ribbon, about 15 minutes. Meanwhile, mix together the crumbs, baking powder, spices and nuts. Gently fold the nut mixture into the beaten eggs, sprinkling it on lightly as you fold. Light handling is very important at this stage because if the mixture loses the air beaten into the eggs, the cake will be heavy. Pour the mixture into a well greased and floured, 10 inch, round cake pan and smoothen the surface. Bake in a 350°F oven for 30-35 minutes. The cake is done when the edges begin to shrink from the sides of the pan, and the top feels springy to the touch. Meanwhile, prepare the syrup. Dissolve the sugar in the water over medium heat then add the lemon juice and boil the syrup for 5 minutes. Cool slightly and stir in brandy. Ladle the syrup over the cooled cake, slowly and evenly. Allow the cake to cool completely and turn it out onto a serving dish. Place a laced paper doily onto the surface and sift confectioners' sugar over it. Carefully remove the paper; the patterns will remain on top of the walnut cake.

Semolina Halva
(Halvas Simigdalenios)

Serves 20
Preparation time 5 minutes
Cooking time 15-20 minutes

4-4½ cups water
2½-3 cups sugar
1   cinnamon stick
      the rind of one lemon
6-8   whole cloves

1   cup melted unsalted butter or vegetable oil
2   cups coarse semolina
1/2   cup coarsely chopped almonds or whole pine nuts
1/2   teaspoon grated lemon rind

The Garnish
cinnamon
3   oz almonds, blanched and roasted

The amount of water depends on the glutenous capability of semolina. Follow the instructions labeled on the package to obtain the correct proportions. Put the water and sugar in a large, heavy pan and stir over medium heat until the sugar is completely dissolved. (The amount of sugar may vary according to your own preference). Add cinnamon, lemon peel and cloves, cover the pan and boil the syrup for 5 minutes. Remove the spices; they may be substituted by vanilla flavoring, if prefered. Heat the butter in a deep, heavy-bottomed pan; add the semolina and brown it over medium heat, stirring constantly until golden. The degree of browning depends on your personal taste. However, keep in mind, the browner the semolina, the heavier the halva. A few minutes before the end of browning, add the almonds. Carefully empty the browned semolina into the hot syrup, stirring constantly. Add the grated lemon rind, and stir the mixture over medium heat until all the syrup is absorbed and the semolina is puffed and soft. Halva is ready when it falls off the spoon cleanly. Remove the saucepan from the heat. Cover the pan with a kitchen towel, then the lid. Allow to stand for 10-15 minutes; then spoon halva into one, large, 3 pint mold or into individual jelly molds. Press to pack tightly; then unmold on to a serving dish and sprinkle with a little cinnamon. Garnish with roasted almonds or pine nuts, if desired. Serve warm or cold. It keeps well at room temperature up to one week.

Walnut Cake with Syrup, page 101

Ravani   (Ravani)

Serves 20
Preparation time 45 minutes
Baking time 35 minutes

1$\frac{1}{3}$	cups fine semolina
1$\frac{1}{3}$	cups self raising flour
1$\frac{1}{2}$	teaspoons baking powder
8	eggs
1$\frac{1}{3}$	cups sugar
4	tablespoons lukewarm milk
2	teaspoons vanilla

The Syrup

3	cups sugar
2$\frac{1}{2}$	cups water
6	tablespoons butter
2	tablespoons lemon juice
1$\frac{1}{2}$	teaspoons grated lemon rind
20	blanched almond halves for garnishing

Mix together semolina, flour and baking powder in a bowl. Beat the eggs and sugar with an electric mixer at high speed for about 15 minutes, until thick and fluffy. Beating continuously, add the milk, a tablespoon at a time; then add the flavoring. Stop beating. Gently fold in mixed, dry ingredients, taking care not to break down the air bubbles beaten into the eggs. The batter should be light and foamy. Pour the mixture, spreading it evenly into a well-greased, 12 inch, round baking pan and bake in a 350°F oven for 30-35 minutes. The cake is ready when the edges begin to shrink from the sides of the pan. Meanwhile, prepare the syrup. Dissolve the sugar in the water over medium heat; then boil for 5 minutes. Add the lemon juice, butter and lemon rind. Remove from the heat, and ladle it over the lukewarm cake, slowly and evenly. When completely cold, cut the ravani into wedges, arrange them on a serving dish, and place one halved almond on each. Keep refrigerated.

Yogurt Ravani   (Ravani me Yiaourti)

Serves 20
Preparation time 15 minutes
Baking time 30 minutes

1	cup sugar
1$\frac{1}{2}$	cups coarse semolina
1	cup yogurt
1/2	teaspoon baking soda dissolved in
1	tablespoon brandy
1	tablespoon grated orange rind or
2	teaspoons vanilla
5	tablespoons melted butter
3	eggs
1/2	cup slivered blanched almonds

The Syrup

1$\frac{1}{2}$	cups sugar
1	cup water
1	tablespoon lemon juice

Mix half the sugar with semolina in a bowl, add the yogurt, brandy with the soda, and flavoring. Mix well, stirring with a spoon. Let the mixture stand for one hour, to puff up the semolina. Add the melted butter and mix well. Beat the eggs with the remaining sugar until thick and light. Gently fold them into the semolina mixture, taking care not to break down the air bubbles beaten into them. Pour the mixture into a greased and floured, 10 inch, cake pan and sprinkle with the almonds. Bake in a 400°F oven for approximately 30 minutes, or until golden and firm to the touch. Remove the ravani from the oven. Let it cool for 5-10 minutes; then cut it into diamond shaped pieces. Boil the syrup ingredients for 5 minutes and ladle it over the cake, slowly and evenly. Let it absorb the syrup and cool completely. Then transfer the pieces to a serving dish. Keep refrigerated. Cover to keep it moist.

Coconut Ravani
(Ravani me Indokarido)

Serves 20
Preparation time 15 minutes
Baking time 1 hour

1$\frac{1}{2}$	cups grated coconut
1$\frac{1}{2}$	cups self raising flour
1	teaspoon baking powder
2/3	cup shortening
1	cup sugar
3	eggs
2/3	cup milk

The Syrup

1$\frac{1}{2}$	cups sugar
1$\frac{1}{2}$	cups water
1	tablespoon lemon juice
	the rind of one lemon

Mix together coconut, flour and baking powder. Cream the shortening, add the sugar, and beat together until the mixture is light and fluffy. Beating continuously, add the eggs, one at a time. Reduce the speed to low, and gradually add the milk in four stages, alternated with the dry ingredients. Do not overbeat. Beat just until all the ingredients are mixed. Pour the mixture into a well-greased and floured turban cake mold, filling it up to $\frac{3}{4}$ full, and bake in a 350°F oven for approximately 1 hour. Allow to cool until lukewarm. Meanwhile, prepare the syrup. Dissolve the sugar in the water, add the lemon rind and boil the syrup for 5 minutes. Ladle the syrup over the lukewarm cake, slowly and evenly. The next day, unmold the cake on a serving dish and garnish with pineapple slices and maraschino cherries, if desired. Keep refrigerated.

Coconut Ravani, page 102
Phoenician Honey Cookies, page 141
Ravani, page 102

Almond Flutes (Flogeres me Amigdala)

Yields 30-40 pieces
Preparation time 1 hour and 30 minutes
Baking time 35 minutes

2½	cups finely ground blanched almonds
1/2	cup sugar
3/4	cup whipping cream
4	tablespoons melted unsalted butter
1	egg
4	egg yolks
1	teaspoon almond extract
1	teaspoon vanilla
1	tablespoon fine semolina
1	lb phyllo pastry
3/4	cup melted unsalted butter or half butter and half margarine

The Syrup

2	cups sugar
1½	cups water
1/2	cup glucose
1	tablespoon lemon juice

Mix the first 9 ingredients in a bowl to make a soft, firm mixture. Cut the entire stack of phyllo sheets lengthwise into 2 long strips. Keep pastry not in use covered with a plastic wrap and a damp cloth. Lightly brush each pastry strip with melted butter and fold in half, widthwise. Brush again with butter. Place 1 tablespoonful of the filling on a short end of the buttered phyllo. Fold in the two, long sides over filling, butter again the folded in sides, and loosely roll up the phyllo enclosing the filling. Arrange the rolls on a greased baking sheet, leaving ¹/₂ inch space in between them, and brush them with the remaining melted butter. At this stage you may freeze the rolls. To bake, let them thaw out first. Bake the "flutes" in a 400°F oven for 35 minutes or until golden. Meanwhile, boil the syrup ingredients for 5 minutes, add the lemon juice and pour the syrup over the "flutes" as soon as they come out of the oven. To keep the phyllo crisp, do not cover the rolls. Keep them refrigerated.

Semolina Dessert (Samali me Gala)

Serves 30
Preparation time 2-3 hours
Baking time 40 minutes

2¼	cups fine semolina
1	cup coarse semolina
2	cups sugar
2½	teaspoons baking powder
2	tablespoons grated lemon rind
1	teaspoon vanilla
1½	cups milk
	blanched almond halves
4	tablespoons melted unsalted butter

Almond Flutes, page 104

The Syrup

1¹/₂ cups water
2¹/₂ cups sugar
1/2 cup glucose
1 tablespoon grated lemon rind
1 teaspoon vanilla

Mix together semolina, sugar, baking powder and flavoring, into a large mixing bowl. Add the milk and stir with a spoon until all semolina is moistened. Pour the mixture into a well-greased, 11 by 15 inch baking sheet, and smoothen the surface with a metal spatula. Let it stand 2-3 hours. Place the almonds on top, symmetrically, so that when the dessert is cut, there will be an almond on every piece. Bake in a 350°F oven for 35-40 minutes or until the surface is golden. Meanwhile, boil all the syrup ingredients for 3 minutes. Remove the cake from the oven and spread the butter on top using a pastry brush. Then pour over the hot syrup. Allow the cake to absorb the syrup and cool completely. Cut it into squares and transfer to a serving dish. To keep moist, cover with a plastic wrap. It keeps well at room temperature for several days.

Constantinople Semolina Dessert
(Samali Politiko)

Serves 30
Preparation time 2-3 hours
Baking time 40 minutes

1¹/₂ cups fine semolina
1 cup coarsely ground semolina
1¹/₂ cups sugar
1 teaspoon vanilla or
1/4 teaspoon ground mastic

1 teaspoon baking powder
1¹/₂ cups yogurt
1 teaspoon baking soda
48 blanched almond halves
4 tablespoons melted unsalted butter

The Syrup

2¹/₂ cups sugar
1¹/₂ cups water
1/3 cup glucose (corn syrup)
2 tablespoons lemon juice
1 teaspoon vanilla or
1/8 teaspoon ground mastic

Mix together semolina, sugar, flavoring and baking powder in a large bowl, and make a well in the center. In a separate bowl, mix the yogurt with baking soda. Pour the mixture into the well. Gradually mix semolina with yogurt, stirring with a spoon until well blended. Pour the mixture into a well-greased, 11 by 15 inch, baking pan or in a 14 inch, round cake pan. Smoothen the surface with a wet spatula. Let it stand for 2-3 hours until semolina is well swollen. Score the surface into pieces and place a half almond on each piece. Bake the cake in a 350°F oven for 35-40 minutes or until golden. Meanwhile, prepare the syrup. Boil all the ingredients together for 5 minutes. Remove the cake from the oven, brush the top with the butter, and ladle over the syrup, slowly and evenly. Allow the dessert to cool completely before transfering to a serving dish. Keep covered with plastic wrap. It keeps well several days at room temperature.

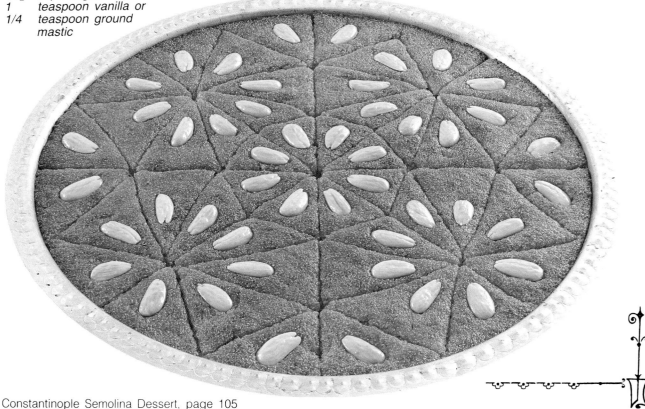

Constantinople Semolina Dessert, page 105

Diples (Diples)

Yields 60 diples
Preparation time 1 hour
Frying time 1 hour

The Dough
2　eggs and 4 egg yolks
6　tablespoons orange juice
1　tablespoon sugar
2　tablespoons olive oil
4　cups all purpose flour
2　tablespoons finely grated orange rind

The Syrup
1/2　cup honey
1　cup sugar
1/2　cup water

The Garnish
2　cups finely chopped walnuts
2　teaspoons cinnamon
　oil for frying

Lightly beat the eggs and egg yolks in a mixing bowl. Stir in orange juice, sugar, oil and grated orange rind. Gradually add enough flour, kneading well until a rather soft and elastic dough is formed. Divide the dough into 8 equal portions and roll them into balls. Cover the balls with plastic wrap and let them stand for 1 hour. On a floured surface, roll out each ball into a sheet as thin as possible. Sprinkle the surface frequently with flour to avoid sticking. Do it easier by substituting cornstarch for the flour. Cut into 12 inch long, 2 inch wide strips. Heat the oil in a deep fryer until it registers 375°F. Place one edge of each strip between the prongs of a fork and fasten it by wrapping around the fork twice. Hold the other edge of the strip with your other hand. Dip the fork with the dough into the boiling oil, swirl the fork around, and wrap the remaining dough strip slowly around the fork as it is frying. Fry until golden all around. Remove them with a slotted spoon and place on absorbent paper to drain. Put the syrup ingredients in a small, deep saucepan. Bring to a boil and skim off the froth. Drop in diples, a few at a time, let them stand for 1-2 minutes, and transfer to a serving dish. Mix the walnuts and cinnamon, and sprinkle over diples as soon as you remove them from the honey. They keep well for several weeks at room temperature.

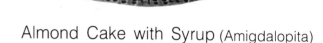

Almond Cake with Syrup (Amigdalopita)

Serves 16-20
Preparation time 45 minutes
Baking time 35 minutes

1　cup all purpose flour
1/2　cup fine rusk crumbs
2　teaspoons baking powder
2　cups finely chopped, unblanched almonds
8　eggs, separated
1　cup sugar
1/2　teaspoon almond extract
1/4　cup brandy

The Syrup
2　cups sugar
1 1/2　cups water
1　tablespoon lemon juice
1/4　cup brandy

The Garnish
1　recipe, Whipped Cream (page 49)
　a few maraschino cherries

Mix together flour, crumbs, baking powder and almonds. Set aside. Beat the egg yolks with half the amount of sugar and flavoring until thick and lemon colored. Whisk separately the egg whites with remaining sugar until stiff and glossy. Add the mixed, dry ingredients in 3-4 stages to the egg yolks, alternated with the brandy and half the beaten egg whites. Then, gently fold in the remaining meringue taking care not to break down the air bubbles beaten into them. Pour the mixture into one large, 10 inch, round cake pan or several individual jelly molds well-greased and floured. Bake in a 350°F oven, 30-35 minutes for the large mold, and 15-20 minutes for the jelly molds. To make the syrup, dissolve the sugar in the water, stirring over medium heat; then add the lemon juice and boil for 5 minutes. Remove from the heat, add the brandy and ladle the syrup over the cakes slowly and evenly. When completely cold, unmold them onto a serving dish. Garnish the cakes with whipped cream and cherries. Keep refrigerated. Cover with plastic wrap to keep it moist.

Diples, page 106
Almond Cake with Syrup, page 106

Honey Dipped Pastry Bites
(Kourkoubinia)

Serves 10
Preparation time 30 minutes
Frying time 15 minutes

1/2   cup unsalted butter or margarine, melted
1   lb ready-made phyllo pastry
     oil for frying

The Syrup

1¹/₂   cups sugar
1   cup water
1   cup honey
1   teaspoon vanilla
1   tablespoon lemon juice

On a working surface, place two phyllo sheets at a time, one on top of the other, brushing with the melted butter in between. Butter the surface and fold in half. Roll them up tightly into long sticks, moistening the long edge at the end of phyllo to seal tight. Cover and refrigerate the rolls until firm. Cut into bite- sized pieces, and deep-fry them in very hot oil (375°F) until golden. Remove from the oil with a slotted spoon and place on absorbent paper to drain off the excess oil. Boil the syrup ingredients together for 5 minutes. Skim off the froth and pour the hot syrup over the pastry bites. Allow to stand until all the syrup is absorbed and they are completely cold. Alternately, drop them into the syrup immediately after removing from the oil. Allow them to absorb syrup for a few minutes and remove with a slotted spoon. Place on a serving dish. Keep uncovered to preserve crispness. They keep well several weeks at room temperature.

Smyrna Bread Cakes (Fetes Smirnis)

Serves 4
Preparation time 5 minutes
Frying time 15 minutes

3   eggs
1   cup milk
     a pinch of salt
8   slices white bread (crusts removed)
     butter or margarine or a mixture of the two for frying
     sugar, honey or syrup
     cinnamon

Beat the eggs, milk and salt together. Dip the bread slices into the egg mixture, and let them soak briefly for a few seconds. Heat the butter into a heavy-bottomed preferably non-stick skillet, and fry the bread quickly, so that the slices are golden-brown and crisp on both sides. Sprinkle the slices with the sugar and cinnamon and serve immediately.
Alternate: Add 1 teaspoon vanilla flavoring into the egg and milk mixture and drench the fried bread slices with a little syrup or honey. Omit sugar and cinnamon.

Honey Puffs (Loukoumades)

Yields 100 puffs
Preparation time 1 hour
Frying time 1 hour

The Dough

2   oz fresh yeast or
2   tablespoons dry yeast
3¹/₄   cups all purpose flour
1   cup tepid water (100°F)
1   cup tepid milk (100°F)
1   tablespoon sugar
1   teaspoon salt
4   tablespoons oil
     oil for frying

The Garnish

honey, cinnamon, finely chopped walnuts

Dissolve the yeast in the tepid water. Put it along with the remaining dough ingredients into the mixing bowl of an electric mixer. Beat them at high speed until a smooth batter is obtained. Cover and let the batter rise in a warm place until it is three times its previous bulk, 1-2 hours. To speed up the procedure, place the dough in a warm oven (90°F). Moisten one of your hands and take a handful of the dough. Clench your fist and gently squeeze out a small ball of dough the size of a walnut. Cut off the dough with a wet spoon, and drop it into the hot oil. Dip the spoon in water every time before cutting the dough to avoid sticking. Fry loukoumades a few at a time in very hot oil, (375°F) pushing them into the oil with a slotted spoon, until the outside of the pastry fries to a crisp, golden-brown. Remove with the slotted spoon and transfer to a serving dish. Pour hot honey over them and lightly dust with cinnamon. Then sprinkle them with chopped walnuts or pistachio nuts. Serve immediately. If the honey is too thick, boil it adding a little water. Skim off the froth before using.

Honey Puffs, page 107
Honey Dipped Pastry Bites, page 107

Honey Choux Puffs (Sviggi)

Yields 30-40 puffs
Preparation time 30 minutes
Frying time 1 hour

1 1/2   cups water
1/2   cup unsalted butter or margarine
1   teaspoon grated lemon rind
1 1/2   cups strong flour
4-5   large eggs
   vegetable oil for frying

The Syrup

1   cup sugar
1/2   cup honey
1   cup water
1   stick cinnamon
3-4   cloves

The Garnish

1   cup finely chopped walnuts

Heat the water, lemon peel, and butter in a heavy-bottomed saucepan until the butter is melted. Bring to a boil. Turn off the heat and add all the flour at once. Follow the procedure according to the recipe for Puffed Honey Choux Strips, to make a glossy and rather stiff dough. Pour 3 inches of oil into a heavy-bottomed pan and heat it to 350°F-375°F. Grease a teaspoon and use it to cut and drop spoonfuls of dough into the hot oil. Fry the choux balls, pushing them with a slotted spoon to cover them with the oil, until the outside of the pastry fries to a crisp, golden brown. To keep the oil at a consistently high temperature, fry only a few pastries at a time. Remove them with a slotted spoon and drain on paper towels. To make the syrup, put the ingredients in a pan and simmer for 5 minutes. Remove the froth and the spices. Serve the choux puffs warm or cold, covered with the syrup and sprinkled with the nuts. Serve them preferably on the day they are made.

Puffed Honey Choux Strips (Touloumbakia)

Serves 10
Preparation time 30 minutes
Frying time 1 hour

1   cup water
1/4   teaspoon salt
1   tablespoon sugar
1/2   cup shortening or vegetable oil
1 1/2   cups country or yellow flour
7   large eggs
1   teaspoon vanilla
   olive oil and corn oil for frying

The Syrup

1 1/2   cups water
2   cups sugar
1/2   cup honey or glucose

The Garnish

1   cup finely chopped walnuts (optional)

Put the water, salt, sugar, and shortening in a small, deep saucepan over high heat and stir until the shortening melts. As soon as the liquid starts to boil, turn off the heat. Add all the flour at once, stirring vigorously with a wooden spoon, for about 1 minute, until the mixture forms a solid mass that comes away cleanly from the sides of the pan. Place the dough in the mixing bowl and cool it for 8-10 minutes. Meanwhile, prepare the syrup. Mix all the ingredients in a saucepan and cook for 5 minutes. Set aside. Beat the dough with the kneading hook of the mixer and add the eggs, one at a time, mixing thoroughly so that the dough absorbs them. Use as many eggs as are needed to make a sufficiently firm paste. Flours vary in their absorbent qualities. Pour 3 inches of oil (half olive

Honey Choux Puffs, page 108
Puffed Honey Choux Strips, page 108

oil and half corn oil) into a heavy-bottomed pan, and heat it to 350°F-370°F. Fit a star nozzle to a piping bag. Fill it with dough. Pipe 3 inch lengths into the oil, cutting off the dough near the nozzle with a wet knife. The dough swells as it comes in contact with the oil. Fry the pastries for 5-7 minutes, pushing them into the oil with a slotted spoon so that the outside of the pastry fries to a crisp, golden-brown all around. Remove the puffs with a slotted spoon and drain on paper towels. Then drop them into the syrup. Allow them to soak for 5 minutes and remove with a slotted spoon onto a serving dish. Repeat the process until all the dough is used. Serve the puffs cold, preferably on the day they are made. Keep any leftovers in the refrigerator, covered with plastic wrap.

Halvas from Farsala
(Halvas Farsalon)

Yields 2¹/₂ lbs halva
Preparation time 15 minutes
Cooking time 1 hour and 30 minutes

3   cups sugar
1/2   lb cornstarch or gluten
2   teaspoons vanilla
5   cups water
1/2   cup halved blanched almonds
2/3   cup melted unsalted butter or vegetable oil
        sugar and cinnamon

Reserve 1 cup of the sugar and mix the remaining with the cornstarch and vanilla into a large bowl. Add the water and stir until well blended. Into a 10 inch wide heavy-bottomed pan, brown the almonds with one tablespoon of the butter or oil. Remove the almonds with a slotted spoon and set aside. Lower the heat and gradually add in the reserved sugar, stirring constantly with a wooden spoon, until it is melted and a dark golden colored caramel is formed. Remove from the heat, and gradually add in the cornstarch mixture. Return to the heat and cook the mixture over medium heat stirring constantly with a wooden spatula, until it is thick, and clear, and comes away cleanly from the sides of the pan. Add the almonds, increase the heat and gradually add the remaining butter or oil, a little at a time, stirring constantly until it is all incorporated. Continue to stir until the mixture begins to fry and forms a crust. Smoothen the surface and cook 5-6 minutes without stirring, until a thick glistening caramelized crust is formed on the bottom. Remove from the heat. Let it cool slightly. Invert a tray over the pan and turn it over. When halva is completely cold cut it into squares. Serve sprinkled with a little sugar and cinnamon. It keeps well at room temperature up to one week.

Squash Pita from Roumeli
(Kolokithopita Roumelis)

Serves 20
Preparation time 1 hour and 30 minutes
Baking time 1 hour

1   lb ready-made phyllo pastry or
1   recipe, homemade Phyllo Pastry Dough(page 28)
1   large white or yellow squash (3 lbs)
1   cup sugar
1/3   cup short grain rice
1   small onion, grated and blanched
1   tablespoon cinnamon
1¹/₂   cups oil or shortening or
        a mixture of the two
        confectioners' sugar and cinnamon for dusting

Peel and cut the squash into pieces. Grate and place it in a collander. Let it drain overnight. The next day, press it between your hands to squeeze out remaining water, and mash it with a fork. Wash the rice, boil and drain well. Combine the squash, sugar and rice into a bowl. Add the onion, cinnamon and one half cup of the fat. If using homemade phyllo pastry dough, divide it into 12 equal portions. On a well-floured surface, roll out the phyllo dough portions into very thin sheets. Brush half part of each phyllo sheet with melted butter; fold other half over the buttered part and butter the surface. Place 2-3 tablespoonfuls of the filling lengthwise on the phyllo sheet. Roll it up into a long stick. On the center of a greased, 14 inch, round baking sheet, coil the roll into a spiral. Repeat the procedure with the remaining phyllo sheets, and coil the rolls around the center spiral until the bottom of the pan is covered. Brush the surface with butter and bake the pita in a 350°F oven for about 1 hour or until the surface is golden brown. Remove from the oven and sprinkle the surface with confectioners' sugar and a little cinnamon. Serve warm or cold.

Squash Pie from Roumeli, page 109

Pastry Dessert from Ioannina
(Yianniotiko se Formakia)

Serves 12
Preparation time 1 hour
Baking time 35 minutes

5	phyllo pastry sheets
2/3	cup melted unsalted butter
1/2	lb kataifi pastry
1	cup coarsely chopped walnuts
1	teaspoon cinnamon
1/8	teaspoon cloves
1	tablespoon rusk crumbs

The Syrup

2	cups sugar
1¼	cups water
1	tablespoon lemon juice

On a working surface lay the phyllo sheets one on top of the other, brushing each one with melted butter. Cut into 12 squares. Line the cavities of a 12-cupcake baking pan and trim the ends to form round cups. Cover with a damp cloth to keep the phyllo pastry moist. Mix together walnuts, cinnamon, cloves and crumbs in a bowl. Set aside. Divide kataifi pastry into 12 equal portions. Keep it covered with a damp cloth while you are working, as it tends to dry out quickly. Take one kataifi portion and fluff it up. Spread it on your palm, shaping it into a small bird 's nest. Put in 1 tablespoonful of nut mixture and roll it into a ball. Place the rolled kataifi ball into a lined cavity. Shape and fill the rest of the kataifi portions the same way. Brush the tops with the remaining butter, using a pastry brush. At this stage you may freeze the pastries. Let them thaw out before baking. Bake in a 350°F oven for 35- 40 minutes or until golden brown. Meanwhile, dissolve the sugar in the water stirring over medium heat, then allow the syrup to boil for 5 minutes. Add the lemon

Almond Cream Turnovers
(Trigonakia me Sfoliata)

Yields 40 turnovers
Preparation time 1 hour
Baking time 20 minutes

1	lb ready-made puff pastry or
1	recipe, homemade Puff Pastry (page 67)
1	egg yolk beaten with 1 teaspoon water

The Filling

1	cup ground blanched almonds
1	tablespoon sugar
1/4	cup whipping cream
2-3	egg yolks
2	tablespoons melted unsalted butter
1/4	teaspoon almond extract or
1	teaspoon vanilla

The Syrup

2	cups sugar
1/2	cup glucose (corn syrup)
1½	cups water

Roll out the puff pastry into a ⅛ inch thick sheet. Cut the sheet into 2 inch squares. Mix together the filling ingredients in a bowl. The mixture should be firm. Place a teaspoonful of the filling on each square and fold it to form a triangle. Press the edges well together. Moisten them with a little water, before folding, to seal better. Place the triangles on a lightly greased baking sheet, brush them with the egg yolk mixture, and bake in a 400°F oven for 15-20 minutes or until golden-brown. Meanwhile, prepare the syrup. Boil all the ingredients together for 5 minutes. Pour the hot syrup over the turnovers as soon as you remove them from the oven. Let them absorb all the syrup, and cool completely. Transfer to a serving dish. Keep uncovered to preserve the pastry 's crispness.

juice and remove from the heat. Ladle the syrup, dividing it equally, over the pastry desserts while hot and allow to cool. To preserve crispness do not cover. The dessert keeps well at room temperature from one to two weeks. **Alternate:** Stack the phyllo sheets on a buttered baking tray. Brush each sheet with melted butter and sprinkle over the walnut mixture. Spread the kataifi pastry on top and brush generously with the butter. Continue following the procedure as for the individual pastries. When completely cold cut the dessert into squares.

Pastry Dessert from Ioannina, page 110

Walnut Puff Pastry Rolls
(Roxakia)

Yields 50-55 rolls
Preparation time 1 hour and 30 minutes
Baking time 25 minutes

2	lbs puff pastry
1	egg yolk beaten with 1 teaspoon water

The Filling

3	tablespoons rusk crumbs
$1^1/_3$	cups finely chopped walnuts
2	tablespoons sugar
1	tablespoon cocoa
2	teaspoons cinnamon
1/4	teaspoon cloves
2	eggs
1/4	teaspoon baking soda dissolved in 1 tablespoon brandy

The Syrup

$3^1/_2$	cups sugar
1/2	cup glucose
$2^1/_2$	cups water

Mix together all the filling ingredients into a bowl. The mixture should be rather firm. On a floured surface roll out the puff pastry into about a $^1/_6$ inch thick sheet. Use a 2 inch plain cookie cutter to cut out rounds of dough. Using a smaller $1^1/_2$ inch cutter cut out the center of half of the rounds. Spoon a little filling into the middle of each round, brush the edges with the egg yolk mixture, then place a ring of dough on top. Lightly press the surface of the ring with your finger, and brush it with the egg yolk mixture, taking care that no egg touches the cut sides and impedes the dough from rising. Arrange the rolls on an ungreased baking sheet and chill for 20 minutes. Bake in a 400°F oven for 20-25 minutes or until the rolls are puffed and golden. Meanwhile, prepare the syrup. Heat sugar, glucose and water in a heavy saucepan allowing the mixture to boil for 5 minutes. Pour it over the pastries as soon as they are removed from the oven. Allow them to absorb the syrup and cool completely. Transfer to a serving dish. Keep them uncovered to preserve crispness. They keep well 2-3 days at room temperature.

Walnut Puff Pastry Rolls, page 111
Almond Cream Turnovers, page 110

a sharp-pointed knife slit open the one side of each triangle and carefully remove some of the inside, to make a cavity. Place them close together in a cake pan, large enough to hold them. Boil all the syrup ingredients together for 5 minutes and pour it over the triangles. Allow them to absorb the syrup and cool completely. Meanwhile, prepare the pastry cream and cool. Spoon or pipe enough cream into the triangles. Keep them refrigerated. A filled pastry will soften in time; do not fill the triangles until shortly before serving to ensure crispness. **Alternate:** Ice cream may be substituted for the pastry cream filling. Ice cream filled triangles should not be kept in the freezer longer than 15 minutes. Preferably fill them just before serving. They may be topped with whipped cream or covered with chocolate sauce (page 49).

Pastry Cream Filled Triangles
(Trigona me Krema)

Yields 14 large triangles
Preparation time 1 hour
Baking time 30 minutes

1	lb phyllo pastry
2/3	cup melted unsalted butter

The Syrup

1$\frac{1}{2}$	cups sugar
1	cup water
2	tablespoons glucose or
1	tablespoon lemon juice

The Filling

1	recipe, Pastry Cream (page 49)

Lay one phyllo sheet on a working surface. Brush half of it lengthwise with melted butter and fold it over the unbuttered half. Repeat the above procedure once more making a long strip. Brush the entire surface with butter. At one end fold over one corner to make a triangle. Fold the triangle over and over again, until the whole strip is folded. Repeat the procedure with the remaining phyllo sheets. Place the triangles, folded edge down, on a greased baking sheet. Brush them all over with butter. Bake in a 380°F oven for 30 minutes or until golden brown. Remove from the oven and cool on a rack. Using

Nut Pastry Pinwheels
(Saragli)

Yields 32-36 pinwheels
Preparation time 1 hour
Baking time 30 minutes

6	cups coarsely ground walnuts (1$\frac{1}{4}$ lbs)
4	teaspoons cinnamon
2	teaspoons cloves
1	cup unsalted butter or
	half butter, half margarine clarified and heated
1	lb phyllo pastry

The Syrup

3	cups sugar
1$\frac{1}{2}$	cups water
1	tablespoon lemon juice
1/2	cup glucose (corn syrup)

Mix together walnuts, cinnamon and cloves in a bowl. Set aside. On a working surface lay 3 phyllo sheets one on top of the other, brushing each one with butter. Sprinkle some of the nut mixture over the surface and lightly roll them up widthwise into a long cylinder. With a sharp serrated knife slice the cylinder at intervals of 1$\frac{1}{2}$ inches and transfer the pinwheels to a greased baking sheet, placing them close together. Follow the same procedure for the rest of the phyllo pastry. Brush the tops with the remaining butter and bake in a 380°F oven for about 30 minutes, or until golden brown. Meanwhile, prepare the syrup. Boil all the ingredients for 5 minutes and ladle it over the pinwheels as soon as they are removed from the oven. Allow them to absorb the syrup and cool completely. Transfer to a serving dish. Keep uncovered to preserve crispness. They keep well at room temperature from one to two weeks.
Alternate: Pistachios or almonds may be substituted for the walnuts.

Pastry Cream Filled Triangles, page 112
Rice Pudding, page 50

Small Savarins
(Babades)

Serves 18-20
Preparation time 1 hour
Baking time 25 minutes

1	oz fresh yeast or 2 teaspoons dry yeast
1/4	cup tepid water (100°F)
1/4	cup tepid milk (100°F)
1/3	cup melted unsalted butter
1/4	cup sugar
3	eggs, lightly beaten
2	cups self raising flour

The Syrup

2$\frac{1}{2}$	cups sugar
1$\frac{1}{2}$	cups water
1	tablespoon lemon juice
2	tablespoons brandy

The Garnish

1	cup apricot jam
1	recipe, Whipped Cream (page 49)
3-4	tablespoons finely chopped pistachio nuts

Dissolve the yeast in the tepid water. Put it along with the remaining ingredients, except for the butter, into the mixing bowl of an electric mixer. First mix all the ingredients together at low speed. Then beat the batter for 2 minutes at medium speed, scraping frequently the sides of the bowl with a rubber spatula. Stop beating. Cover the bowl with a plastic wrap and leave the dough rise in a warm place for 30 minutes to 1 hour or until doubled in bulk. Beat the melted butter into the raised dough until smooth. Spoon the dough into well greased, preferably non- stick, custard molds filling them up to $^1/_3$ full. Arrange them on a baking sheet, cover with a damp cloth and let them rise in a warm place until the molds are almost full, about 1 hour. The batter should not reach the rims of the molds otherwise it will stick to the cloth. Bake in a 380°F oven for 20-25 minutes. Meanwhile, prepare the syrup. Heat the sugar and water over low heat until the sugar dissolves. Boil the syrup for 5 minutes. Remove from the heat and stir in the brandy. Remove savarins from the oven and prick them several times with a wooden skewer. Ladle the syrup equally over them, allow to cool, and unmold. Heat the jam and strain through a sieve. Brush savarins all over with the jam. After 1 hour brush them again with the remaining jam. With a sharp knife make a diagonal slit in each savarin. Lift the upper part a little, and pipe some whipped cream into the slit. Pipe a rosette on top of each savarin and sprinkle them with pistachio nuts. Store in the refrigerator, covered with plastic wrap.

Saragli Rolls
(Saragli Souroto)

Prepare the filling as in the recipe, Nut Pastry Pinwheels (page 112). Spread each phyllo sheet on a working surface and brush it generously with butter. Place a thin wooden dowel, widthwise, at one end of the phyllo sheet and fold the edge over the dowel. Sprinkle some of the nut mixture over the surface and lightly roll up the sheet around the dowel. Plait the phyllo sheet as you pull out the dowel. Repeat the same procedure with the rest of the phyllo sheets. Place the plaited rolls on a greased baking sheet, brush with butter and continue the procedure as for nut pastry pinwheels. After they have been soaked in syrup cut the rolls into 3 inch pieces.
Alternate: You may roll the sheets without using the dowel. Coil the rolls into spirals. Arrange on a greased baking sheet, brush with butter and continue as for the nut pastry pinwheels. Illustrated on page 94, 95.

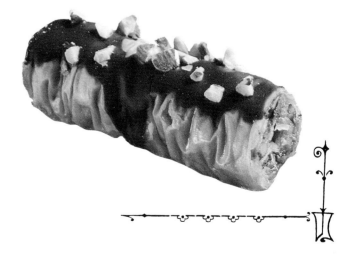

Baklava   (Baklava)

Yields 30 small pieces
Preparation time 1 hour and 15 minutes
Baking time 40 minutes

2   cups coarsely chopped almonds
2   cups coarsely chopped walnuts
2   teaspoons cinnamon
1/2   teaspoon cloves
1¹/₂   cups unsalted butter, clarified and heated
1   lb ready-made phyllo pastry or
1   recipe, homemade Phyllo Pastry Dough (p. 34)
        whole cloves for garnishing (optional)

   The Syrup

3   cups sugar
2   cups water
1/2   cup glucose or honey
1   teaspoon vanilla (optional) or
        the rind of one lemon (optional) or
2   tablespoons brandy (optional)

Mix together walnuts, almonds, cinnamon and cloves in a bowl. Set aside. It is preferred to use a baking sheet the size of the phyllo pastry. If not available cut the entire stack of phyllo sheets into rectangles or rounds to fit in your baking pan. The trimmings should be interspersed between the layers also brushed with butter. Generously grease the baking pan with butter. Lay 4 phyllo sheets over the bottom of the pan, one on top of the other, brushing each one with butter. Sprinkle some of the nut mixture evenly over pastry. The multiple layer effect of a baklava is achieved by spreading the nut filling on every second couple of phyllo sheet. Layer the phyllo sheets, buttering between each layer and sprinkling the nut mixture in between every second layer until all the nut mixture is used, ending with 4 layers of phyllo sheets on top. Score the top layers with a sharp-pointed knife into small diamond or triangle shaped pieces. Stick a clove in the center of each, if desired. Brush with the remaining melted butter and sprinkle the surface with some drops of warm water to prevent the phyllo from curling up while it is baking. Bake the baklava in a 350°F oven for 30-40 minutes or until golden brown. Meanwhile, prepare the syrup. Heat all the ingredients in a heavy pan allowing the mixture to boil for 5 minutes. For extra flavor you can add vanilla, lemon rind or brandy to the syrup. If using lemon rind boil it with the syrup ingredients. Vanilla or brandy should be added after removing the syrup from the heat. Ladle the hot syrup over the baklava slowly and evenly, as soon as it is removed from the oven, and let it absorb the syrup and cool completely. You may keep baklava at room temperature from one to two weeks.

Baklava

Custard Pastry
(Galaktoboureko)

Serves 14
Preparation time 30 minutes
Baking time 50 minutes

4	cups milk
3	eggs and 2 egg yolks
1/2	cup sugar
1/3	cup and 1 tablespoon fine semolina
2	teaspoons vanilla
1/2	lb phyllo pastry
1/2	cup hot melted, clarified unsalted butter

The Syrup

1 1/2	cups sugar
1	cup water
1	tablespoon lemon juice
1	teaspoon vanilla

Boil the milk and cool slightly. Beat the eggs and sugar with an electric mixer, until light and creamy. Add the semolina and mix well stirring with a wooden spoon. Transfer the mixture into a large heavy saucepan. Stirring constantly pour in the hot milk. Cook the mixture stirring, over low heat, to maintain a smooth textured cream, about 10 minutes. Remove from the heat, stir in the flavoring and 3-4 tablespoons of the butter. Grease an 8 by 12 inch pyrex cake pan. Cut the phyllo sheets into rectangles the size of the pan. Spread half the phyllo sheets over the bottom of the pan brushing each one with melted butter. Intersperse any pastry trimmings in between the layers also brushed with butter. Pour in the cream and spread it evenly over the pastry. On a working surface lay the remaining phyllo sheets, one on top of the other, brushing each one with melted butter. Cut them lengthwise into 4 strips, without cutting through the edges to prevent them from separating. Lift the strips of phyllo carefully and place them lightly on top of the custard. Brush the surface with butter and sprinkle with some drops of warm water to prevent the phyllo from curling up while baking. Bake in a 375°F oven for about 15 minutes then lower the temperature to 325°F and bake for about 35 minutes longer or until the top is golden brown. To make the syrup, put the ingredients in a saucepan and bring to a boil. Let it boil for 7 minutes. Ladle the syrup slowly over the pastry as soon as you remove it from the oven. Allow it to absorb the syrup and cool slightly. Cut the Galaktoboureko in pieces and serve warm or cold, preferably on the day it is made. Keep any leftovers in the refrigerator, uncovered to preserve crispness.

Custard Pastry

Bougatsa with Cream
(Bougatsa me Krema)

Serves 8-10
Preparation time 30 minutes
Baking time 30 minutes

1/2	cup butter
2/3	cup fine semolina
4	cups milk, scalded
2/3	cup sugar
2	eggs
2	egg yolks
1	teaspoon vanilla
1	lb phyllo pastry
2/3	cup melted unsalted butter
	confectioners ' sugar and cinnamon for dusting

Melt the butter in a heavy saucepan. Add semolina and stir over medium heat 1-2 minutes. Pour in the hot milk at once, stirring vigorously. Then add the sugar and simmer, stirring until the cream is thick, the consistency of a custard. Remove from the heat and allow to cool slightly, stirring occasionally to avoid a skin forming. Beat the eggs and egg yolks slightly and stir into the cream along with the flavoring. Press a piece of plastic wrap against its surface to prevent a skin from forming and set aside. Spread half the phyllo pastry over the bottom of a greased baking pan (the size of the phyllo sheets) one on top of the other, brushing each one with butter. Pour the custard on top and cover with the remaining sheets, brushing again with butter. Bake the bougatsa at 400°F oven for approximately 30 minutes or until the surface is golden brown. With a sharp knife cut it into bite size pieces and serve hot sprinkled generously with confectioners ' sugar and a little cinnamon.

Bird 's Nests (Folitses)

Yields 40-50 pieces
Preparation time 1-2 hours
Baking time 30 minutes

5	egg whites
1	cup confectioners ' sugar
1	teaspoon almond extract
1	lb almonds, blanched and ground
1	lb phyllo pastry
3/4	cup melted unsalted butter

The Syrup

3	cups sugar
2	cups water
1	cup honey
1	teaspoon grated lemon rind

Beat the egg whites until they form soft peaks. Beating continuously add the sugar a little at a time, until all is used and the meringue is stiff and glossy. Add the flavoring and stop beating. Gently fold in the almonds. Add as much as necessary being careful not to make the

Cream or Ice Cream Topped Kataifi
(Kataifi me Krema i Pagoto)

Serves 8-10
Preparation time 45 minutes
Baking time 35 minutes

1/2	lb kataifi pastry
1/2	cup melted unsalted butter
2	lbs vanilla ice cream or
1	recipe, Pastry Cream (page 49)

The Syrup

1 1/2	cups sugar
1	cup water
1	teaspoon lemon juice

The Garnish

1	recipe, Whipped Cream (page 49)
	chopped pistachio nuts

Fluff up the kataifi pastry and spread it over the bottom of a greased, 10 inch, round cake pan. Dribble with the melted butter and bake in a 350°F oven for 30-35 minutes or until golden brown and crisp on top. Meanwhile, prepare the syrup. Boil all the ingredients together for 5 minutes and pour it over the pastry while still hot. Let it cool and spread over either the pastry cream or the vanilla ice cream, as preferred. Whichever is used, garnish with the whipped cream and pistachio nuts. Keep the kataifi with pastry cream refrigerated and store the kataifi topped with ice cream in the freezer. Let it soften 10-20 minutes in the refrigerator before serving.

mixture too thick. Cut the phyllo sheets into 3-5 inch wide strips. Brush each strip generously with butter and fold in half lengthwise. Wind each folded strip around 2 fingers to form a cup. Tuck about 2 inches of the end underneath forming the cup 's base. Arrange the cups one next to the other. Dribble the remaining butter over them. Fill each cup with about one tablespoon of the filling. Bake in a 350°F oven for about 30 minutes or until golden. Meanwhile, boil the syrup ingredients for 5 minutes and pour it over the nests as soon as they are removed from the oven. Allow them to absorb the syrup and cool completely. Transfer to a serving dish and keep uncovered to ensure their crispness.

Alternate: You may substitute walnuts or pistachio nuts for the almonds. Using 2 teaspoons cinnamon and a little nutmeg instead of the almond extract.

Kataifi
(Kataifi)

Yields 30-35 pieces
Preparation time 1 hour and 30 minutes
Baking time 1 hour

1	lb chopped walnuts
1/4	cup rusk crumbs
2	tablespoons cinnamon
1	teaspoon grated lemon rind or
1	teaspoon cloves
3	tablespoons brandy
1	lb kataifi pastry
1	cup unsalted butter
1	cup unsalted margarine

The Syrup

$3^{1}/_{2}$	cups sugar
2	cups water
1/2	cup glucose
1-2	sticks of cinnamon or
1	teaspoon grated lemon rind
	chopped pistachio nuts for topping

Mix together the first 6 ingredients into a bowl and sprinkle with the brandy. Fluff up the kataifi pastry and divide it into 30-35 portions. Keep covered with a damp cloth while you are working as the pastry dries quickly. Take one portion of kataifi pastry and spread it to form a long strip. Put 1 tablespoonful of nut mixture at one end and roll it up loosely into an oblong roll. It is important to roll loosely because the kataifi pastry tightens as it bakes. Continue the same procedure with the rest of pastry portions. Place the rolls closely in a greased baking pan. Melt the butter and dribble it slowly and evenly over all the rolls. At this stage you may freeze the kataifi rolls. Allow them to thaw out before baking. Cover the pan with aluminum foil and bake in a 350°F oven for 30 minutes. Remove the foil and bake 30 minutes longer or until tops and sides are crisp and golden brown. Meanwhile, prepare the syrup. Heat all the syrup ingredients in a heavy pan and allow the syrup to boil for 5 minutes. Remove the rolls from the oven. Ladle a little syrup over each roll and as it is absorbed, pour over a little more syrup and continue until all the syrup is used. Allow the kataifi rolls to cool completely and transfer to a serving dish. Sprinkle the tops with chopped pistachios. Keep the rolls uncovered to ensure their crispness. They keep well at room temperature from one to two weeks.

7

Cookies and Confections
(Koulouria ke Zacharota)

Cookies and confections are to be enjoyed at any hour, whether served between meals as a little tender sweet treat or as a graceful accompaniment to our morning coffee or tea. A tempting array of cookies served with a steaming cup of coffee or of tea breaks the day deliciously. Most Greek cookies have traditional associations with holiday celebrations and are of great importance. No Greek Christmas is complete without Melomakarona (Honey Dipped Cookies) as no Greek Easter is complete without Koulourakia Paschalina (Greek Easter Cookies) and Kourabiedes. Moustokouloura (Grape-Must Cookies) are baked and served during the fasting period before Christmas and Skaltsounia are the lenten cookies eaten on fasting days before Easter. On Christmas and New Year's Eve when children wonder around the neighborhood singing the carols, they are carrying little baskets which, by the end of the day, are filled with a variety of seasons special goodies.

Cookie making is an experiment in imaginative sculpting and molding. The dough, made by mixing very simple and common ingredients (flour, sugar, honey, butter, eggs and flavorings), is soft and pliable. Cookies, baked almost until dry, keep for a long time.

A variety of biscuits are those made with eggs or egg whites, beaten with sugar and mixed with flour or various nuts. Such as sponge biscuits, walnut macaroons, coconut macaroons, and almond macaroons. These biscuits usually contain either a little or no butter.

Cookies may be flavored with a variety of spices or flavorings. Experiment to find your favorite combination. To bring out the more fresh, strong aroma of spices, buy them whole and keep in airtight containers. Grind the required amount in a mortar or in the blender just before using. Biscuits and cookies are the best assortment for a cup of Greek coffee.

General Instructions:

The basic ingredients for a cookie or biscuit dough are flour, butter and sugar. By mixing these ingredients with some liquid (milk or eggs), an easy-to-handle dough is obtained. Baking a few minutes in a hot oven transforms the dough into crisp cookies. For light, crisp and crumbly biscuits and cookies, follow the proportions specified in your recipe, keep the ingredients cool and lightly mix them together. Overworking the dough strengthens the gluten in the flour and makes the cookies tough. The final texture depends on the amount of fat and the manner in

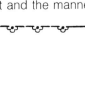

which the ingredients are mixed.

There are three methods of mixing the ingredients together.

According to the first method, the butter is creamed alone, then it is beaten vigorously with sugar so that air bubbles are trapped in the mixture, inflating it. The airy mixture is then mixed lightly with eggs and flour. The resulting dough is pliable and elastic enough to be rolled and cut out into cookies, with a cookie cutter, or to be shaped by hand. The cookies may be rolled in chopped nuts before baking, or sandwiched together with a filling in between, before or after baking. Cocoa may be substituted for part of the flour to make chocolate biscuits or a part of the dough may be colored with food coloring to make multi-colored biscuits.

According to the second method, the butter is cubed cold and rubbed with flour and sugar until the mixture resembles coarse meal. Then eggs, milk or other liquids are added, in small amounts, just enough to make the dough cohere. The dough is not as pliable as the dough in the previous method. Cover and chill for 30 minutes before using. The dough can be rolled out and cut with cookie cutters. Also the rolled out dough can be sprinkled with sweet or savory ingredients, like ground walnuts or grated cheese, rolled up and sliced into thin biscuits.

According to the third method, all the ingredients are mixed together and rubbed lightly by hand to cohere. Honey or syrup cookies usually are made with the third method.

Greek Coffee

Coffee, still known by its Arabic name "Kahwah" which means the appeaser of appetites, was brought to Europe by Venetian merchants in the 16th century. Nowadays in Greece coffee is prepared in different ways. However, the favorite coffee remains the strong, sweet brew made by the Arabs four centuries ago.
In Greece the habit of drinking coffee is a way of life. Coffee lovers can sit for hours in the cafes, called "Kafenia", sipping small cups of coffee, and enjoying it quietly or talking about politics. Nowadays there remain throughout the country only a few old-time coffee shops that have not been modernized. At such a "Kafenio" the visitor would be transferred to another world and experience the charming atmosphere of the past. Only men were allowed to visit the old kafenia. Women enjoyed their coffee at home, two or three times a day, most of the times with the company of a friend or neighbor. There were some among the neighbors who aspire to foretell the future by "reading" the coffee-grounds left in the cup after drinking. The cups were turned over onto the saucers and the grounds were allowed to dry. A large irregular splash would mean problems ahead, an even black line indicated a trip ahead.
The best coffee is made by freshly roasted and ground coffee beans. In every household, there used to be a coffee roaster and a mill for grinding the coffee beans. The whole house was filled with the lovely coffee aroma every time my mother roasted coffee beans. Coffee was roasted once a week and was ground two or three times a day just before coffee time.
Coffee is brewed in a copper or brass long-handled, lipped classic coffee pot known as a "Briki". For best results the briki must not be filled more than half full of water. Every household had a display of "brikia", from a tiny one for just one cup of coffee to a very large one which could hold up to 6 cups.

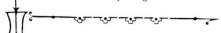

The proportions for two persons are:

2   *demitasse cups water ($^2/_3$ cup)*
2   *teaspoons sugar*
2   *heaping teaspoons coffee*

Pour the water into the briki and heat it to the boiling point. Add the coffee and sugar and stir well. Heat over low heat until the coffee is frothy but not boiling. Immediately remove from the heat and divide the froth between two demitasse cups. Return the remaining coffee to the heat and let it boil. Pour it carefully into the cups without disturbing the froth. For a light foamy froth pour the coffee into the cups from a high to a low motion. If too much froth is not wanted, let the coffee boil at the beginning. The individual taste of coffee lovers varies. The most common, orders when you are ordering a Greek coffee are "Metrio Vrasto" which means you prefer your coffee medium boiled and medium sweetened. "Vari gliko" which means strong and sweet and "Sketo vrasto" indicates that you would like it without sugar. There are other variations depending on the personal taste and mood. The strangest order I heard was at Mount Pilion at an old "Kafenio", where a customer asked for a coffee with "foustaneles" (the skirts worn by Evzones). The cafe 's owner explained to me that the customer wanted his coffee with lots of bubbles.

Greek Coffee

Walnut Macaroons, Island Style
(Karidata Nissiotika)

Yields 30-40 pieces
Preparation time 35 minutes
Baking time 10 minutes

2	lbs coarsely chopped walnuts
4	tablespoons rusk crumbs
6	tablespoons sugar
3	egg whites
1	tablespoon grated orange rind
1	cup orange juice
	confectioners ' sugar

Mix the walnuts and crumbs into a bowl. Lightly mix the egg whites with sugar and add to the walnut mixture, together with grated orange rind and half the orange juice. Mix lightly by hand, adding the remaining orange juice, a little at a time, until the mixture just begins to cohere and can be easily molded. Take small pieces of the mixture and form them into fig shaped cookies. Arrange on baking sheets lined with greased baking paper. Bake in a 350°F oven for 10 minutes. Turn off the oven and let the Macaroons stand inside for 5-6 minutes longer. Cool on a rack. When completely cold, dip them in rose water and roll in confectioners ' sugar.

Skaltsounia (Lenten Cookies)
(Skaltsounia)

Yields 22-24 cookies
Preparation time 1 hour
Baking time 15 minutes

3	cups blanched, finely ground almonds
1	small potato, peeled and boiled
1	cup sugar
1	tablespoon rose water or brandy
1/2	teaspoon vanilla

The Filling

1/2	cup coarsely chopped walnuts
1/2	cup sultana raisins
1/2	cup dried prunes or apricots, finely cut
2	tablespoons apricot jam
	confectioners' sugar and cinnamon for dusting

Blend the almonds and remaining ingredients in a food processor or blender, until they form a firm easy to handle mixture. Cover and chill for about 2 hours. Mix separately the walnuts, raisins, dried fruit and jam to bind. On a floured working surface, roll out pieces of dough into 3 inch rounds, about $1/8$ inch thick. Spoon one tablespoon filling on one side of dough rounds and fold the other side over to form a crescent. Dip your fingertips into confectioners' sugar and lightly press the edges to seal. Place skaltsounia on a baking sheet lined with greaseproof baking paper. Bake in a 350F oven for 10-15 minutes, until lightly golden. Remove from the oven. Let

them cool for 5 minutes, and carefully tranfer to a greaseproof paper dusted with confectioners' sugar. Through a large sieve, generously dust them with confectioners' sugar and sprinkle with cinnamon. Keep in tightly covered container as they tend to dry quickly.

Skaltsounia with Sesame Seeds
(Skaltsounia me Sousami)

Yields 30-40 cookies
Preparation time 2 hours
Baking time 30 minutes

The Filling

2	cups finely cut walnuts
1	cup finely cut blanched almonds
1/4	cup sesame seeds
1/2	teaspoon ground mastic
1/2	teaspoon baking powder
2-3	tablespoons honey or jam

The Dough

3	cups all purpose flour
1/2	teaspoon baking powder
1/2	teaspoon baking soda
1/4	teaspoon salt
1	cup sesame oil or vegetable oil
2/3	cup orange juice
1/4	cup sugar

The Garnish

1	cup rose water
1	cup confectioners ' sugar

Mix first 5 ingredients of the filling into a bowl. Add enough honey or jam to bind. Sift together the flour, baking powder, soda and salt into a large bowl and make a well in the center. Blend the remaining ingredients of the dough for 1-2 minutes and pour into the well. Gradually fold in the flour from the sides of the well, working by hand, until a soft and pliable dough is formed. Avoid overworking. On a lightly floured surface roll out the dough into an $1/8$ inch thick sheet. Use a plain 4 inch cutter to cut out rounds. Place a tablespoon of the filling into the middle of each round and fold in half to create a crescent shape. Press edges with your fingers to seal, and arrange skaltsounia on well greased baking sheets.

Bake in a 350°F oven for 25-30 minutes until lightly golden. Remove from the oven and while lightly warm, quickly dip them, one at a time, in rose water and roll in confectioners ' sugar. Keep them in a cookie tin.

Almond Biscuits (Biskota Amigdalou)

Yields 40-50 biscuits
Preparation time 1 hour and 30 minutes
Baking time 12 minutes

1	cup unsalted butter or margarine, softened
1	cup confectioners' sugar
2	eggs
1/4	teaspoon almond extract
3	cups all purpose flour
3	teaspoons baking powder
1 1/2	cups roasted ground almonds

Cream the butter and sugar with an electric mixer until pale and fluffy. Beating continuously, add the eggs one at a time. Then add the flavoring. Stop beating. Sift flour and baking powder together. Fold it gently into the creamed butter in 3-4 stages alternated with ground almonds. Knead lightly until a smooth and pliable dough is formed. Avoid overkneading. Roll out the dough to an $^1/_8$ inch thick sheet and cut out biscuits with a fluted biscuit cutter. With a metal spatula, transfer the cut biscuits to a lightly greased baking sheet and bake in a 350°F oven for about 12 minutes. Cool on a rack. To keep crisp, store in a cookie tin.
Alternate: Substitute roasted sesame seeds for the ground almonds, and vanilla flavoring for the almond extract. Sprinkle the unbaked biscuits with sesame seeds.

Skaltsounia (Lenten Cookies), page 122

Walnut Tarts
(Formakia me Karidia)

Yields 16 tarts
Preparation time 1 hour
Baking time 25 minutes

5	phyllo pastry sheets
1/4	cup melted margarine
5	eggs
2	tablespoons custard powder
1	cup sugar
5	tablespoons melted unsalted butter
3	cups coarsely chopped walnuts
2	tablespoons grated orange rind
	confectioners' sugar and cinnamon for dusting

Stack the phyllo sheets on a working surface, one on top of the other, brushing each one with melted margarine. Use a plain 4 inch biscuit cutter to cut out rounds and line 16 well greased individual tart molds. Beat the eggs with custard powder and sugar until thick and foamy. Gently fold the nuts into beaten egg mixture, sprinkling them on lightly as you fold. Then fold in the butter, a tablespoon at a time. Sprinkle a little grated orange rind in each tart and fill them up to $^3/_4$ full with the walnut mixture. Bake tarts in a 350°F oven for 20-25 minutes. While still warm, sprinkle with confectioners' sugar and cinnamon.

Walnut Macaroons
(Karidata tis Fotias)

Yields 30-35 macaroons
Preparation time 45 minutes
Baking time 15 minutes

1 1/2	cups sugar
2	tablespoons cocoa
2	tablespoons all purpose flour
1/2	teaspoon cinnamon
2	cups ground walnuts
4	egg whites
	Chocolate Icing (page 59) optional

Sift together sugar, cocoa, flour and cinnamon into a saucepan. Add the walnuts and egg whites. Stir the mixture over a water bath or over direct, very low heat until hot. Remove from the heat and cool slightly. The mixture thickens as it cools. When it is thick enough to pipe, spoon it into a piping bag fitted with a 1/2 inch wide plain nozzle. Pipe 1 1/2 inch dots onto a greased baking paper placed on a baking tray. Leave about 1 inch between dots to allow room for expansion. Let them stand for about 10 minutes to cool and stiffen, before baking. Bake in a 350°F oven for 15-18 minutes. Let macaroons cool for 5 minutes. Then remove carefully with a spatula and cool on a rack. You may sandwich pairs of walnut macaroons together with chocolate icing. Keep in tightly covered container as they tend to dry quickly.

Walnut Cookies (Karidata)

Yields 30-35 cookies
Preparation time 1 hour
Baking time 8 minutes

3	large eggs
1	cup sugar
1	teaspoon vanilla
2 1/2	cups coarsely chopped walnuts
2/3	cup rusk crumbs
2	oz baking chocolate, grated
1/2	teaspoon baking powder
1/2	recipe, Buttercream (page 53) optional

Beat eggs and sugar with an electric mixer at high speed until thick and lemon-colored. Add vanilla. Mix together walnuts, crumbs, grated chocolate and baking powder. Gently fold the nut mixture into beaten eggs. Batter must be thick enough to be shaped. One to two additional tablespoons of crumbs or nut may be added, if necessary. Shape the dough into balls the size of a small walnut and place them on a baking sheet lined with greased baking paper. Leave enough space between them to allow room for spreading. Bake in a 350°F oven for 6-8 minutes. You may sandwich pairs of cookies together with buttercream. Store in a cookie tin.

Almond and Coconut Macaroons
(Karides)

Yields 40 macaroons
Preparation time 30 minutes
Baking time 20 minutes

5	eggs, separated
2	cups sugar
4	cups grated coconut (1 lb)
1	cup finely chopped almonds
1	teaspoon vanilla
1	teaspoon grated lemon peel
1	tablespoon flour
1	tablespoon butter

Beat the egg yolks with half the amount of sugar, until thick and lemon-colored. Mix in the remaining ingredients. Whisk the egg whites with remaining sugar until stiff and glossy. Gently fold it into the egg yolk mixture. Spoon the batter into a piping bag fitted with a plain 2/3 inch nozzle and pipe strips of batter about 4 inches long on to a greased baking sheet. Use a knife to stop the flow of batter at the end of each strip. Leave a 1 inch space between each strip to allow for expansion. Bake the cookies in a 350°F oven for 20 minutes, or until lightly golden. Cool them for 5 minutes. Then remove carefully from the paper. Cool on a rack. Store the cookies in a cookie tin as they dry out rather quickly.

Chocolate Filled Cookies
(Biskota me Sokolata)

Yields 20-25 double cookies
Preparation time 1 hour and 30 minutes
Baking time 15 minutes

1 1/2	cups unsalted butter, softened
2 1/2	cups confectioners' sugar
2	eggs or 4 egg yolks
2	teaspoons vanilla
1/4	teaspoon salt
6	cups all purpose flour
	Chocolate Icing (page 49)

Cream the butter with an electric mixer. Add the sugar and beat them together until the mixture is pale and fluffy. Beating continuously, add the egg yolks one at a time. Then add the flavoring. Sift the flour with salt and gently fold into the butter mixture. Add enough flour and knead lightly to form a soft, pliable dough. Avoid overkneading. On a well floured working surface, roll out the dough into an 1/8 inch thick sheet. Use a plain 2 inch cookie cutter to cut out round cookies. Place the cookies on a baking sheet lined with baking paper and bake in a 400°F oven for about 10 minutes, until lightly golden. Cool them on a rack. Meanwhile, prepare the chocolate icing as in the recipe for Praline Parfait Torte, and sandwich pairs of cookies together with the icing in between. Garnish each cookie with a dab of chocolate. Store in a cookie tin.

Coconut Macaroons
(Indokarida)

Yields 25-30 macaroons
Preparation time 1 hour
Baking time 20 minutes

2	tablespoons all purpose flour
3	cups grated coconut
1	cup sugar
1	tablespoon glucose (corn syrup)
2	tablespoons butter
3	eggs, slightly beaten
15	crystallized cherries, halved

Mix the flour and coconut into a bowl. Put sugar, glucose, butter and eggs into a heavy saucepan and stir over low heat until they are heated through. Remove from the heat. Add flour and coconut. Mix lightly and cool. Spoon the mixture into a piping bag fitted with a $^2/_3$ inch star nozzle, and pipe large rosettes onto greased baking paper placed on a baking tray. Place a halved cherry on top of each cookie and bake in a 350°F oven for about 20 minutes, until lightly golden. Cool and store in a cookie tin as they tend to dry out quickly.

Almond Clusters
(Anomala Sokolatakia me Amigdala)

Yields about 100 pieces
Preparation time 2 hours

2	lbs roasted whole almonds or hazelnuts
4	tablespoons butter
1	lb baking chocolate
4	tablespoons vegetable oil
1/4	teaspoon almond extract or
1	teaspoon vanilla

Spread some butter on your palms and rub the almonds or hazelnuts between them lightly, to grease them before roasting. Put chocolate and oil into a saucepan and melt over a water bath or over direct very low heat. Remove from the heat. Add flavoring and roasted almonds or hazelnuts. Stir the mixture to blend the chocolate thoroughly with the nuts. Remove teaspoonfuls of the chocolate mixture and using a metal spatula, push the mixture off spoon onto a baking tray lined with greased baking paper. Allow chocolates to set in a cool place. Put each one in small candy cups or wrap in aluminum foil. You may substitute pralines for the almonds. Store in a cool place.

Coconut Macaroons, page 125
Chocolate Filled Cookies, page 124

Hazelnut Filled Kourabiedes
(Kourabiedakia me Foundouki)

Yields 70-80 small kourabiedes
Preparation time 1 hour
Baking time 20 minutes

2   cups unsalted butter, clarified and softened
1/2   cup confectioners ' sugar
3   teaspoons vanilla
5-6   cups all purpose flour
      roasted whole hazelnuts or almonds
      confectioners ' sugar for dusting

Cream the butter and sugar with an electric mixer until the mixture is pale and fluffy. To ensure that all the sugar is blended in, scrape the sides of the bowl with a rubber spatula from time to time. Add the flavoring and stop beating. Fold in enough flour, a little at a time, blending it gently by hand to form a soft and easy to handle dough. Avoid overworking as this would strengthen the gluten, making the dough tough when baked. Roll a piece of dough, the size of a walnut, into a small ball. Press your finger into the ball to make a cavity and place a hazelnut or almond into it. Press the dough over the nut to seal it and roll again to a ball. Place the balls on a greased baking sheet and bake in a 350°F oven for about 20 minutes or until lightly golden. Remove from the oven and immediately transfer with a spatula to a greaseproof paper, liberally dusted with confectioners ' sugar. While still hot, liberally sift confectioners ' sugar on them until they are completely covered. Cool thoroughly and place in individual candy cups. Stored in a cookie tin, they keep well up to a month.

Kourabiedes (Kourabiedes)

Yields 50-60 kourabiedes
Preparation time 20 minutes
Baking time 20 minutes

1   cup unsalted soft butter, clarified
1   cup shortening
1/2   cup confectioners ' sugar
3   teaspoons vanilla
4-5   cups all purpose flour
1   cup blanched almonds, coarsely
      chopped and roasted
      rose-water (optional)
      confectioners ' sugar for dusting

Cream the butter, shortening and sugar with an electric mixer until light and fluffy. Add the flavoring and stop beating. Fold in 2 cups flour a little at a time, blending lightly by hand. Then fold in the almonds, and knead lightly adding more flour until the dough is light and does not stick to the fingers. Avoid overworking the dough. This would strengthen the gluten, making the Kourabiedes tough when baked. Roll the dough into crescent shapes, or cut it with a star shaped cookie cutter, and place on a baking sheet. Bake in a 350°F oven for about 20 minutes, or until lightly golden. Remove from the oven and immediately transfer with a spatula to a greaseproof paper, liberally dusted with confectioners ' sugar. If desired, sprinkle with rose-water. Then sift lots of confectioners ' sugar on them, which will cling to their surfaces. Let the Kourabiedes cool. Then transfer to a serving dish. Stored in a cookie tin, they keep well up to one month.

Almond Bonbons
(Fondan me Amigdala - Venizelika Limnou)

Yields 50-60 pieces
Preparation time 2 hours

$1\frac{1}{2}$ lbs unblanched almonds, ground
3   cups confectioners ' sugar
1/2   lb baking chocolate, grated
1   tablespoon cocoa
1   cup brandy
      vanilla fondant icing

Mix together almonds, sugar, chocolate and cocoa into a bowl. Add brandy. It may not be necessary to use all the amount of brandy. Add $^2/_3$ at the beginning. Then gradually add the remaining until the mixture is easy to handle. Take small pieces of it and roll each one between your fingers, shaping them into balls. Dip bonbons one at a time into white or colored vanilla fondant icing. Keep in tightly covered cookie tins, as they tend to dry out.
Vanilla Fondant Icing: Melt 1 lb vanilla fondant (page 12) over a water bath or over direct very low heat. Whisk 1 egg white with 2-3 drops lemon juice to a stiff meringue. Add it to the vanilla fondant and mix well. Keep the icing hot. Dip the almond bonbons in it, threaded one by one on to wooden picks. Slip them off picks onto greaseproof paper to dry. Use food coloring to color the glaze, if desired.

Almond Bonbons, page 126

Honey Dipped Cookies (Melomakarona)

Yields 40-50 cookies
Preparation time 30 minutes
Baking time 30 minutes

8	cups all purpose flour
1	teaspoon baking soda
2	teaspoons baking powder
$1\frac{1}{2}$	cups oil
1/2	cup shortening
1	cup sugar
3/4	cup orange juice
1/4	cup brandy
2	teaspoons grated orange rind

The Syrup

2	cups honey
2	cups sugar
2	cups water

The Garnish

$1\frac{1}{2}$	cups finely chopped walnuts
1	teaspoon cinnamon
1/2	teaspoon cloves

Sift together flour, soda and baking powder into a kneading basin, and make a well in the center. Blend the remaining ingredients at high speed in a food processor or blender. Pour the mixture into the well. Gradually incorporate the flour from the sides of the well into the liquid and knead lightly until a soft and greasy dough is formed. Avoid overkneading. On a wooden surface, roll out the dough into a $\frac{1}{3}$ inch thick sheet. Use cookie cutters to cut out the dough into ovals, squares or rounds. Arrange them on ungreased baking sheets and decorate the tops by drawing and pressing the prongs of a fork across the surface. Bake in a 350°F oven for about 30 minutes or until golden browned. Meanwhile, combine the syrup ingredients into a large pan and bring them to a boil. Decrease the heat and simmer for 7 minutes. Skim off the froth and pour the syrup over the cookies as soon as they come out of the oven. When all the syrup is absorbed, turn them over and allow to cool completely. Mix together walnuts, cinnamon and cloves in a bowl. Picking up, one cookie at a time, turn them over and sprinkle the tops with the walnut mixture. Place the cookies on a serving dish and keep covered with plastic wrap to prevent from drying out. They keep well in room temperature up to 3 weeks.

Almond Cream Triangles
(Bourekakia me Amigdala)

Yields 42 triangles
Preparation time 1 hour
Baking time 20 minutes

3   cups ground, blanched almonds
1½   cups sugar
2   tablespoons rose water
1   teaspoon vanilla
2-3   egg yolks, lightly beaten
1   lb ready made phyllo dough sheets
1   cup melted, unsalted butter

Mix the first 4 ingredients in a bowl. Add as many egg yolks as are needed to make a soft mixture. Gently unfold the phyllo sheets on a board. With a sharp knife, cut them lengthwise into 2½ inch wide strips. To avoid drying, cover the strips with a damp cloth. Place two strips, one on top of the other, generously brushing each one with melted butter. Put a teaspoonful of the almond mixture in one corner, then lift the edge of the strip and fold it over the filling to form a triangle. Fold the triangle over and over again until the whole strip is folded. Arrange the triangles on a greased baking sheet and brush the tops with melted butter. (At this point you may freeze them, if desired). Bake in a 350°F oven for 15-20 minutes, until lightly golden. Dust with confectioners ' sugar and cinnamon as soon as they come out of the oven. Serve them on the day they are baked.

Walnut Bonbons (Fondan me Karidia)

Yields 64 bonbons
Preparation time 2 hours

2   cups sugar
3/4   cup whipping cream
1/4   cup milk
1   tablespoon glucose (corn syrup)
1/8   teaspoon salt
1   teaspoon vanilla
3/4   cup finely chopped walnuts
1/2   lb baking chocolate, melted
       crystallized fruits or walnut halves

Mix the sugar, cream, milk, glucose and salt in a medium sized, deep saucepan. Bring slowly to the boil, stirring to dissolve the sugar. Then cook the mixture undisturbed until it reaches the soft ball stage or registers 240°F on a candy thermometer. Remove the pan from the heat. Immediately dip in cold water to stop the cooking. Let the mixture cool to 115°F. Add the vanilla and beat until the mixture becomes thick and opaque. Mix in the finely chopped walnuts, and pour into a well greased 8 inch square baking pan. Spread the melted chocolate on top. Cool until it is completely stiff and cut into bite sized squares. Decorate each bonbon with half walnut or pieces of crystallized fruit. Store in a cookie tin.

Kourabiedes from Kozani
(Kourabiedes Zematisti Kozanis)

Yields 60 kourabiedes
Preparation time 1 hour
Baking time 30 minutes

1/2   cup fine semolina
6   cups all purpose flour
1   cup sugar
1   cup water
1   lb unsalted butter
2   egg yolks
1   tablespoon ammonium bicarbonate,
       dissolved into 2 tablespoons milk
30   almonds, blanched and halved

The Syrup

3   cups sugar
2   cups water
1   tablespoon lemon juice

Sift together semolina and flour. Set aside. Cook the sugar and water until it is condensed to 1 cup syrup. Let it cool. Cream the butter with an electric mixer at high speed until light and fluffy. Beating continuously, add the egg yolks, one at a time. Lower the speed and beating with the dough hook, add the ammonium bicarbonate, then the syrup in 3-4 stages alternated with the sifted semolina and flour. Add as much of the mixture as needed to make a soft, easy to handle dough. Roll small pieces of dough into balls and place them on a baking sheet lined with greased baking paper. Place half almond on each piece. Bake the Kourabiedes in a 200°F oven for about 30 minutes, or until golden brown. Meanwhile, boil all the syrup ingredients for 5 minutes and pour it over the Kourabiedes as soon as they come out of the oven. Allow them to absorb the syrup and cool. Transfer to a serving dish. They keep well at room temperature up to one week.

Almond Cream Triangles, page 128

Kourabiedes with Syrup
(Kourabiedes me Siropi)

Yields 40 Kourabiedes
Preparation time 30 minutes
Baking time 20 minutes

1/2	lb margarine
1/2	cup sugar
2	whole eggs, or 3 egg yolks
2	teaspoons vanilla
3	cups all purpose flour
	blanched almonds

The Syrup

2	cups sugar
1$^1/_2$	cups water
1	tablespoon lemon juice

Cream the butter and sugar with an electric mixer until pale and fluffy. Beating continuously, add the eggs or egg yolks one at a time. Then add the flavoring. Stop beating. Gently fold in the flour, a little at a time, kneading lightly until a soft, pliable dough is formed. Avoid over-kneading. Shape small pieces of dough into balls, and place on a greased baking sheet spaced well apart to allow room for spreading. Top each cookie with a blanched almond. Bake in a 350°F oven for 15-20 minutes or until lightly golden. Meanwhile, prepare the syrup. Put the sugar and water in a saucepan over low heat and stir until the sugar is dissolved. Add the lemon juice, increase the heat and boil the syrup for 5 minutes without stirring. Pour the syrup over Kourabiedes as soon as they come out of the oven. Let them absorb the syrup and cool. Transfer to a serving dish. They keep well at room temperature for up to one week.

Small Truffles
(Troufakia)

Yields 60 truffles
Preparation time 2 hours

1	cup milk
1/2	lb baking chocolate, cut in pieces
1/4	cup brandy
1	cup unsalted butter
1	cup confectioners' sugar
4	egg yolks
4	cups Graham cracker crumbs
1/2	lb chocolate sprinkles
2$^1/_2$	cups coarsely chopped walnuts

Boil the milk, add the chocolate and stir over low heat until the chocolate is melted and well blended with the milk. Remove from the heat and cool. Stir in brandy. Set aside. Cream the butter and sugar until light and pale. Beating continuously, add the egg yolks one at a time. Stop beating. Gradually pour the chocolate mixture into the creamed butter and mix gently. Fold in the crumbs and walnuts. Refrigerate the mixture for a few hours, until firm. Dip your palms into a little brandy or liqueur and shape the mixture into small balls. Roll them in chocolate sprinkles and place into small candy cups. Arrange on a serving dish and dust the tops with confectioners' sugar. Keep refrigerated. They keep well one week in the refrigerator and several months in the freezer.

Kourabiedes with Syrup, page 129

Savory Salty Bites (Almires Boukitses)

Yields 90-100 bite sized cookies
Preparation time 2 hours
Baking time 15 minutes

4-5   cups all purpose flour
2   teaspoons salt
2   teaspoons baking powder
1/2   cup olive or vegetable oil
1/2   cup shortening
1/2   cup milk
2   teaspoons sugar
1/2   cup grated cheese (optional)
1   egg, lightly beaten
100   hazelnuts

Sift the flour, salt and baking powder into a large bowl and make a well in the center. Blend together oil, shortening, milk and sugar for 2 minutes in a food processor or blender. Pour the mixture into the well. Stir in the cheese. Then gradually incorporate the flour from the sides of the well into the liquid, working by hand, until a soft and easy to handle dough is formed. Avoid overworking. Pinch pieces of dough and roll them into cylinders the size of your little finger. Form cylinders into U shapes, twist the ends and place a nut in the opening. Also cylinders may be shaped into circles, figure eight or any desired shapes, placing nuts in the openings. Place small cookies onto baking sheets greased or lined with baking paper and brush the tops with beaten egg. Bake in a 400°F oven for 15- 20 minutes, until golden. Cool on a rack. Store in a cookie tin. They keep well up to one month.

Feta Cheese Biscuits
(Biskotakia me Feta)

Yields 20 biscuits
Preparation time 30 minutes
Baking time 15 minutes

2   cups all purpose flour
1/4   teaspoon salt
3   teaspoons baking powder
1   tablespoon sugar
3   oz unsalted butter, cubed
1/2   cup finely crumbled Feta cheese
1/4   cup milk
1   egg yolk beaten with 1 tablespoon water

Mix the first 4 ingredients into a mixing bowl. Add the butter and rub it with the flour, using your fingertips and thumbs, until the mixture resembles coarse bread crumbs. Add cheese and mix lightly. Sprinkle the milk over the mixture, and mix lightly until it just begins to cohere. The dough should feel crumbly. Do not knead. Just gather all the crumbs into a ball, pressing them with your hands. Roll out the dough on a floured surface into a $^1/_3$ inch thick sheet. Use a 2 inch fluted cookie cutter and cut out round biscuits. Place on lined baking sheets. Brush the tops with the egg yolk mixture and bake in a

Chios Mastic Flavored Cookies
(Koulourakia Chiotika)

Yields 30-35 cookies
Preparation time 1 hour and 30 minutes
Baking time 20 minutes

1/2   cup unsalted butter or margarine, softened
1/2   cup sugar
2   eggs
1   teaspoon ammonium bicarbonate, dissolved in
      2 tablespoons milk
1/4   teaspoon ground mastic from Chios
4   cups self raising flour
1   egg yolk mixed with 1 teaspoon water
      sesame seeds

Cream the butter and sugar until light and fluffy. Beating continuously, add the eggs one at a time alternated with a tablespoon of flour to prevent the mixture from curdling. Stop beating. Add ammonium bicarbonate and flavoring. Then add the flour, a little at a time, folding it gently into the creamed butter until a smooth and easy to handle dough is formed. Avoid overworking. Roll small pieces of dough into 4 inch long finger thick strips. Form strips into U shapes, and twist the ends. Place the cookies on a baking sheet lined with baking paper. Brush the tops with egg yolk, and sprinkle with a few sesame seeds. Bake the cookies in a 350°F oven for 15-20 minutes. Remove from the oven and cool on a rack. Store in a cookie tin.

400°F oven for about 15 minutes. Serve the biscuits the day they are made, preferably within minutes of their baking. They keep well in the freezer. To defrost, place them on a baking sheet and heat in a 350°F oven for 5-7 minutes until warm.

Chios Mastic Flavored Cookies, page 130

Cinnamon Cookies
(Koulourakia Kanelas)

Yields 40 cookies
Preparation time 1 hour and 30 minutes
Baking time 20 minutes

1	lb all purpose flour
1	teaspoon baking soda
1	teaspoon baking powder
1½	teaspoons cinnamon
1/4	teaspoon cloves
1/4	teaspoon nutmeg
3/4	cup sugar
1	cup vegetable oil
1/4	cup sparkling water (club soda)
1	tablespoon brandy
1/4	cup orange juice
1	teaspoon grated orange rind

Sift together flour, soda, baking powder, cinnamon, cloves and nutmeg into a large bowl and make a well in the center. Blend the remaining ingredients for 1-2 minutes in a food processor or blender. Pour the mixture into the well. Mix in the flour, pulling it gradually from the sides of the well and working by hand until a soft, pliable dough is formed. Avoid overworking. On a working surface, form pieces of dough into 8 inch long finger thick strips by rolling backwards and forwards under your fingers. Then fold in half and twist. Place on lined baking sheets and bake in a 350°F oven for about 16 minutes. Cool and store in a cookie tin.

Savory Salted Cookies
(Koulourakia Almira)

Yields 40 cookies
Preparation time 1 hour and 30 minutes
Baking time 20 minutes

3	cups all purpose flour
3	teaspoons baking powder
1	teaspoon salt
1/2	cup shortening
1/3	cup olive oil
2	teaspoons sugar
1/2	cup yogurt

Sift together flour, baking powder and salt. Beat the butter, oil and sugar with an electric mixer until creamed. Beating continuously with the dough hook, add the sifted ingredients in 3-4 stages alternated with yogurt. Add enough flour to make a soft, easy to handle dough. Refrigerate the dough for 2 hours. Roll out small pieces of dough into 6 inch long, finger thick strips, fold in half and twist. Arrange them on a lined baking sheet and bake in a 375°F oven for 15-20 minutes or until lightly golden. Cool on a rack and store in a cookie tin.

Walnut Bars
(Biskota me Karidia)

Yields 48 pieces
Preparation time 30 minutes
Baking time 30 minutes

1	recipe, Rich Shortcrust Pastry Dough (page 31)
2	cups coarsely chopped walnuts
2	tablespoons all purpose flour
2	teaspoons cinnamon
1	teaspoon cloves
2	eggs, separated, and
2	egg whites left over from the pastry dough
3	tablespoons unsalted butter
1/2	teaspoon cream of tartar
1	cup sugar

Prepare the Shortcrust Pastry according to the recipe. Roll out the dough into a rectangle and line a well greased 10 by 14 inch baking pan. Pierce the pastry all over with a fork and bake in a 375°F oven for about 10 minutes. Meanwhile, mix together walnuts, flour and spices into a large bowl. Add the egg yolks and butter and stir the mixture until well blended. Whisk the egg whites with cream of tartar until foamy. Gradually add the sugar and continue to whisk until the meringue is stiff and glossy. Stir a few spoonfuls of meringue into the walnut mixture to loosen it and enable the rest of the meringue to be folded in gently. Spread the mixture over the dough evenly. Return to the oven and bake for about 20 minutes until firm. Remove from the oven, cool slightly and cut into 1 by 3 inch bars. You may keep it in the refrigerator up to one week.

Assortment of Cookies

Honey Cookies
(Koulourakia Melenia)

Yields 30-35 cookies
Preparation time 1 hour and 30 minutes
Baking time 15 minutes

2	cups all purpose flour
1	teaspoon baking powder
1/4	teaspoon salt
1$\frac{1}{2}$	teaspoons cinnamon
1/2	teaspoon cloves or nutmeg
1/2	cup unsalted butter or margarine, softened
1/4	cup sugar
1/4	cup honey
1/4	teaspoon baking soda dissolved in one tablespoon brandy
2	tablespoons yogurt

Sift together flour, baking powder, salt and spices. Cream the butter and sugar at high speed until light and fluffy. Add honey, baking soda and yogurt and mix with a spoon. Then gradually add the sifted ingredients and mix lightly, working by hand until a soft and pliable dough is formed. Roll out small pieces of dough into long, finger thick strips and form them into various shapes. Arrange the cookies on a baking sheet lined with baking paper and bake in a 350°F oven for approximately 15 minutes. Cool and store in a cooking tin.

Wine Cookies
(Koulourakia Methismena)

Yields 30-40 cookies
Preparation time 20 minutes
Baking time 20 minutes

1/2	cup sesame seeds
1/2	cup vegetable oil
1/2	cup margarine
1/2	cup white wine
1/2	cup sugar
3$\frac{1}{2}$	cups self raising flour
1	egg white, sesame seeds

Spread the sesame seeds in a baking pan and brown lightly in a 350°F oven. Cool and mix with the flour. Blend together oil, margarine, wine and sugar for 1-2 minutes in a food processor or blender until light. Pour the mixture into a large bowl. Gradually mix in the flour and sesame mixture and knead lightly to form an easy to handle dough. Avoid overkneading. Roll it by hand or use a cookie cutter to form the dough into various shapes. Brush the cookies all over with lightly beaten egg whites and roll them in sesame seeds until well coated. Place the cookies on a lightly greased baking sheet and bake in a 400°F oven for about 20 minutes. Cool the cookies and store in a cookie tin. They keep well up to a month.

Smyrna Cookies
(Koulourakia Smirneika)

Yields 40 cookies
Preparation time 1 hour and 30 minutes
Baking time 20 minutes

1	cup unsalted butter
4$\frac{1}{2}$	cups all purpose flour
1	teaspoon baking powder
1/4	teaspoon baking soda
3/4	cup sugar
2	egg yolks
1/4	cup milk
1/2	teaspoon mastic from Chios, ground
1-2	egg yolks, beaten with 2 teaspoons water

To clarify the butter, melt it over low heat, cool and refrigerate overnight. The next day lift off the solidified butter and discard the water. To speed up the procedure freeze the butter for 1-2 hours. Sift together the flour, baking powder and soda. Cream the butter and the sugar until light and fluffy. Beating continuously add the egg yolks one at a time; then add the milk and flavoring. Beating with the dough hook or by hand, gradually fold in the sifted ingredients and knead lightly to form a soft pliable dough. Roll pieces of dough into 10 inch long, finger thick strips. Shape each strip into a capital letter **N** figure. Press the edges tightly together to form the cookies into small boat shapes. Arrange them on lightly greased baking sheets and brush the tops with the egg yolk mixture. Bake in a 350°F oven for about 20 minutes. Cool and store in a cookie tin.

Almond Praline
(Pralina - Karamelomena Amigdala)

Yields about 1 lb
Preparation time 10 minutes

1/2	lb sugar
1/2	teaspoon lemon juice or cream of tartar
1/2	cup water
1/2	lb almonds, blanched and lightly roasted

Put the sugar, lemon juice and water in a heavy-bottomed pan and cook, stirring constantly, over very low heat, until the sugar is dissolved. Place the lid on the pan for a few moments. Then remove it and cook the syrup, undisturbed, until its color turns amber caramel. Drop in the almonds and stir gently with a wooden spatula to mix them into the syrup. When the mixture begins to boil again, remove from the heat and pour it onto a well greased metal or marble slab. Spread it out with a spatula and let it cool thoroughly. Break the praline into small or large pieces and store it in a tightly sealed jar. In a dry, cool place, praline can be kept for several months. Other hard nuts can be substituted for the almonds.

Muhlep Cookies
(Koulourakia me Mahlepi)

Yields 45-50 cookies
Preparation time 1 hour
Baking time 15 minutes

3¹/₂   cups self raising flour
1   teaspoon salt
1   teaspoon ground muhlep
3/4   cup soft margarine or vegetable oil
2/3   cup yogurt
3/4   cup sugar
1   egg yolk beaten with 1 teaspoon water
        sesame seeds

Sift together flour, salt and muhlep into a large bowl and make a well in the center. Put in margarine, yogurt and sugar. Mix lightly by hand, pulling in the flour from the sides of the well, gradually, until all the flour is incorporated and the dough is soft and pliable. Roll small pieces of dough into a short, broad cigar shape. Turn tapered ends in opposite directions to form a letter **S**. Arrange the cookies on a lightly greased baking sheet, brush the tops with the egg yolk mixture and sprinkle with sesame seeds. Bake in a 400°F for 15 minutes until golden. Cool and store in a cookie tin. They keep well up to one week.

Lemon Flavored Cookies
(Koulourakia me Aroma Lemoni)

Yields 35-40 cookies
Preparation time 1 hour and 30 minutes
Baking time 10-15 minutes

4-4¹/₂ cups all purpose flour
2   tablespoons baking powder
3/4   cup unsalted butter
1¹/₄   cups sugar
2   egg yolks
2   tablespoons grated lemon rind
1/4   cup milk

Sift the flour with the baking powder. Cream the butter with the sugar until smooth and fluffy. Beating continuously, add the egg yolks one at a time. Stop beating. Add the flavoring. Then gradually fold in the flour in 3-4 stages, alternated with the milk, and knead lightly until the dough is soft and easy to handle. Refrigerate the dough for 30 minutes. Cut the dough into small equal pieces the size of a small egg. Roll each piece back and forth on a board to make a long, even strip the thickness of your little finger. Tie each strip of dough into a loose knot and place on a greased baking sheet. Brush the tops with lightly beaten egg white and bake the cookies in a 400°F oven for 10-15 minutes, until lightly golden. Cool and store in a cookie tin.

Smyrna Cookies, page 132
Muhlep Cookies, page 133

Sifnos ' Sweet Cheese Tarts
(Melitinia Sifnou

Yields 40 tarts
Preparation time 1 hour and 30 minutes
Baking time 20 minutes

The Dough

1	lb all purpose flour
1/4	teaspoon salt
3	tablespoons melted unsalted butter
1/2	cup lukewarm water

The Filling

1	lb Mizithra cheese (Cottage cheese)
1/2	lb ricotta cheese
5	cups confectioners sugar
4	eggs, lightly beaten
2	cups self raising flour
1/4	teaspoon ground mastic or
2	teaspoons vanilla

Sift together flour and salt into a large mixing bowl. Make a well in the center. Put the butter, and water into the well. Gradually fold in flour from the sides of the well, mixing by hand, until all the flour has been incorporated. Then knead lightly until the dough is smooth and elastic. It may be necessary to add some more water. Divide the dough into 40 small balls. Place them on a well floured surface, cover with a damp towel and let them stand 1-2 hours. Meanwhile, prepare the filling. Put together both cheeses and sugar into a mixing bowl. Beat until well blended. Add the eggs one at a time, then add the flavoring. Gradually fold in the flour. On a floured surface roll out the dough balls into 4 inch rounds. Place one tablespoon of the filling in the center of each round and spread it leaving a 1/2 inch margin. Using your thumb and index finger turn up the margin to make a border. Pinch the raised border around to form a fluted tart. Place the tarts on a greased baking sheet and bake in a 350°F oven for about 20 minutes until the surface is golden. Cool on a rack and store in a cookie tin. Keep refrigerated. They keep 1 week in the refrigerator and several months in the freezer.

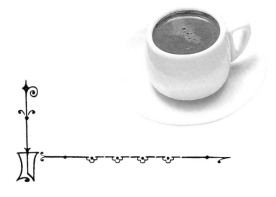

Sweet Cheese Tarts (Tartes Mizithras)

Yields 24 tarts
Preparation time 1 hour
Baking time 30 minutes

The Pastry

1/2	cup butter or margarine
1/2	teaspoon salt
2	tablespoons sugar
1	egg
2	tablespoons brandy
1	teaspoon grated lemon rind
1 1/2-2	cups self raising flour

The Filling

1	lb Mizithra cheese (Cottage cheese)
3	tablespoons unsalted butter or margarine
3/4	cup sugar
4	eggs
1	tablespoon grated lemon rind or
1	teaspoon vanilla
1/2	cup milk
1	tablespoon cornstarch
1/2	cup whipping cream
1/2	cup blanched almonds, coarsely chopped

Beat the butter with the sugar and salt until smooth and creamy. Beating continuously, add the egg and then add brandy and flavoring. Stop beating. Gradually fold in sifted ingredients, working by hand, until a smooth and easy to handle dough is formed. Roll it out into 1/8 inch thick sheet. Use a floured pastry cutter and cut out 24 dough rounds. Use them to line 24 small individual tart pans. Beat the cheese with butter and sugar until light and well blended. Beating continuously, add the 3 eggs one at a time, then add flavorings. Dissolve the cornstarch in milk and gradually add it into the cheese mixture. Pour the mixture, dividing equally, into the tarts. Lightly beat the cream with remaining egg. Pour 1 tablespoon into each tart, spreading it evenly on top. Sprinkle with chopped almonds and bake in a 350°F oven for about 30 minutes. When completely cold, dust with confectioners ' sugar and cinnamon, if desired.

Greek Easter Cookies
(Koulourakia Paschalina)

Yields 60-80 cookies
Preparation time 2 hours
Baking time 30 minutes

1	cup soft unsalted butter or margarine
1¹/₂	cups sugar
6	egg yolks
3	teaspoons vanilla
1/2	cup milk
2	teaspoons ammonium bicarbonate
2	lbs all purpose flour
2	egg yolks mixed with 2 teaspoons water

Cream the butter and sugar with an electric mixer. Beating continuously, add the egg yolks one by one. Then add the flavoring. Dissolve the ammonium bicarbonate in the milk. Beating with the kneading hook, add the ammonium mixture into the butter in 2-3 stages alternated with the flour. Knead the dough with the hook, or by hand, adding as much flour as necessary to form a smooth, easy to handle dough. Avoid overworking. On a working surface, form pieces of dough into 8 inch long, finger thick cylinders by rolling them backwards and forwards under your fingers. Then fold the cylinders in half and twist. Place on a greased baking sheet, spaced well apart to allow room for expansion. Brush the tops with the egg yolk mixture and bake in a 400°F oven for 20-30 minutes. Cool on a rack and store in a cookie tin.

Grape-Must Cookies (Moustokouloura)

Yields 30 cookies
Preparation time 1 hour and 30 minutes
Baking time 20 minutes

4	cups all purpose flour
1¹/₂	teaspoon baking soda
4	teaspoons baking powder
2	teaspoons cinnamon
3/4	teaspoon cloves
1	tablespoon cocoa
1/2	teaspoon nutmeg
1/2	cup olive or vegetable oil
1	cup grape syrup
2	tablespoons brandy
1/4	tablespoons orange juice
2	tablespoons lemon juice
1/2	cup blackcurrant raisins

Sift together flour, soda, baking powder, salt and spices into a kneading basin. Make a well in the center. Blend the remaining ingredients, except for the raisins, 1-2 minutes in a food processor or blender. Pour the mixture into the well. Gradually incorporate the flour from the sides of the well into the liquid, working by hand, until a soft and pliable dough is formed. Avoid overworking. Add the raisins and mix well. Pinch walnut sized pieces of dough and roll them into 6 inch long finger thick cylinders. Shape the cylinders into rings and place on well greased baking sheets spaced well apart to allow room for expansion. Bake the cookies in a 350°F oven for 20 minutes. Cool and store in a cookie tin.

Grape Must Cookies, page 135

Rusks
(Paximadakia)

Yields 40-50 rusks
Preparation time 1 hour
Baking time 45 minutes

5	cups all purpose flour
2	teaspoons baking powder
1	teaspoon baking soda
1/4	teaspoon salt
1	cup vegetable oil
1¹/₂	cups sugar
5	eggs, sligtly beaten
1	teaspoon vanilla or
1/2	teaspoon anise extract
1	cup chopped walnuts
1	egg yolk beaten with 2 teaspoons water
	sesame seeds

Sift together flour, baking powder, soda and salt into a kneading basin. Make a well in the center. Add oil, sugar, eggs and flavoring. Start by stirring with a wooden spoon, folding the flour a little at a time into the other ingredients. When the mixture becomes too stiff to stir, mix in the flour by hand and knead lightly until the dough is soft and easy to handle. Divide the dough in half. On a floured working surface roll out each half into a ¹/₂ inch thick rectangle. Sprinkle with nuts and roll them up tightly. Place the rolls on a baking sheet. Brush the tops with the egg yolk mixture, sprinkle with sesame seeds and bake in a 350°F oven for about 30 minutes or until pale golden. Slide the baking paper off the sheet and place on a rack. Allow to cool of 15 minutes and slice the rolls with a sharp knife. Lay the slices flat and closely on the baking sheet and bake in a 300°F oven, 15 minutes on each side until golden. Cool on a rack and pack in airtight containers. They will keep for a month.
Alternate: Substitute 1 cup unsalted butter for the oil. Beat the butter with the sugar until light and pale, add the eggs one at a time, then fold in the sifted dry ingredients. Continue as directed in the recipe.

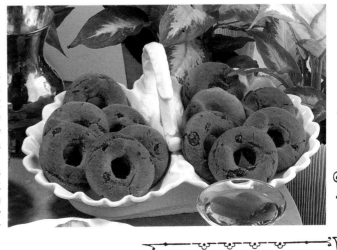

Apple Filled Cookies, page 137

Apple Filled Cookies
(Milopitakia)

Yields 30 cookies
Preparation time 1 hour
Baking time 35 minutes

The Dough

3½   cups self raising flour
1   cup unsalted butter, chilled
      and cubed
4-5   tablespoons yogurt

The Filling

4   large apples, coarsely grated
2   tablespoons lemon juice
1/4   cup sugar
1/2   teaspoon cinnamon
1/2   teaspoon cloves
1/4   teaspoon nutmeg
1   cup coarsely chopped walnuts
      confectioners ' sugar
      cinnamon for dusting

Sift the flour into a large bowl. Add the butter and rub it with the flour between your fingers until the mixture resembles coarse crumbs. Add the yogurt and mix lightly until it just begin to cohere. The dough should feel crumbly. Do not knead. Just gather all the crumbs from the sides of the bowl into a ball, pressing them together with your hands. Cover and refrigerate the dough for half hour. Meanwhile, place the apples, lemon juice and sugar in a small saucepan. Stir over low heat until all the liquid has been evaporated. Remove from the heat and mix in the remaining ingredients. Divide the dough into 30 equal portions. Roll each one into a ball. Pressing your thumbs into the ball form a cavity and spoon a little filling into it. Press the dough over the filling to seal. Place the balls, seam side down on a greased baking sheet, and bake in a 350°F oven for approximately 35 minutes, until lightly golden. As soon as they come out of the oven, sift a little confectioners ' sugar and cinnamon over the cookies. Can be kept 2-3 days at room temperature and several months in the freezer.

Sponge Biscuits
(Biskota Savouayiar)

Yields 24 large or 40-50 small biscuits
Preparation time 30 minutes
Baking time 10 minutes

1   cup self raising flour
4   eggs, separated
1/2   cup castor sugar
1   teaspoon vanilla
      confectioners sugar

Sift the flour. Beat the egg whites at high speed with an electric mixer. When the whites begin to form soft peaks, gradually add the sugar. Continue to whisk until the meringue forms stiff peaks and becomes smooth and glossy. Add the egg yolks, one by one, then add the flavoring. Lower the speed to minimum and gradually add the flour. Or stop beating; sift the flour over the eggs, folding it carefully, until it is thoroughly incorporated into the egg mixture. Take care not to break down the air bubbles. Alternatively, beat the egg yolks with half the amount of the sugar until thick and lemon-colored, about 5 minutes. Then beat the egg whites to a stiff meringue, gradually adding the remaining sugar while beating constantly. Fold sifted ingredients into beaten egg yolks. Stir in a few spoonfuls meringue to loosen the batter and help the rest of the meringue to be folded in gently. Spoon the mixture into a piping bag fitted with a ½ inch plain nozzle; then pipe, onto greased baking paper, strips or rounds of any size desired, leaving enough space in between to allow room for spreading. Generously dust the tops with confectioners ' sugar. Bake in a 400°F oven for 8-10 minutes until lightly golden. Cool the biscuits and remove them carefully from the paper. They keep one week in a biscuit tin, and several months in the freezer. You may sandwich pairs of biscuits together with jam and butter in between or use to make Cream Filled Round Sponge Biscuits, illustrated on page 83.

Almond Macaroons (Amigdalota-Ergolavi)

Yields 18-20 macaroons
Preparation time 20 minutes
Baking time 20 minutes

1/2	lb blanched almonds
12	oz sugar
3-4	egg whites
1	teaspoon vanilla
20	almonds, blanched and halved

Finely grind the almonds, together with 1 of the egg whites and vanilla, in a food mill or processor. Gradually add more egg white and process or stir until it is completely incorporated and the mixture is loose but not runny. Spoon the mixture into a piping bag, fitted with a $^1/_2$ inch plain nozzle, and pipe rosettes or put spoonfuls of the mixture on a greased sheet of baking paper placed on a baking sheet. Leave plenty of space between macaroons as the batter will spread during baking. Brush the tops with a little egg white and place half almond on each. Bake in a 350°F oven for 20 minutes or until lightly golden. Remove from the oven, allow them to stand 5 minutes, then peel off the paper. Place on a serving dish or store them, slightly warm, in a tightly closed container, to keep moist. They keep two weeks at room temperature, about a month in the refrigerator and several months in the freezer.

Alternate: Decrease the amount of egg white so that the dough can be molded by hand into individual shapes. For a finer texture use confectioners ' sugar in place of granulated. One tablespoon jam added gives extra and more lasting moisture to the macaroons. Roll small pieces of the paste into about 3 inch long sticks. Brash all over with lightly beaten egg white and roll them in chopped almonds until completely covered. Bend the sticks into crescent shapes and bake. Because of their shape this macaroons are called "garides" shrimp. Other nuts, or a mixture of several kinds, can be used instead of almonds.

Hazelnut Biscuits
(Biskota me Foundouki)

Yields 30-40 biscuits
Preparation time 30 minutes
Baking time 30 minutes

1	cup unsalted butter or margarine, softened
3/4	cup sugar
1	egg
3	cups self raising flour
1	cup ground hazelnuts
40	whole hazelnuts

Cream the butter and sugar with an electric mixer. Beating continuously add the egg. Lower the speed and gradually add the flour a little at a time until all is incorporated. Gently fold in the ground hazelnuts. Spoon the mixture into a piping bag fitted with a $^1/_2$ inch plain nozzle. Pipe rosettes onto a baking sheet lined with baking paper. Leave about 1 inch between them to allow room for spreading. Place a hazelnut on top of each cookie and bake in a 400°F oven for about 30 minutes, or until golden. Allow to cool 5 minutes, then carefully transfer with a spatula to a rack and cool completely. Store in a biscuit tin. They keep up to one month.

Jam Filled Cookies
(Biskota me Marmelada)

Yields 20 double cookies
Preparation time 1 hour and 30 minutes
Baking time 15 minutes

$1^1/_2$	cups unsalted butter
3/4	cup sugar
2	teaspoons vanilla
1/4	teaspoon salt
2	egg yolks
2	tablespoons brandy
5	cups all purpose flour
	several kinds of jams or marmalades

Beat the butter, sugar and salt with an electric mixer until light and fluffy. Beating continuously add the egg yolks one at a time, then add brandy and flavoring. Stop beating. Gently fold in the flour a little at a time working by hand until a soft and pliable dough is formed. Avoid overworking. On a wooden board roll the dough out into a $^1/_8$ inch thick sheet. Use a 2 inch cookie cutter and cut out rounds. Using tiny star, heart, tree or bird shaped cutters cut out the centers of $^1/_3$ of round cookies. Arrange all cookies on a baking sheet lined with baking paper and bake in a 400°F oven for 10-15 minutes, until lightly golden. When they are completely cold, spread round cookies with jam and press the ones with the opening on top. Place tiny cookie figures onto the remaining rounds. Store them in a biscuit tin, can be kept for 2 weeks.

Almond Macaroons, page 137

Chestnut Chocolate Balls
(Fondan me Kastano)

Yields 30-40 balls
Preparation time 2 hours

2	lbs chestnuts, shelled and boiled
1/2	cup confectioners ' sugar
6	tablespoons melted unsalted butter
3	tablespoons evaporated milk
3	tablespoons liqueur or brandy

The Chocolate Icing

1/4	lb baking chocolate
4	tablespoons confectioners ' sugar
2	tablespoons unsalted butter
1-2	tablespoons milk
1	tablespoon brandy
1	egg yolk

While stil warm, puree the chestnuts along with the sugar in a food processor. Gradually stir in the melted butter, milk and brandy. Grease your hands, and shape the mixture into chestnut sized balls. Arrange them on a sheet of baking paper placed on a tray and refrigerate for 2-3 hours until firm. Meanwhile, prepare the chocolate icing. Melt the chocolate over a water bath or over direct very low heat. Add the remaining ingredients all at once, stirring vigorously, until the chocolate is well blended with the other ingredients and the mixture is smooth and thick. Keep the chocolate warm over low heat. Pick up the balls one at a time with a wooden skewer, and dip into the melted chocolate, to cover them completely. Drain over the pan for a few seconds, then stick the skewers into a large grapefruit. Allow to stand until the chocolate icing is firm. Then remove the skewers carefully and place the balls into small individual candy cups. Put in a cookie tin and refrigerate the chestnuts for up to one week.

Sweet Delights
(Loukoumia)

Yields 48 pieces
Preparation time 6 hours
Cooking time 15 minutes

2	cups sugar
1/8	teaspoon salt
1/2	cup warm water
1/2	cup cold water
2	tablespoons gelatine
1/2	cup orange juice
2	tablespoons lemon juice
1/2	teaspoon vanilla or almond extract
2	tablespoons grated lemon or orange rind
2/3	cup coarsely cut and roasted, blanched almonds
	confectioner 's sugar for dusting

Put the sugar, salt and warm water in a heavy-bottomed pan over medium heat and cook for about 10 minutes to make a thick syrup. Stir the gelatine into cold water and allow to soften, about 5 minutes. Pour in the hot syrup and stir until gelatine is completely dissolved. Add the orange and lemon juices, desired flavoring, and almonds. Lightly grease a 7 by 10 inch baking pan and pour in the mixture. Refrigerate for about 6 hours until set. Loosen edges with a sharp knife and turn out on a sheet of baking paper generously dusted with confectioners ' sugar. Cut it into 1 inch cubes and roll them in confectioners ' sugar. Store in a cookie tin to keep loukoumia fresh. Keep at room temperature for up to a month.
Alternate: Hazelnuts or pistachios may be substituted for the almonds. Also rose-water may be used for the orange juice. In this case omit other flavorings. The mixture may be colored with a few drops of food color.

Salted Cookies, page 131
Jam Filled Cookies, page 138

Marzipan (Almond Paste)
(Pasta Amigdalou)

Yields 1¹/₂ lbs
Preparation time 15 minutes

3¹/₂	cups blanched, finely ground almonds
2¹/₂	cups confectioners' sugar
1	teaspoon vanilla or
1/4	teaspoon almond extract
1	tablespoon lemon juice
2	tablespoons rose water or
1	tablespoon apricot jam
2	egg whites, lightly beaten

Mix the almonds, sugar and flavoring into a bowl. Sprinkle the mixture with the lemon juice and rose water or add the jam. Pour in the beaten egg whites, a little at a time, stirring the mixture with a fork. When the mixture is moist, mix it by hand until all the white has been added. Add as much egg white as necessary to produce a smooth, rather stiff paste. Gather the mixture into a ball and knead it lightly on a working surface sprinkled with confectioners' sugar. Avoid overkneading as this would bring out natural oil from the almonds and make the marzipan oily. Cover it with a plastic wrap to prevent drying and refrigerate. Marzipan can be kept for 2 weeks. If dried, knead it with a little rose water, until it becomes soft and pliable again. It freezes well for several months. Marzipan can be used in making various cookies as Island Almond Cookies, illustrated on page 147 and sweets as Cream Filled Marzipan Rolls, illustrated on same page above.

Cream Filled Marzipan Rolls
(Rodinia)

Yields 20 rolls
Preparation time 1 hour

1	recipe, Marzipan (page 140) or
1¹/₂	lbs ready made almond paste
1/2	recipe, Buttercream (page 53)
1/2	cup finely cut crystallized orange confectioners' sugar whole cloves for decoration

Prepare Buttercream according to the recipe. Fold in crystallized orange pieces. Keep refrigerated. Sprinkle a sheet of baking paper with confectioners' sugar and roll out the almond paste into ¹/₈ inch thick 4 inch wide strips. Spoon buttercream into a piping bag fitted with ¹/₂ inch plain nozzle and pipe a thick stick of buttercream lenghtwise in the center of a margipan strip. Lift up the paper, both sides along the strip and bring the edges together over the buttercream. Using your fingertips press them together to seal, enclosing the filling and forming a long cylinder. Lay the cylinders, seam side down, and dust with confectioners' sugar. Refrigerate until firm. With a very sharp serrated knife cut the cylinders into diamond shaped pieces and arrange on a serving dish. Stick a whole clove on top of each, if desired. Keep in the refrigerator covered with plastic wrap. You may keep for one week.

Phoenician Honey Cookies, page 141
Cream Filled Marzipan Rolls, page 140

Phoenician Honey Cookies (Finikia)

Yields 100-110 small Finikia
Preparation time 2 hours
Baking and frying time 35 minutes

The Dough

$3^1/_2$	cups all purpose flour
1/4	teaspoon salt
1/4	cup sugar
3	tablespoons oil
1	tablespoon grated lemon rind
1	teaspoon vanilla
2/3	cup water
3	tablespoons ammonium bicarbonate
	olive or vegetable oil for frying

The Syrup

$2^1/_2$	cups sugar
$2^1/_2$	cups water
1	cup honey

It has been said that the Phoenicians introduced these delicious honey dipped cookies to the people of Greece.

Sift the flour and salt into a large bowl and make a well in the center. Add the sugar, oil and flavorings. Dissolve the ammonium bicarbonate in the water and pour the mixture into the well over the other ingredients. Start by stirring with a spoon, folding the flour a little at a time into the other ingredients. When all the flour is incorporated, knead the dough lightly until soft and easy to handle. It may be necessary to add more water. Roll the dough into cylinders the size of your little finger. Press them lightly to flatten and place on a greased baking pan, spaced well apart to allow room for expansion. Otherwise, roll out the dough into a $^1/_3$ inch thick sheet and cut out $^1/_2$ inch wide strips. Cut each strip into 3 inch long pieces. Place them on baking sheets. Bake finikia in a 400°F oven for 20-25 minutes or until lightly golden. Remove from the oven. Boil all the syrup ingredients together for 5 minutes. Pour 3 inches of oil (half olive, half corn oil) into a heavy bottomed pan and heat it to 350°- 375°F. Drop batches of cookies into the hot oil and fry until golden brown. Using a slotted spoon take them out of the oil, drain well and drop into the hot syrup. Allow finikia to absorb enough syrup, approximately 3-4 minutes. Draining them with a slotted spoon transfer to a serving dish.

Sesame Seed Honey Bars
(Pasteli me Meli)

Yields $1^1/_4$ lbs
Preparation time 10 minutes
Cooking time 10 minutes

1	lb sesame seeds
1	cup honey
1	cup sugar

Spread sesame seeds in a baking pan and toast in a 350°F oven until slightly golden. Mix the sugar and honey into a heavy-bottomed, non-stick pan and cook for about 10 minutes. Add the sesame seeds and stir the mixture over low heat, until it is amber-colored, or registers 475°F on a candy thermometer. Pour the mixture onto a well greased work surface, preferably metal or marble and spread it into a $^1/_4$ inch thick rectangle. While still warm, score with a sharp knife into pieces and allow to cool completely. Break apart by placing a knife in scores and tapping gently with a spoon. Wrap the pieces in plastic foil. Keep in a cool dry place. It keeps up to a year.

Mandarin Fondant
(Mandarinata)

Yields 50-55 balls
Preparation time 1 hour

1	lb ground walnuts
1/2	lb confectioners' sugar
	the rind of 4 mandarins ground
2	tablespoons brandy
1	egg white, lightly beaten or
1-2	tablespoons orange marmalade
	extra brandy and sugar for dusting

Mix together walnuts, confectioners' sugar and ground mandarin rind into a bowl. Add brandy. Mix lightly by hand, adding as much egg white or orange marmalade as necessary to produce an easy to handle mixture. Dip your palms into a little brandy and shape the mixture into chestnut sized balls. Roll them in sugar and place into small candy cups. Keep them in a cookie tin. They keep well at room temperature up to one week and in the refrigirator one month. They also freeze well for several months.

Sesame Honey Bars, page 141

8

Religion and Tradition
(Thriskia ke Paradosi)

Greek tradition is linked closely with the Greek Orthodox religion. Orthodox Greeks as devout and God-fearing people follow the dogmas of the Church.

The Church always has been the center of all Greek life events, such as weddings, christenings and funerals. The full circle of life goes through the Church. For 2000 years the four long fasting periods of the year preceding Christmas, Easter, Feast day of the Apostles (June 30) and Assumption of the blessed Virgin Mary (August 15) regulated the Greeks' diet. Greek people were fasting and receiving the Holy Communion very often.

When the church bell tolled on Sundays, in Florina, where I spend part of my childhood, the doors of all the houses opened and families wearing their best clothes walked to the church. People from the first to the last house of the village headed for St. George's church. When the congregation had gathered, our priest, Father Nicholas, stood in front of the Holy Doors of the Altar wearing his worn sacerdotal vestments and began the Divine Liturgy. I can recall clearly his venerable figure as he was praying for us in his serene peaceful voice, giving his blessing and distributing the Antidoron bread to everybody, as a sign of brotherly love, at the end of each service. I remember his religious devotion as he chanted in his feeble voice while blessing the five loaves of bread my mother brought to the church on our name days for the Artoklasia service: "Fortunes may be lost and people may starve. They that seek the Lord will not want for anything". He would give, then, one of the breads to my mother and the remaining to the deacon to slice and divide among the congregation at the end of Divine Liturgy. Father Nicholas blessed weddings, christenings and the harvesting, sharing all our joys and sorrows.

The role of bread in the Greek Orthodox Church always has been very important. In every Divine Liturgy, the priest commemorates, reenacts, relives the Last Supper of Christ with his disciples. The Altar Bread called "Prosforon", which means offering, is offered by the believers to God and symbolizes the bread offered by Christ to his disciples, saying: "Take, eat: this is my body which is broken for you; this do in remembrance of me". Prosforon is used in the preparation of the gifts of Holy Communion and distributed to the congregation after the Divine Liturgy. Prosforon consists of two parts, the top and the bottom part, to signify the two natures of Christ, heavenly and earthly. The Altar Bread is stamped on top with a religious seal "Sfragida", which is divided into four parts with the sign of the cross, and the Greek symbols IC XC, NIKA marked on it are abbreviations of the words "Jesus Christ conquers".

Sharing of "Artoklasia" the five loaves brought by the faithful to the church, to be blessed on their name day, is in memory of the five breads blessed by Christ in the desert to feed 5000 men along with their wives and children.

"Koliva" is a traditional, religious dish, made with boiled wheat and brought to the church to be blessed in memory of a deceased relative or friend, forty days after the death. The special memorial service is called "Mnimosino".

Wheat symbolizes the eternal life and resurrection. Just as the wheat kernel is

Altar Bread for Artoklasia, page 146

buried in the earth, sprouts and bears fruit again, so do our lives. The human body buried in the earth after death, holds the promise of the Risen Christ. The offering of the wheat is a request to the congregation to join in prayer for the salvation of the departed soul. In memory of all our loved ones, trays or bowls of koliva are blessed in church on the last Saturday of the Mardigras, on three Saturdays during the Great Lent and on the Saturday before Pentecost Sunday. These Saturdays are called "Psihosavata" (Saturdays of the Souls).

The wedding ceremony in an Orthodox church is so beautiful that it reminds one of a royal coronation. Engagement rings are exchanged and the bride and the groom sip wine from a golden cup. Beautifully worked lemon blossom wreaths, joined together with a white satin ribbon, are placed on the heads of the couple, then exchanged three times by the priest, calling upon the Holy Trinity in prayer to bless the bride and the groom. While still wearing the wreaths, the couple follow the priest in a wedding walk around in a circle three times in front of the Altar, as the priest chants the hymn of Isaiah. Friends and relatives throw rose petals and rice at them. The rice regarded as a symbol of an unbroken union and fertility. Upon leaving the church, the guests are offered "koufeta", candy-coated almonds wrapped in tulle and tied with white satin ribbons forming a little bouquet "boubouniera". Also often offered is a small snow-white meringue. Both denote a wish for sweetness in the couples' life.

Christening, another of the seven Holy Sacraments of the Orthodox Church, is also a beautiful and impressive ceremony. The naked infant is anointed by the godfather or godmother with oil. Then the priest submerges the child three times in a huge brass or silver "Kolibithra" (a large basin with warm water which the priest has invoked the Holy Trinity to bless). The child is then dried and anointed by the priest with the Holy Myron (Chrism) so that it may enter to the new Kingdom, the kingdom of God. The godparents then dress the child in completely new clothes and bring a gold cross on a chain which the priest asks God to bless and then puts around the child's neck, all gifts to the small new Christian.

After the christening, "Martiria" a tiny cross decorated with a small bow (pink for the baby girl and blue for the boy) is offered to each guest, plus a boubouniera and a small sweet. In Hydra and other islands, small marzipan cookies are given to the guests.

Besides all these religious ceremonies, there are also a lot of other customs linked to the church. Farmers used to bring their first crops to be blessed by the priest. On August 6th, Transfiguration Day, worshippers carry baskets overflowing with first-cut grapes to be blessed before the harvest. This is similar to the "Aparches", a ceremony that took place in ancient Greece. At Easter time the believers bring little baskets filled with red eggs and Tsourekia (Easter sweet breads). They are placed under the icons next to the Altar. The eggs and sweets are later distributed by the priest among the not-so-wealthy families of the neighborhood. On the 27th of August, St. Fanourios namesday, unmarried girls prepare "Fanouropita", a cake containing nine ingredients, and bring it to the church to be blessed so that St. Fanourios will disclose their future.

On New Year's Eve, just before midnight, in each home the head of the household cuts the Vasilopita (New Year's Sweet Bread). He makes the sign of the cross over the pita and cuts the first slice in the name of Christ. Slices are then cut for the family members in order of age and then for the relatives and friends present. If the coin should be found in the slice offered to Christ, it denotes blessings and happiness for the whole family. Otherwise, the slice with coin in it specifies personal blessings for the individual for whom the slice was cut.

Meringue (Marenga)

Yields 30-40 individual meringues
Preparation time 15 minutes
Baking time 1-2 hours

6	egg whites
1/2	teaspoon cream of tartar or
1	tablespoon lemon juice
1¹/₂	cups castor sugar
1/4	teaspoon vanilla

Put the egg whites and cream of tartar in a large mixing bowl of an electric mixer. Beat them at high speed until they form soft peaks. If using lemon juice, add it gradually while beating the egg whites. Beating continuously, add half the sugar, a very little at a time until the mixture holds stiff peaks. Decrease the speed to low and fold in the remaining sugar in 3-4 stages, sprinkling it over the egg whites with a spoon. Otherwise, stop beating and gently fold in the remaining sugar with a spoon. Spoon the meringue into a piping bag and pipe it into bite sized meringues, small tart shapes, large meringue cases or any other desired shapes on baking sheets lined with greased baking paper. Bake the meringues in a 240°F oven until they are completely dry. To let the steam escape from the oven and help the meringue dry easier, wedge the door open with a wooden spoon. If a crusty top and a soft textured inside is desired, bake the meringues in a 300°-325°F oven. Time required for the meringues to dry depends on their shape and size. When ready, turn off the oven and let the meringues cool inside it. When completely cold, gently lift each meringue and peel off the paper. They can be kept for 2-3 weeks in a dry cupboard or up to 6 months in the freezer, tightly sealed in plastic bags.

Cream Filled Meringues
(Marenges i Bezedes)

Yields 20 double meringues
Preparation time 30 minutes
Baking time 1 hour

1	recipe, Meringue (page 145)
1	recipe, Whipped Cream (page 49)
3	oz pistachio nuts, chopped

In many regions of Greece, especially on the islands, meringues are offered at weddings, together with the "koufeta" candy-coated almonds.
Prepare the meringue according to the recipe. Spoon the mixture into a piping bag fitted with a star-shaped nozzle and pipe into 2¹/₂ inch zig-zag strips on a baking sheet lined with greased baking paper. Leave a 1 inch space in between the strips to allow room for expansion. Bake in a 240°F oven for about one hour, or until completely dry. Turn off the oven and let the meringues cool inside it. Remove them carefully from the paper. Then sandwich pairs of meringues together with the whipped cream in between. Sprinkle the sandwiched edges with pistachio nuts and place the meringues in individual candy cups. Filled meringues should be served within a few hours of their completion. Refrigerate until served. Keep them unfilled in an airtight container for two to three weeks.

Cream Filled Meringue, page 145

a well-floured baking pan. Dip the religious seal in flour, shake off the excess and press it firmly onto the floured surface. Let the seal remain on dough for about 5 minutes and carefully remove it. Place the other two rounds, the same way, onto a separate pan. Cover and leave in a warm place to rise until doubled in bulk. Just before baking, prick inside and outside corners of cross with a wooden skewer to attain a flat-top appearance of the breads. Bake in a 400°F oven for 15-20 minutes, taking care not to burn them. As soon as they are removed from the oven, brush them with a little water, using a pastry brush. Cover the altar breads with a cotton towel and leave them to cool on a rack.

Altar Bread (for "Artoklasia")
(Artos gia Artoklasia)

Yields 5 small loaves
Preparation time 2-3 hours
Baking time 20 minutes

3	oz fresh yeast or
3	tablespoons dry yeast or
2	recipes, Traditional Sourdough Starter (page 23)
1	cup tepid water (100°F)
5	lbs strong flour
2	tablespoons salt
1 1/2	cups sugar
1	teaspoon ground mastic
1/2	cup shortening or vegetable oil
6	eggs (optional)
1	cup tepid milk or water (100°F)
	a little confectioners' sugar

If using sourdough starter, reactivate it the night before. Otherwise dissolve the yeast in tepid water and add enough of the flour to form a thick paste. Cover and let it stand in a warm place until doubled in bulk, about 20 minutes. Sift the flour with the salt in a basin, and make a well in the center. Put in sugar, mastic, oil, eggs, yeast mixture and milk. (Add double the amount of milk, if not using eggs). Gradually incorporate flour from the sides of the well into the liquid until all the flour is moist. Knead the dough hard for 5-10 minutes, until it is soft and elastic. Cover and leave it in a warm, humid place until doubled in bulk, 1 1/2-2 hours. Divide the dough into 5 parts and shape them into round loaves. Place them in greased baking pans, cover, and let them rise in a warm, humid place until doubled in bulk. Brush the tops with a little milk and bake in a 400°F oven for approximately 20 minutes. In a circulating air oven, you may bake 3 loaves together, occasionally turning them as necessary for even baking. Cool them on a rack. While still warm, dust the tops with confectioners' sugar.
Alternate: Anise extract may be substituted for the mastic. Just before baking, the loaves may be slashed across the top in the sign of a cross, with a razor blade, brushed with a little milk, and sprinkled with sesame seeds.

Altar Bread (Litourgia - Prosforo)

Yields 2 Altar Breads
Preparation time 40 minutes
Baking time 20 minutes

6	cups country or all purpose flour
1	teaspoon salt
2	cups tepid water (100°F)
1	recipe, Traditional Sourdough Starter (page 23) or
1	oz fresh yeast or
2	teaspoons dry yeast

If using sourdough starter, reactivate it the night before. Otherwise, dissolve the yeast in one half cup of the tepid water. Add 3-4 tablespoons flour and mix well. Let it stand for about 10 minutes or until doubled in bulk. Meanwhile, sift the flour with the salt into a kneading basin and make a well in the center. Pour in the sourdough starter or the yeast mixture and the remaining tepid water. Gradually incorporate flour from the sides of the well into the water until all the flour is moist, and knead until a smooth and elastic dough is formed. Cover the dough with plastic wrap, and let it rise in a warm place until doubled in bulk, about 2 hours. Knead the dough again for about 5 minutes and divide into 4 equal parts. Shape each part into a ball. Slightly flatten the balls into rounds, pressing with your palms, and flour them generously. Put the two rounds, one on top of the other, in

Siatista's Walnut Filled Cookies
(Saliaria Siatistas)

Yields 40-50 cookies
Preparation time 2 hours
Baking time 30 minutes

8   cups all purpose flour
2   cups olive or vegetable oil
1   cup ash water or
1   cup water plus

     1 teaspoon baking soda and
     2 teaspoons baking powder
1   cup sugar
1   teaspoon lemon juice

The Filling

2   cups coarsely chopped walnuts
2   tablespoons sugar
1   tablespoon cinnamon
1   teaspoon cloves

The Syrup

1¹/₂ cups sugar
2   cups water
1   lb confectioners' sugar for dusting

In the town of Siatista, in Macedonia, girls on their engagement day, make these cookies and send them to their future mother-in- law, to show off their skills, and flatter her.
Mix all the filling ingredients into a bowl. Set aside. Sift the flour into a kneading basin and make a well in the center. If baking powder and soda are used, sift them along with the flour. Heat the oil. To check if it is heated to the right temperature, drop a small bread cube into it. Bread should be fried in one minute. Put the sugar into the well and pour in the hot oil. Stir with a wooden spoon, then gradually pull the flour from the sides of the well, and mix with the oil until all the flour is greased. Sprinkle the ash or plain water and lemon juice over the mixture and knead lightly. Avoid overkneading. Roll a piece of dough, the size of a walnut, between your palms and flatten it into a round. Spoon one teaspoon of the filling into the center and press the dough over the filling to seal. Roll it lightly between your fingers into a short, cigar shape and place on an ungreased baking sheet, seam side down. Lightly press the cigar under your palm to flatten into an oval. Fill and shape the rest of the dough pieces the same way. Bake in a 350°F oven for about 30 minutes or until golden. Cool on a rack. Meanwhile, dissolve the sugar into the water over low heat and boil the syrup 5 minutes. Dip the cookies into the syrup, one at a time, for a few seconds and roll in confectioners' sugar. They keep well at room temperature for several weeks. Alternatively, you may roll the cookies in confectioners' sugar as soon as they are removed from the oven without dipping them in syrup, just like kourabiedes.

Island Almond Cookies
(Amigdalota Nisiotika)

Yields 80 pear shaped cookies
Preparation time 30 minutes
Baking time 15 minutes

1   recipe, Marzipan (page 140)
     crystallized orange rind, cut in small
     pieces or whole crystallized cherries
     whole cloves

These cookies made on the Island of Hydra and other Greek islands are served at christenings. A tiny bow, pink for the girls and blue for the boys, is secured on top of each cookie with a clove.
Dip your fingertips into confectioners' sugar, break off small marzipan pieces, and shape into small pears, enclosing a piece of orange rind or a cherry in the center. Roll small, marzipan pears in sugar, pressing lightly with your fingers to make the sugar stick around. Pin a clove on top of each cookie to represent the stalk of the pear. Keep them in airtight containers, as they tend to dry rather quickly. They keep at room temperature up to one week.
Alternate: Preparing the marzipan mixture add 5-6 tablespoons rose water and 2 tablespoons fine semolina along with the other ingredients. Arrange the cookies after shaping on a greased baking sheet and bake in a 350°F oven for about 15 minutes. Remove them from the oven, and cool completely. Quickly dip the cookies, one by one, into rose water and roll in confectioners' sugar. After 2 hours, roll them again in sugar.

Koliva
(Koliva)

Serves 50
Preparation time 12 hours
Cooking time 1 hour and 30 minutes - 5 hours

2	lbs wheat kernels
3	cups sultana raisins
3	cups coarsely chopped walnuts
2	cups slivered, blanched almonds
4	tablespoons cinnamon
2	teaspoons cloves
2	cups all purpose flour

The Garnish

2	lbs confectioners' sugar
	silver candy
	candy-coated almonds
	halved walnuts

Wash the wheat kernels well and put in a large, heavy-bottomed pan. Cover with cold water and let stand overnight. The next day, drain and cover with fresh water. Cook for about 4-5 hours or until tender. (In a pressure cooker it takes 1 hour and 30 minutes). Stir occasionally to prevent burning. Add hot water as needed. Remove from the heat and rinse off all starch. Drain in a colander. Spread the kernels on kitchen towels to absorb excess moisture. Meanwhile, put the flour in a frying pan and stir over medium heat until it is lightly brown. Let it cool. Mix the dry wheat kernels with one half cup browned flour and the remaining ingredients. Line a large tray with paper doilies and mound the wheat mixture on it. Press down with waxed paper to smoothen the surface. Sift the remaining browned flour on top and press once more with the paper. Sift the confectioners' sugar on top and smoothen with the paper. Trace a cross on a piece of cardboard and cut it out. Press it on the center and make an impression. Fill the impression of the cross with the silver candy and decorate with the candy-coated almonds and halved walnuts. On either side of cross, form initials of deceased with silver candy.

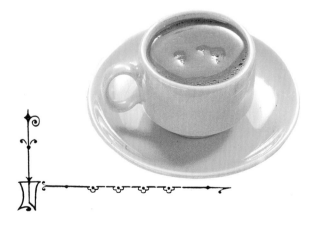

Boiled Wheat Pudding
(Assoures - Varvara)

Serves 8-10
Preparation time 12 hours
Cooking time 3 hours

1	lb wheat kernels
4	pints warm water (8 cups)
1	cup sugar
1	cup sultana raisins
1	cup coarsely chopped walnuts
2	teaspoons cinnamon
1/2	teaspoon cloves
1/4	teaspoon nutmeg
1/8	teaspoon salt
4	tablespoons cornstarch or flour

The Garnish
finely chopped walnuts
cinnamon

On December 4th, feast day of St. Varvara, Greek housewives prepare this Wheat Pudding and offer it to the neighbors.
Wash the wheat kernels well and put them in a large, heavy-bottomed pan. The next day, place over low heat and simmer for 3-4 hours until wheat kernels break and liquid becomes starchy. (In a pressure cooker it takes only 1 hour and 30 minutes). Drain and reserve the liquid. Rinse the wheat kernels with water, adding it to the reserved liquid until it measures up to 7 cups. Place the liquid in a saucepan over low heat, add one cup of the boiled wheat kernels and all the remaining ingredients. (Dissolve the flour or corn flour in a little of the liquid, before adding. If using flour, brown it slightly over medium heat). Boil the varvara 7-10 minutes until slightly thickened. Divide it into individual bowls. Cool, and refrigerate until set. Sprinkle with finely chopped walnuts and a little cinnamon.

Boiled Wheat Pudding, page 148

Saint Fanourios Pita 1 (Fanouropita 1)

Serves 20
Preparation time 15 minutes
Baking time 45 minutes

1½   cups self raising flour
1½   cups coarsely chopped walnuts
1   teaspoon cinnamon
1/2   teaspoon cloves
1/2   cup olive or vegetable oil
1/2   cup orange juice
1/4   cup brandy
4   eggs
1½   cups sugar

These flavorfull cakes even nowadays are brought to the church on August 27th, feast day of St. Fanourios, by the unmarried girls to be blessed, with the hope that St. Fanourios will disclose their fortune.
Mix the flour with the walnuts, cinnamon and cloves into a large mixing bowl. Mix separately in a bowl the oil, orange juice and brandy. Set aside. Beat the eggs with the sugar until light and fluffy. Pour the oil mixture over the nut mixture and stir with a spoon until dry ingredients are sufficiently moistened. Gradually add the beaten eggs, folding them in gently, until all are incorporated and the mixture is light and fluffy. Pour it into a greased and floured 10 by 12 inch baking pan and bake in a 350°F oven for about 45 minutes. Cool the cake and cut it into squares. Arrange the pieces on a dish and sprinkle them with a little confectioners ' sugar.

Saint Fanourios Pita 2 (Fanouropita 2)

Serves 20
Preparation time 15 minutes
Baking time 1 hour

3   cups self raising flour
1   teaspoon baking soda
1/2   teaspoon cloves
1½   teaspoons cinnamon
2/3   cup olive or vegetable oil
1   cup sugar
1   cup orange juice, water or milk
1/2   cup coarsely chopped walnuts
1/2   cup blackcurrant raisins
       confectioners ' sugar

Sift together flour, soda, cloves and cinnamon into a large mixing bowl, and make a well in the center. Blend oil, sugar and orange juice in a blender for 1-2 minutes. Pour the mixture into the well, add the walnuts and raisins, and mix stirring with a spoon until all the ingredients are well combined. Pour the batter, spreading it evenly into a well greased and floured, 11 inch, round cake pan and bake in a 350°F oven for about 1 hour. Cool the cake 5 minutes in the pan; then turn it onto a serving dish. Place a laced paper doily on the surface of the cake and sieve confectioners ' sugar over it. Remove the paper doily carefully. The design will remain on the cake. Alternately, just dust the top of the cake with confectioners ' sugar.

Saint Fanourios Pita 2, page 149

Smyrna New Year's Sweet Bread
(Vasilopita Smirnis)

Preparation time 30 minutes
Baking time 35 minutes

1	cup unsalted butter or margarine (1/2 lb)
1 1/4	cups sugar
2	tablespoons grated orange rind
1	teaspoon baking soda dissolved in 2 tablespoons brandy
6	cups all purpose flour
2/3	cup orange juice
1	egg yolk beaten with 1 teaspoon water
1	oz pine nuts or whole cloves
2	tablespoons onion seeds

Cream the butter with an electric mixer. Add the sugar and beat them together until the mixture is pale and fluffy. Stop beating. Add the orange rind and baking soda mixture. Then gradually add the flour in stages, alternated with the orange juice, folding in gently and working by hand to form a soft and easy to handle dough. Roll out the dough into a cylinder about 36 inches long and coil it into a spiral on a greased baking paper, placed on a baking sheet. Slip in a coin, wrapped in aluminum foil, so that it is well hidden. Brush the top with the egg yolk mixture, then stick in the pine nuts following the spiral's pattern. Sprinkle with the onion seeds, if desired. You may also pat the dough in a 12 inch round baking pan lined with greased baking paper. Smoothen the surface with your palms and pinch with two forks to make a pattern. Pin on top a few cloves and brush with egg yolk mixture. In Smyrna, housewives used to stamp the bread with the double headed eagle, symbol of the Byzantine Empire. Bake in a 380°F oven for 30-35 minutes or until the surface is golden brown. Cool on a rack. To keep it moist, store the bread covered with plastic film.

Crunchy New Year's Bread
(Vasilopita Trifti)

Preparation time 45 minutes
Baking time 35 minutes

6	cups all purpose flour
1 1/2	cups unsalted butter or margarine, chilled and cubed
1 1/2	teaspoons baking soda
1	teaspoon cream of tartar
2	tablespoons brandy
1/3	cup milk
3	teaspoons vanilla
3	eggs
1 1/2	cups sugar
1	egg yolk, beaten with 1 teaspoon water

Sift the flour into a large mixing bowl. Add the cubed

butter and rub the mixture with your fingertips until it resembles coarse meal. Dissolve the soda and cream of tartar in brandy. Set aside. Lightly beat together milk, flavoring, eggs and sugar. Pour the mixture into the flour along with the brandy and knead lightly, to form a soft, flaky dough. Avoid overkneading. Set a small piece of dough aside. Push in a coin, wrapped in foil, and press the remaining dough into a 12 inch, round baking pan lined with greased baking paper. Roll out the reserved dough on a floured surface. Using tiny cookie cutters, cut out season's decorative shapes and stick on bread's surface, brushing with a little egg yolk mixture. Brush whole surface with the remaining egg yolk mixture and bake in a 350°F oven for 30-35 minutes or until golden brown. Cool on a rack. To preserve bread's texture, keep it covered with a plastic wrap, until used.

Constantinople's New Year Bread
(Vasilopita Politiki)

Preparation time 3 hours
Baking time 30 minutes

2	oz fresh yeast or
2	tablespoons dry yeast
1	lb strong or all purpose flour
1/2	teaspoon baking powder
1/2	teaspoon salt
1/2	teaspoon mastic from Chios or
2	teaspoons vanilla
1	tablespoon ground muhlep
1	cup sugar
2	eggs and 2 egg yolks, slightly beaten
1/3	cup warm evaporated milk
1/3	cup warm melted unsalted butter
1	egg yolk beaten with 1 teaspoon water
3	oz almonds, blanched and halved

Dissolve the yeast in 1/3 cup tepid water (100°F). Add 1-2 tablespoons flour and stir well. Cover and let it stand 10 minutes to rise. Meanwhile, sift the flour, baking powder, salt and flavorings into a kneading basin and make a well in the center. Put in sugar, milk, slightly beaten eggs and yeast. Gradually pull the flour from the sides of the well into the liquid until it is all incorporated. Knead until a soft, elastic dough is formed. Cover with plastic wrap and let it rise in a warm place until doubled in bulk, about 2 1/2 hours. Punch down the dough. On a floured surface, roll out the dough into about a 36 inch long cylinder and coil it into a spiral on a baking paper placed on a baking sheet. Slip in a coin wrapped in foil. Cover with a kitchen towel and leave the bread in a warm, humid place until doubled in bulk, about 30 minutes. Brush the top with the egg yolk mixture; then stick in the halved almonds following the spiral's pattern. Bake in a 400°F oven for 20-30 minutes, until golden brown. Cool the bread on a rack. To keep it moist, store covered with plastic wrap, until used.

Constantinople New Year's Bread, page 150
Smyrna New Year's Sweet Bread, page 150
Crunchy New Year's Bread, page 150

New Year's Yeast Bread
(Vasilopita me Mayia)

Preparation time 3 hours
Baking time 30 minutes

1	lb strong or all purpose flour
1/2	teaspoon salt
2	oz fresh yeast or
2	tablespoons dry yeast
1/2	cup unsalted butter
3/4	cup sugar
1	tablespoon grated orange rind
1	tablespoon grated lemon rind
1/2	cup milk, scalded
3	eggs
1	egg yolk beaten with 1 teaspoon water almond halves or sesame seeds

Sift the flour and salt. Dissolve the yeast in 4 tablespoons tepid water (100°F). Add 1-2 tablespoons flour mix and let it stand 10 minutes to rise. Melt the butter and heat until very hot. Put the sugar and flavorings in a kneading basin. Pour in the scalded milk and stir with a spoon. Break in the eggs and add the yeast. With your fingers, crush the yolks and combine the eggs with the other ingredients. Gradually add the flour and knead lightly. Add the hot butter and fold it into the dough. Avoid overkneading. Traces of butter remaining in the dough will be absorbed during the rising. The dough should be warm, light and buttery. Cover and let the dough rise in a warm place until it is three times its previous bulk, $1^{1}/_{2}$-2 hours. Punch down the dough. Shape it into one large or several small round loaves, one for each family member. (In this case, put a foil covered coin in one of the loaves). Cover and let them rise until doubled in bulk, about 30 minutes. Brush the tops with the egg yolk mixture, and decorate with the almond halves or sprinkle with sesame seeds. Bake in a 400°F oven for 20 minutes. Cool on a rack. To keep the bread moist, store covered with plastic wrap, until used.

Soda Leavened New Year's Bread, page 153
New Year's Yeast Bread, page 152

Soda Leavened New Year's Bread
(Vasilopita me Soda)

Preparation time 15 minutes
Baking time 1 hour and 15 minutes

1	cup soft unsalted margarine
2 1/2	cups sugar
9	eggs
1 1/2	teaspoons baking soda dissolved in 2 tablespoons brandy
2	tablespoons lemon juice
1	tablespoon grated lemon rind
1	cup yogurt
6	cups self raising flour
	confectioners' sugar

Cream the margarine and sugar with an electric mixer. Beating continuously add the eggs, one at a time, alternated with a tablespoon of flour to prevent curdling. Lower the speed to minimum. Add soda with brandy, lemon juice and rind. Then add the flour in 3-4 stages, alternated with the yogurt. Put the dough into a well greased, 14 inch, round cake pan and bake in a 350°F oven for approximately 1 hour and 15 minutes, or until a wooden pick inserted in the center of the bread comes out clean and dry. Let the bread cool 5 minutes in the pan. Then unmold and transfer to a serving dish. While still warm, place a laced paper doily on top and sift confectioners' sugar over it. Carefully remove the paper. The designs will remain on the top of the bread. Wrap a clean silver coin in foil and push it up into the bread from the bottom.

Wedding Bread from Roumeli
(Preventa Roumelis)

Yields 2 large loaves
Preparation time 2-3 hours
Baking time 40 minutes

2	recipes, Traditional Sourdough Starter (page 23)
3	cups tepid water (100°F)
10	whole cloves and one stick cinnamon
4	lbs strong or all purpose flour
1	teaspoon salt
1/2	teaspoon ground mastic
1 1/2	cups sugar
2	teaspoons vanilla
1/3	cup banana liqueur, or other liqueur banana liqueur
	confectioners' sugar for dusting

These wedding breads made by the mother-in-law, even nowadays, in Roumeli, are placed on a tray, lined with a hand crocheted or embroidered lace, and taken to the church. They are offered to the guests at the wedding dinner.
To reactivate the starter, mix it into a bowl with 1 cup of the tepid water and 2 cups of the flour. Cover and leave it in a warm place overnight. The next day, put the remaining water, cloves and cinnamon stick in a saucepan, cover and simmer for 10 minutes. Drain and discard the spices. Sift the flour, salt and mastic into a kneading basin, and make a well in the center. Put in the sugar, vanilla, liqueur, starter and most of the spiced water. Gradually pull the flour from the sides of the well into the liquid until it is all incorporated. Knead, adding as much water as necessary, to form an elastic, easy to handle dough. Cover the basin and leave the dough rise in a warm place until doubled in bulk, 1-2 hours. Punch down the dough and shape it into two large, round loaves. Place them in well greased baking pans, cover and leave them to rise until doubled in volume. Before baking, pinch and decorate the surface of each bread with two forks. Bake in a 400°F oven for 30-40 minutes. Transfer to a rack and let the breads cool for a few minutes. While warm, brush the tops with a little liqueur and dust with confectioners' sugar.

New Year's Pita Epirus Style
(Vasilopita Ipirou)

Preparation time 2-3 hours
Baking time 40 minutes

2	lbs ready-made puff pastry or
1	recipe, homemade Puff Pastry (page 67)

The Filling

3	large onions, sliced
2	leeks, chopped
1/4	cup butter or margarine
1/4	cup olive oil
4	lbs boneless cuts of pork or veal salt, pepper and cinnamon to taste
6	eggs, lightly beaten

Prepare the filling. Blanch the sliced onions and chopped leeks and drain well. Heat the butter with the oil in a heavy pan, and saute the meat cuts over high heat, turning them to brown all over. Add the drained onions and leeks, salt, pepper and a little cinnamon, if desired. Cover and simmer until the meat is tender and juices are reduced to about one cup. When cool, cut the meat in small pieces and mix with the eggs. Set aside. Grease a 14 inch round baking pan. Divide the puff pastry into two equal portions and roll them out into two thick sheets the size of the pan. Place one of them over the bottom of the pan and spread the meat mixture on top. Put in a coin wrapped in foil. Cover the filling with the remaining puff pastry sheet, moisten the edges and press firmly together to seal. Prick the surface with a fork, in a designed pattern, to decorate and to allow the steam to escape while the pita is baking. At this stage, you may freeze the pita, if desired. Thaw it before baking. Bake the pita in a 350°F oven for 35-40 minutes. Serve warm.

Unkneaded Bread
(Psomi Keik Azimoto)

Yields one loaf
Preparation time 10 minutes
Baking time 45 minutes

Recipe 1

3   cups strong or all purpose flour
1/4   cup honey
1   tablespoon dry yeast
1   egg
$1\frac{1}{4}$ cups tepid water (100°F)
$1\frac{1}{4}$ teaspoons salt

Recipe 2

$1\frac{1}{2}$ cups beer
2   tablespoons honey
2   tablespoons oil
$3\frac{1}{2}$ cups self raising flour

This bread is not kneaded, it is made like a cake. Place all the ingredients of recipe 1 or recipe 2 into a mixing bowl and mix thoroughly. Pour the mixture into a well greased loaf pan, filling it up to half of its depth. Cover the pan and let the dough rise in a warm place until it reaches the rim of the pan. Bake in a 400°F oven for 15 minutes; then lower the oven temperature to 350°F and continue baking for another 30-35 minutes. Remove the pan from the oven and turn the bread out on a rack to cool. It is a delicious, easy to make bread. Keep covered with plastic wrap as it tends to dry out rather quickly.

Easter Bread Rings, page 155

Easter Bread Rings
(Lambrokouloures)

Yields three breads
Preparation time 2-3 hours
Baking time 20 minutes

1   *recipe, Easter Sweet Bread (page 31)*
8   *red died eggs*
2   *egg yolks beaten with 2 teaspoons water*
    sesame seeds
    almonds, blanched and flaked

Prepare an Easter bread dough according to the recipe. Let it rise, then divide it into 3 equal parts. Divide the first part in half. On a floured working surface roll out each half into a 24 inch long cylinder. Twist the two cylinders together and place on a greased baking sheet, curving into a ring as you set it down. Join the two ends carefully. Arrange 5-6 red eggs in the spaces between the twisted dough cylinders. Divide the second part of the dough into 3 equal portions, and roll them out on a floured surface into 24 inch long strands. Braid them together and place on a greased baking sheet, curving into a ring as you set it down. Join the two ends carefully. Place a red egg on the joint. Divide the third part of dough into 4 equal portions and roll them out into 12 inch long strands. On a greased baking sheet place the strands one on top of each other, crossing them as shown in the diagram, and twist the edges slightly. Make a cavity in the middle and place a red egg in it. Cover the breads and leave them in a warm humid place to rise until doubled in bulk. Brush them with the egg yolk mixture and sprinkle with sesame seeds or almonds, as desired. Bake in a 400°F oven for approximately 20 minutes. Do not overbake, as they tend to dry. Store the Easter breads covered with plastic wrap to keep them fresh and moist. Do not freeze as this would cause the eggs to crack.

Mini-dictionary of culinary terms

antidoron: means "instead of the gifts of the Body and Blood of Christ" and is a piece of blessed bread given to those who do not receive communion that day at the Divine Liturgy.

ash water: a kind of leavening used hundreds of years ago by the Greeks. To make ash water, boil 1 cup wood ashes with 3 cups water for about 10 minutes. Remove from the heat, allow to settle and carefully transfer the clear water into a jar.

blanch: to immerse food quickly in boiling water.

blend: to combine two or more ingredients with a spoon or with an electric blender until the ingredients are indistinguishable.

clarified butter: melt the butter over low heat, cool and refrigerate overnight. The next day lift off the solid butter and discard the water and impurities.

colander: a perforated metal or plastic basket for draining liquids.

concentrate: to minimize the bulk and thicken a liquid by boiling.

crystallized fruits: boiled fruits which have been dipped in heavy syrup, then dried. Chopped can be mixed in fillings, cake batters or sweet bread doughs. Whole are used to garnish various cakes and tartes. Also referred to as glazed or candied fruit.

custard powder: custard pudding mix.

double boiler: a utensil which consists of two pans. Water is boiled in the bottom pan and the food is cooked over the steam in the top pan.

drain: to separate solid food from liquid. When solids are finely chopped, draining is done with a sieve. When solids are coarsely chopped, they are drained through a colander.

dredge: to coat food with flour or crumbs, until the surface is completely covered.

drench: to moisten a pastry thoroughly with the syrup.

flaked: thinly sliced.

fold: to mix food from the bottom of the bowl to the top, in an under-over motion that distributes ingredients without breaking down the air bubbles.

glaze: to apply a transparent mixture on food before or after cooking, such as dissolved gelatine, syrup, beaten egg, milk or butter. The glaze adds flavor as well as a glossy appearance to food.

grated rind: the natural rind or skin of a fruit grated for flavoring.

knead: to fold, press and stretch dough, until it becomes smooth and elastic.

mastic: a flavoring from the sap of the mastic tree, which grows on the island of Chios, Greece. Also called mastiha.

mince: to chop food very fine.

muhlep: a spice from Syria, finely ground, used for flavoring.

nougat: a mixture of roasted ground hazelnuts or almonds mixed with sugar and sometimes cocoa. Used as a filling for biscuits, cakes or tortes.

panfry: to cook in a shallow pan over high heat with a small amount of shortening or fat. Food has to be turned over to fry on both sides.

pastry cutters: metal or plastic cutters in various shapes to cut out cookies and biscuits. Also referred to as cookie cutters.

phyllo dough: very thin pastry sheets for pites and desserts. Sometimes called strudel leaves or filo. Phyllo can be purchased in super markets or specialty shops.

pie: usually a deep pastry case with a filling covered with whipped cream, meringue or pastry.

pips: the fruit fibers.

praline: blanched or unblanched almonds or other nuts caramelized in boiling sugar.

puree: to force food through a strainer, a food mill or a blender.

raising or rising: the process of baking goods increasing in volume, by adding leavenings such as yeast, baking powder or baking soda.

rose water: commercially produced flavoring from rose petals; available from pharmacies or specialty stores.

rusks: hard toasted dried bread acquired by baking in oven, under the grill or in a toaster.

rusk crumbs: acquired by crushing rusks into fine crumbs.

saffron: a spice made out of the dried stigma of the saffrom plant or the cultivated crocus plant. Used to produce a yellow color and distinctive musky flavor to foods.

salep: a flavoring from a plant. Available from specialty stores.

scald: to dip foods quickly in boiling water or to heat a liquid to just below boiling.

score: to make cuts across the surface of food before roasting or baking.

sesame seeds: tiny flat oily seeds used whole or ground in cakes and biscuits. Also sprinkled on top of breads, cakes or cookies.

sieve: an open vessel with meshed or perforated bottom for sifting dry ingredients such as flour, confectioners' sugar, etc.

simmer: to cook slowly over low heat.

skewer: a long pin or rod of metal, small wooden or bamboo sticks used to pierce food on before grilling.

skim: to remove the froth that comes up to the surface of a liquid when heated or boiled, usually done with a spoon.

soak: to let food steep in liquid (usually water) for a certain period of time to become soft and moist.

soggy: to loose crispness and become moist (particularly pastries or cakes) as the excess moisture from the filling soaks into them.

sprinkle or dust: to coat with confectioners' sugar, flour, or other fine substance.

tahini: an emulsion made from ground sesame seeds. It can be found at Greek, Asian, health food stores or in the foreign food sections of super markets.

tart: a shallow pastry case with a filling rarely covered on top.

thicken: to add cornstarch (corn flour), flour, egg or fresh cream to thicken sauces, stock or other liquids.

vanilla: a flavoring used in cooking and baking; prepared from the vanilla bean.

whip: to beat rapidly, inflating the volume of the ingredients.

zwieback: a bread which is baked, sliced, and toasted until crisp.

Helpful information for the accurate measuring of ingredients and right baking temperatures

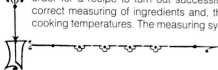

Apart from experience and the use of high quality ingredients, there are two factors that have to be taken into consideration in order for a recipe to turn out successfully: the accurate and correct measuring of ingredients and, the correct baking and cooking temperatures. The measuring systems used in cooking vary from country to country. The basic systems used in the world are the following:

1. Imperial: according to this system, dry ingredients are measured in ounces (oz) and liquids are measured in fluid ounces (fl. oz.). Used mainly in England and Australia.

2. Metric: according to this system dry ingredients are measured in grams (gr), and liquids in cubic centimeters (ml). Used in France, Greece, Germany and other European countries.

3. American: according to this system all ingredients whether dry

or liquid are measured in the standard measuring cup, which is equal to 240 ml. The measuring cup measures volume and all ingredients are measured according to volume. The weight of one cup of different types of ingredients varies.
For example:

1 cup flour weighs	125 gr.
1 cup sugar weighs	225 gr.
1 cup confectioners' sugar weighs	160 gr.
1 cup grated almonds weighs	150 gr.
1 cup grated walnuts weighs	125 gr.
1 cup bread crumbs weighs	105 gr.
1 cup dry cocoa weighs	100 gr.
1 cup milk weighs	240 gr.
1 cup whipped cream weighs	125 gr.
1 cup oil weighs	220 gr.
1 cup water weighs	240 gr.
1 cup fresh cream weighs	225 gr.
1 cup butter weighs	225 gr.
1 cup rice weighs	225 gr.
1 cup grated cheese weighs	110 gr.

1 cup honey weighs	350 gr.
1 cup semolina weighs	170 gr.

The standard measuring cup is divided into thirds and fourths. For quantities less than 1/4 cup the standard measuring spoon is used. 1/4 cup is equal to 4 level tablespoons, consequently 1 cup is equal to 16 level tablespoons. 1 level tablespoon is equal to 3 level teaspoons. The equivalent of 1 level tablespoon is 15 ml. in the metric system. For measuring liquid ingredients there are glass measuring cups that hold 1 to 2 individual cups each with its own subdivisions. For measuring dry ingredients there are measuring cups that hold 1 individual cup, 3/4 cup, 2/3 cup, 1/2 cup etc. Flour and other such ingredients have to be piled lightly into the measuring cup and not packed firmly. Fill to the rim and level off. The same applies for tablespoons and teaspoons. They are always measured as level tablespoons or teaspoons unless stated otherwise. Do not measure ingredients in a regular cup or glass, since it is uncertain if it holds the same volume as a standard measuring cup. There are big and small cups as well as glasses. All ingredients for the recipes in this book are carefully measured in the standard measuring cup and the standard measuring spoons. Whenever a little vanilla is mentioned, it is equivalent to $1/4$ teaspoon. One pinch of spices equals $1/8$ teaspoon.

The juice of a medium size lemon is equal to 2 tablespoons. Half the success of a recipe depends on careful baking. Successful baking needs skill and experience, which you will achieve experimenting on your own oven. It is very important to use the right size and type of baking pan specified in the recipe, filling it up to $2/3$ full. Baking time varies according to the size of the pan. The same amount of batter placed in a deep, high pan requires longer baking time than if it was spread in a wide, shallow pan. The oven should be preheated, to the temperature stated in the recipe unless otherwise specified. The inside oven temperature

Measuring equivalents

measures	symbol	metric system	symbol
1 teaspoon	tsp	5 cub. centimeters	ml
1 tablespoon	tbsp	15 cub. centimeters	ml
1 fluid ounce	fl.oz.	30 cub. centimeters	ml
1 cup	c	0,24 litres	l
1 pint	pt.	0,47 litres	l
1 quart	qt.	0,95 litres	l
1 ounce	oz.	28 grams	gr.
1 pound	lb.	0,45 kilogram	kg.

should be exactly the same as the temperature shown on the thermostat. The accuracy of your thermostat can be checked by placing a metal thermometer inside the oven. Temperature registered on the thermometer should be the temperature registered on the ovens thermostat, when the light turns off. If it is higher or lower, the thermostat is not accurate. It should be adjusted or changed by an expert. Until this is done, you may bake by calculating the difference and setting the oven at a higher or lower temperature according to the thermometer used when checking it. In this cookbook, the temperatures are given in Fahrenheit (°F) degrees. The chart below shows how to change or calculate temperatures in Celsius degrees (°C) or how to regulate the temperatures in a gas range, whether slow, moderate, or hot. When baking cakes or sponge cakes, they should be placed on the lower shelves so that their surface reaches the middle part of the oven. Cookies, kourabiedes or other small cakes are usually placed on the middle shelves or even higher.

Oven temperature chart

	electric		gas range
	°F	°C	regulator
very slow oven	225	110	1/4
	250	120	1/2
slow	275	140	1
	300	150	2
moderate	325	160	3
	350	180	4
moderately hot	375	190	5
	400	200	6
hot	425	220	7
	450	230	8
very hot	475	250	9

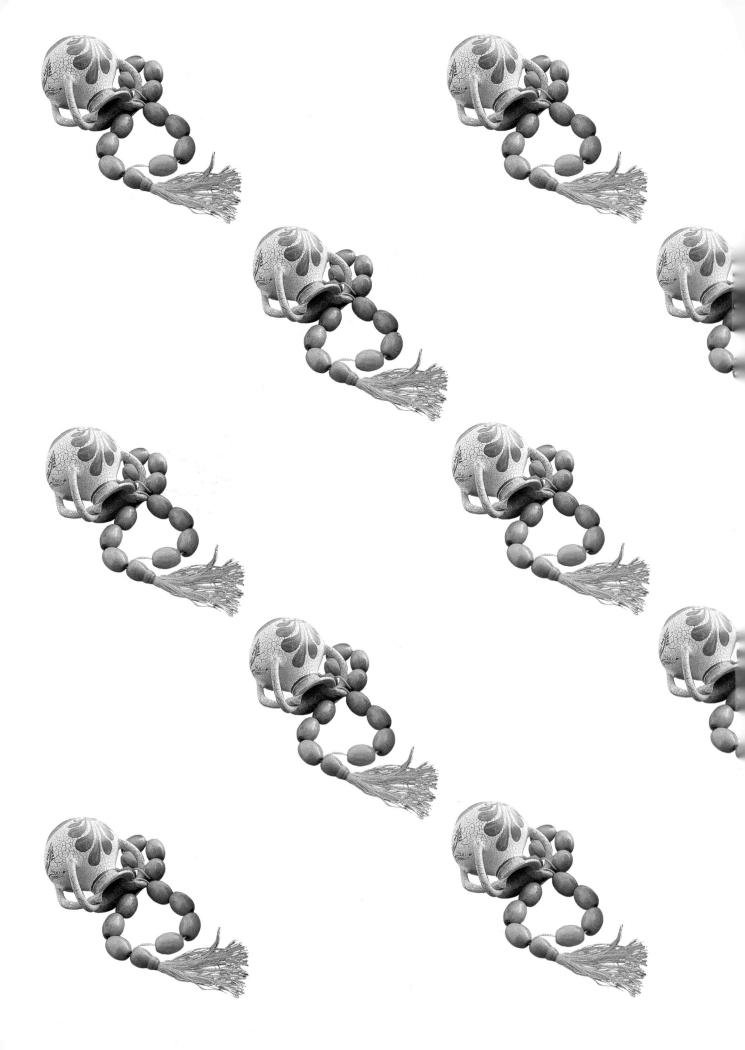